GLOBALIZATION

GLOBALIZATION

THE HIDDEN AGENDA

DENNIS SMITH

polity

First published in 2006 by Polity Press

Polity Press
65 Bridge Street
Cambridge CB2 1UR, UK

Polity Press
350 Main Street
Malden, MA 02148, USA

ISBN-10: 0-7456-1702-6
ISBN-13: 978-07456-1702-6
ISBN-10: 0-7456-1703-4 (pb)
ISBN-13: 978-07456-1703-4 (pb)

1007585587

A catalogue record for this book is available from the British Library.

Typeset in 10.5 on 12 pt Sabon
by SNP Best-set Typesetter Ltd, Hong Kong
Printed and bound in Great Britain by MPG Books Ltd, Bodmin, Cornwall.

The publisher has used its best endeavours to ensure that the URLs for external websites referred to in this book are correct and active at the time of going to press. However, the publisher has no responsibility for the websites and can make no guarantee that a site will remain live or that the content is or will remain appropriate.

Every effort has been made to trace all copyright holders, but if any have been inadvertently overlooked the publishers will be pleased to include any necessary credits in any subsequent reprint or edition.

For further information on Polity, visit our website: *www.polity.co.uk*

Contents

Figure and Boxes

Preface and Acknowledgements

What processes are driving the world of globalized societies coming into existence? How will the West fit into this world it can no longer dominate? What dynamic forces are shaping national societies in Eurasia, America and Africa? This book is the latest instalment of an inquiry guided by these questions that has been under way for more than a quarter of a century.

This inquiry began with *Conflict and Compromise* and *Barrington Moore*, and continued with *The Chicago School, The Rise of Historical Sociology* and *Capitalist Democracy on Trial*. These books are mainly about how individuals and groups fit into national societies, especially in the West. In *Zygmunt Bauman: Prophet of Postmodernity*, and *Norbert Elias and Modern Social Theory* that focus continues but more attention is paid to how nation-states fit into globalizing international structures. Now, in *Globalization: The Hidden Agenda*, global issues are paramount. Nation-states, groups and individuals are considered within this larger context.

This book has benefited from a global fund of goodwill on which its author has drawn freely. It is time to thank Evelin Lindner (Human Dignity and Humiliation Studies), Johan Galtung (TRANSCEND), Huang Ping, Li Peilin, Luo Hongguang, Cher Xin, Guang Xia, Michael Han, Zheng Jing, Zhao Weihua, Ma Chunhua, Zhao Bin and Sun Xiaolong (Beijing), Gao Jianguo, Juren Lin, Fu You-de, Liming Fan, Li Qiyun, Qin Feng Ming, Lin Hong, Donghui Zhang, Zhongming Ge and Zhu YanPing (Jinan), Li Youmei, Wang Wei, Tao Feiya, Zhang Jinghua and Liu Yuzhao (Shanghai), Peter Baehr and Michael Bond (Hong Kong), Vladimir Pankratiev, Anatoli Khazanov,

Elena Melkumian, Alexey Demchenko, Maria Gornostaeva, Vladimir Kultygin, Boris Suslakov, Rudolf Yanovsky, Teodor Shanin, Vassily Zhukov, Vladimir Dobrenkov, Rudolf Yanovsky, Larisa Ruban and Galina Osadchaya (Moscow), Ira Katznelson, Jack Snyder, Alan Brinckley, Bob Kerry, Janet Abu-Lughod, Aristide Zolberg, Nidhi Srinivas, Wolf Schaefer, Said Arjomand, Barbara Walters and Charles Tilly (New York), Bruce Mazlish, Neva Goodwin, Elliott Morss, Dominic Sachsenmaier, Akira Iriye, Susan Rooseveldt Weld and Linda Brownson (Cambridge, Mass), J.-P. Roos, Jean-Charles Lagrée, Ilona Ostner, Elzbieta Halas, Margareta Bertilsson, Yasemin Soysal, Jiri Musil, Capitolina Díaz, Anna Rotkirch, Ulla Bjornberg and Elena Zdravomyslova (European Sociological Association), Ari Sitas, Carlos Fortuna, Devorah Kalekin-Fishman, Syed Farid Alatas, Sujata Patel, Julia Evetts, Susan MacDaniel, Bernd Hornung, Raquel Sosa, Tina Uys, Henry Teune, Dasarath Chetty and Bernd Hornung (International Sociological Association), Oscar Gonzalez and Morna Macleod (Mexico City), Hing Ai Yun, Habibul Haque Khondker and Jennifer Jarman (Singapore), Abebe Zegeye, Vino Reddy, Ramesh Bharuthram, Priya Narismulu, Kovin Naidoo and Avadhna Singh (South Africa), Denis O'Hearn, Eoin O'Broin, Claire Hackett, Mike Tomlinson and David Dunseith (Belfast), Nils Brunnson, Rune Premfors, Christina Garsten, Göran Ahrne and Apostolis Papakostas (Stockholm), Reiner Grundmann, Sue Wright, Georgios Varouxakis and Henry Miller (Aston), Kanakis Leledakis, Surendra Munshi, Chaime Marcuello, Abby Peterson, Robert Fine, Zygmunt Bauman, Barbara Misztal, John Urry, Ruth Lister, Teresa Whitaker and Roberto Franzosi, as well as the friendly patrons of the *Café Culturel* at the *Wax Bar*, Nottingham.

Maria Gornostaeva made valuable comments on key chapters. I also owe thanks to my colleagues at the Department of Social Sciences at Loughborough University, including the technical, administrative and secretarial staff. Thanks to Vivian Dhaliwal for help with the diagrams. Thanks to all my family for their support and forbearance. I am also grateful to the anonymous readers, to Emma Longstaff of Polity Press and to the copy editor Ruth Thackeray. I do not implicate any of the people I have mentioned in the analysis made in this book. For better or worse, I must take full responsibility. Readers may go to *www.globalhelix.org* if they wish to comment on the book.

Dennis Smith

I

Key Themes

What is at stake?

If globalization does not change direction, the cost in terms of freedom and human rights will be high. If we go on as we are, there is a high risk of a major world war occurring by mid-century. It all depends on who wins the current political struggle.

The crucial struggle is not between the West and 'terrorism'. It is *within* the West. On one side, there are supporters of decent democracy, delivering substantial benefits, such as dignity, freedom and fair treatment, to all citizens; on the other, proponents of liberated capitalism, enforced by the domineering state, excluding many from its benefits. The outcome of this struggle will shape the world for the rest of the twenty-first century.

How far will the European Union go to defend its historic commitment to combining the pursuit of prosperity with a strong version of human rights that takes seriously the duty of care to the poor and disadvantaged? How long will it tolerate the United States' determined promotion of a ruthless 'logic of the market' throughout the world without regard to the wishes of others, including its old allies?

How long before Europe builds up its military strength to match its massive economic clout? Will the EU and the United States eventually find themselves intervening on opposite sides in armed conflicts? Unthinkable? So was a Europe without military aggression between France and Germany. So was a world without the Soviet Union. So was a capitalist China.

As the West divides, what lessons will its internal struggles give to the restless, exploding populations of the world's cities throughout Eurasia, America and Africa? These people are the real arbiters of our shared future. If decent democracy loses out in the West to liberated capitalism and the domineering state, this will give the world the following message: don't be a victim, victimize others. That was Hitler's creed.

If urban citizens throughout the world are denied decent democracy, if they are humiliated by the logic of the global market, then they will be tempted to follow new Hitlers, promising the rewards of revenge. It has happened before. If it happens again, we will be on our way to a third world war involving the American state, terrified of humiliating decline, and its increasingly powerful global neighbours in Europe and Asia.

Understanding what the future might hold for us unless we prevent it means looking behind globalization's public agenda to investigate the processes and mechanisms shaping its hidden agenda.

Sensitive issues

Globalization's public agenda is well known. It is focused on market opportunities, business interests and access to key material resources. The benefits of foreign direct investment are frequently mentioned. So are the 'healthy' disciplines imposed by multilateral agencies such as the International Monetary Fund. We hear a great deal about competition for energy resources such as oil and gas, including stratagems to deprive geo-political rivals of such access. 'Orange' political revolutions usually get a round of applause in the Western press. Since the attack on the World Trade Center on 11 September 2001 ('9/11') another item has been added to this public agenda: the 'war on terrorism'.

Behind this public agenda lies globalization's hidden agenda. These are items that touch on too many vested interests to be discussed too openly too often. Five items on the hidden agenda between now and 2035 are:

1 How will the United States and other leading powers cope with the forthcoming relative decline in America's global influence?
2 How will global governance be managed as American power wanes?

3 Now that capitalism has finally triumphed, what *kind* of capitalist political order will become dominant? Whose interests will it serve, and how?

4 What are the future global prospects for the version of human rights supported by the European Union with its emphasis on strong social rights?

5 As the world's population becomes increasingly urbanized with practically half its people in cities already, and half the developing world's population due to be city-dwellers by 2030, how will this newly urbanized population be incorporated within national and global socio-political orders and whose political lead will they follow?

Over the next few decades globalization's hidden agenda will become much less hidden than it is at present. By the time its key questions are obvious to everyone, they may have been answered in ways we do not want. To stand some chance of getting our interests taken into account we must think through those interests in a constructively self-critical spirit. We must also acknowledge the existence of globalization's hidden agenda, and get a better understanding of what globalization is and how it 'works'.

This book identifies a 'triple helix' of historical processes shaping globalization's hidden agenda. If they continue in their current direction, we may expect violent and destructive outcomes before the middle of this century.

The tsunami of globalization

Globalization was 'discovered' in the 1980s. It took a while for the news to get out. For most of the 1980s, references to globalization were infrequent, but during the 1990s they became a stream and then a flood. Journalists, businesspeople, politicians and scholars seized upon the term and made it part of their core vocabulary. Discourse about 'globalization' rapidly increased. Look at the bar chart in figure 1.1.[1] We see a steeply rising curve, like a massive ocean wave. That picture mirrors the way globalization was experienced, especially by Westerners.

During the 1990s globalization felt like a tsunami racing up the beach, transforming our landscape whether we liked it or not. The globalizing world seemed to be 'risk-ridden', 'liquid' and 'runaway'.[2] The evidence was everywhere:

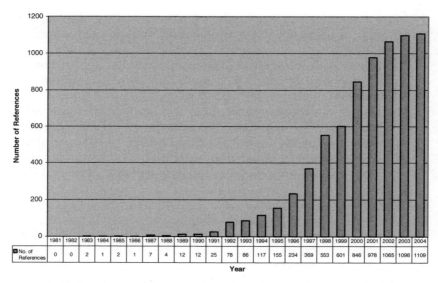

Figure 1.1   References to globalization in social science journals 1981–2004

- international money moving rapidly into and out of different national currencies, causing economic devastation in its wake;
- multinational corporations searching restlessly for new energy sources, scarce raw materials and cheap, flexible labour wherever these things could be found, and rapidly departing if it became more convenient to try somewhere else;
- information technology destroying jobs, penetrating protective shells of all kinds, and laying waste to the old to make space for the new;
- citizens losing confidence in bureaucrats and technocrats, and being forced to come to terms with risks they had not realized existed;
- the determined migration of people from poor countries to the West, hoping to get their feet on a higher rung of the economic ladder; and
- the cosmopolitan jostling of different cultures, nationalities and ethnicities, bringing fear, disruption and conflict.

Read, for example, Anthony Giddens on the runaway world, Zygmunt Bauman on liquid modernity, Manuel Castells on the information age, Ulrich Beck on risk society, Samuel Huntington on the clash of civilizations and Thomas Friedman on globalization's rampaging 'electronic herd' of global investors.[3]

Those themes helped make sense of how we *experienced* global-ization during the 1990s and into the 2000s, especially in the West. These authors did two things. First, they distilled how we felt: disoriented, anxious, vulnerable, angry and in need of reassurance. Second, they gave us organizing concepts linking these feelings to various master trends: decreasing control, growing speed, increasing liquidity, the advancing importance of information technology, heightened awareness of risk, the decline of the West, the resurgence of the market and so on.

These works gave us a vocabulary to describe our condition, iden-tified various factors we could blame, and produced very insightful descriptions of the new countryside we are passing through. But now we need much more. We need a map, a compass and a way of choos-ing among possible routes through this countryside. We also need to look beyond the present, not just forward but also backward.

Looking backwards and forwards tells us that globalization is a long and complex historical process, weaving continents together. It is cultural, political and technological, as well as economic. It has been under way for centuries. It stretches back to the Vikings and much earlier.[4]

It also tells us that for most of those centuries, business or trade was globalization's passenger, hitching a ride. It was rarely the driver, though sometimes the navigator.[5] Furthermore, seen in this historical context, the United States has been globalization's 'star player' for only a very short time, and the 'American' phase of globalization is likely to come to an end in the next few decades.

Why history?

A historical approach is vital, not a scholarly luxury. We use this approach in our daily lives when important assessments and decisions have to be made. Do we buy a road vehicle without looking at its service record? Would we appoint an employee without asking about his or her previous career? Or set up house with another person if we did not know something about his or her past life?

We *are* our history. We are the result of the way processes of personal development have worked out. Furthermore, we become particular kinds of adults, citizens, consumers and cultural beings because of the influence of several groups and institutions (for example family, ethnic group, nation and faith group) that are themselves undergoing processes of development.

There are dangers: retrospective myth-making about the past, false impressions of the present and wishful thinking about the future. To avoid this we need self-knowledge, healthy scepticism, high standards of proof, a willingness to look at as many kinds of evidence as possible, openness to the ideas of others and a readiness to change our minds if rationality and evidence demand it.

So it is when analysing globalization. Applying this approach, we discover through empirical analysis that it is a complex socio-historical process closely interwoven with other processes, each driven by distinctive mechanisms whose workings reveal themselves through long stretches of historical time. Discovering these things about globalization gives us a better chance of working out where we are in the process and what future options are open to us.

What is globalization?

Globalization means the gradual forging of links between groups and societies until they finally reach around the globe in several directions. These links have become increasingly dense, extensive, complex and dynamic over several centuries. How has this long historical process been structured? What kinds of network and hierarchy has it produced?

The globalizing ventures of explorers, opportunists and deal-makers create large, loose networks of social relations. Such networks are liable to fracture and break up as they get more extensive and complex. Networks survive rapid expansion by developing sites of surveillance and hierarchical control. Imperial capital cities play this role. So do institutions like the International Monetary Fund (IMF) and World Trade Organization (WTO).

The term 'globalization' conveys two things:

- the way economic, technological, military, political and cultural forces and mechanisms '*become* global', i.e. become anchored in institutions at the global level, over historical time; and
- the way interests and institutions at the global level *exert downward pressure* upon those below, especially national governments and their citizens, reducing the latter's freedom of action and telling them what to do in some respects.

'Going global' is one way of 'becoming less local'. Over the centuries, village inhabitants have learned to look upward to the big city, whose denizens have increasingly felt the pull of the national metropolis, whose citizens have increasingly found that capital, credit and the market are operating in global circuits.[6] Meanwhile, local dynasties have bowed down to the rulers of national states, which have found themselves part of transcontinental empires.[7]

Societal forces and mechanisms have been getting 'less local' since human societies began, although not without a struggle. There has been continual tension between, on the one hand, localizing pressures to settle, cultivate and defend a specific 'homeland' and, on the other, opposing pressures to expand outwards and upwards beyond the local, capture more land and resources, and construct a higher tier of control from which to survey and control the captured realm.

These latter pressures have tended to prevail after repeated reverses. Becoming less local and more global has happened in a 'two steps forward, one step backward' manner, rather like the way ocean waves advance and recede as the tide comes in.

That tide turned into a tsunami during the 1990s. Why? Because the structure of hierarchical control directing and restraining global flows suffered a catastrophic breach. A major levée holding back the flood collapsed. In other words, the Soviet Union and the Soviet Bloc broke up. This event signalled the final demise of the ancient imperial dream, the end of empires as a viable modern form of government.

The end of empires

By empire I mean a politico-military hierarchy intended to express the superiority of the individual, dynasty, group or nation sitting enthroned at its summit, and the inferiority of all others below. Empires were part of globalization almost from the beginning. They provided regulation, political cover and legitimacy for globalizing ventures by warriors, diplomats, traders, missionaries, fixers and opportunists of many kinds. They were killed by the rise of democracy, citizenship and human rights, backed up with the power of the United States.

The demise of the Soviet Union in 1989 finished the work of humbling Europe's arrogant imperial capitals that began when Americans guns destroyed the Spanish fleet in 1898. In fact, it took almost a century to teach Madrid, Berlin, Vienna, Istanbul, London, Paris and Moscow that they could not make imperialist absolutism stable and permanent in a democratic age.

This was a hard lesson to learn. The imperial impulse does not want to wither and die. It still rages in Washington, which is now paying the price of letting it get the upper hand, especially in Iraq.

One of the biggest questions confronted in the twentieth century was: what global system would replace the European empires? One response was the creation of the United Nations with the ratification of its charter in 1945. However, the world found it hard to break with its old ways.

The European empires were replaced during the Cold War order by two massive global empires, based in Moscow and Washington respectively. These Cold War politico-military structures took over the space occupied by the old European empires. They inherited their fundamental weakness: trying to combine absolutism or top-down assertiveness with the claim to be egalitarian, libertarian and democratic.

The Cold War empires were much bigger than the old inefficient European ones, and tried to be more rationalized and systematic. They were always trying to prove themselves in the eyes of the world by displaying exemplary performance. Ironically, this made them much more vulnerable than the old empires to the political impact of structural contradictions, whose effects tended to be highly visible, especially in the form of liberation movements and acts of repression (as in Vietnam and Afghanistan).

Now the Russian global empire is gone and the American one is practically the lone survivor of an ancient breed.

The collapse of the Berlin Wall and the implosion of the Soviet Union were major and decisive breaches in the rickety structure of empire, leaving the American 'strut' standing alone amid the wreckage. A large political vacuum was suddenly created in Eastern Europe and Central Asia. These factors, acting in combination, released powerful forces, sending capital, commodities, crowds and cultures racing round the world, crashing through borders on every continent.

This was a shift *within* the globalization process. Previously, economic forces and demographic flows had been forced to work their way through and around the overriding global strategic concerns of government and the military. During the 1990s international movements of capital and labour were 'liberated' and given a new lease of life. They made the most of that fact, especially in the ex-Soviet Union and the countries of the old Soviet Bloc.

Beyond the market

But to understand globalization we must look beyond the market-place, taking account of three things:

1 Historically, globalization has been driven at least as much, and often more, by the motive of glorifying gods and magnifying rulers as by the pursuit of business opportunities.
2 Globalization causes people to be displaced or excluded in ways that make them feel outraged and resentful.
3 The model of profit-seeking human beings making rational choices about their material interests is inadequate as a tool for understanding the way in which people participate in globalization. They are also moved by how other people's actions affect their sense of who they are and where they fit into society, and how they feel about this.

Empowered with a historical perspective, and the broadened view of how human beings 'work' that has just been described, we can now turn to three socio-historical processes that are shaping globalization's hidden agenda. These are globalization and two other closely related processes: one shaped by the dynamics of humiliation,[8] the other focused on regulation of modernity (see box 1.1). These are analysed and explained in the rest of this chapter.

The triple helix

Each of the three socio-historical processes just mentioned has its own discernible *internal* logic. It is possible to make empirical generalizations about the distinctive parameters within which each process operates, respectively, the frames of globalization; the modes of response to humiliation; and the codes of modernity.

Relations *among* the three processes are also close. For example, globalization is a major cause of humiliation for many people, and the codes of modernity (the honour code, the human rights code or some mixture of the two) have a great influence on the ways in which this humiliation is experienced and understood. Some aspects of globalization, such as the imperial impulse, are driven by the desire of those engaged in empire-building to escape from humiliation in their homeland and impose domination upon others. In its turn,

Box 1.1 Processes, drivers and parameters		
PROCESSES	DRIVERS	PARAMETERS
Globalization	The pursuit of • Power • Prestige • Profit	Frames of globalization: Imperial impulse Logic of the market Cosmopolitan condition
Regulation of modernity	The regulation of • Social competition • Treatment of the vulnerable • Access to social benefits	Codes of modernity: Honour code Human rights code Mix of codes
Dynamics of humiliation	The imposition of • Conquest • Relegation • Exclusion	Modes of response to humiliation: Escape → Fear cycles Acceptance → Victimization cycles Rejection → Revenge cycles

imperialism is radically undermined by the spread of the human rights code.

Because of feedback mechanisms of this kind between globalization, the regulation of modernity and the dynamics of humiliation, we can treat these closely intertwined socio-historical processes as a kind of triple helix (see box 1.2). Understanding the triple helix will help us to clarify some possible answers to the questions on globalization's hidden agenda. That means reaching back into the past to get a clearer view of the present and a stronger purchase on the future.

Process one: globalization

The major dynamics of globalization are the pursuit of power, prestige and profit as well as the wish to ensure survival. As winners beat losers and incorporate their assets, as networks become more extensive and complex, and as surveillance and rule enforcement

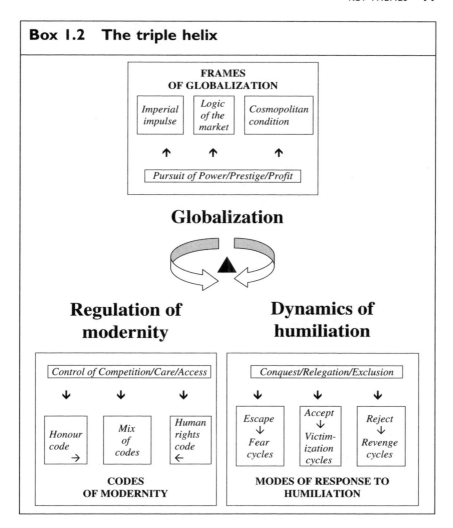

Box 1.2 The triple helix

FRAMES
OF GLOBALIZATION

| *Imperial impulse* | *Logic of the market* | *Cosmopolitan condition* |

↑   ↑   ↑

Pursuit of Power/Prestige/Profit

Globalization

Regulation of modernity

Dynamics of humiliation

Control of Competition/Care/Access

↓   ↓   ↓

| *Honour code* → | *Mix of codes* | *Human rights code* ← |

**CODES
OF MODERNITY**

Conquest/Relegation/Exclusion

↓   ↓   ↓

| *Escape* ↓ *Fear cycles* | *Accept* ↓ *Victim- ization cycles* | *Reject* ↓ *Revenge cycles* |

**MODES OF RESPONSE TO
HUMILIATION**

climb up the agenda, so hierarchies develop whose fields of operation eventually become global in extent.

Globalization makes victims as well as victors. People get wounded. These include victims of the *imperial impulse*. Those at the receiving end of this urge to dominate and destroy are forced to bow down before alien masters. They lose their assets and their sense of independence. They see their homes destroyed and their futures ruined. Then there are the victims of the *logic of the market*, turned into losers by the rules of a game they usually did not ask to join. Finally, there are the estranged victims of the *cosmopolitan condition*, uprooted by processes of socio-political transformation, left stranded between the old and the new. They are liable to feel both liberated and humiliated at the same time: liberated by the weakening of constraints on their behaviour; humiliated by the loss of support for their sense of identity and purpose.

The period since 1600 may be divided into three historical phases:

1 *European imperialism.* This phase came to an end during the decades immediately after the end of the Second World War, when it overlapped with the second phase.
2 *Global imperialism.* The Cold War confrontation pitted the Russian-led 'Communist Bloc' and the American-led 'Free World' against each other. By the 1990s only the American empire remained standing although it was beset by deep internal conflict, especially between Europe and the United States. It overlapped with the third phase.
3 *Global multi-polarity.* The uni-polar world dominated by the United States is coming to an end. In the first decade of the twenty-first century, the third phase is beginning to take shape with the increasing independence of the European Union, the rise of China, the revival of Japan, the resurgence of Russia, the emergence of India and the clear signs of American weariness with, and distaste for, its present role as 'global monarch'.

Process two: regulation of modernity

Globalization needs to be understood and assessed in terms of whether it is going to improve or damage the chances for the majority of the global population to enjoy decent and fulfilled lives in the foreseeable future. That means exploring how the process of globalization intersects with the interplay between two codes of modernity: the *honour code* and the *human rights code*.

Alexis de Tocqueville drew attention to this issue at the centre of his argument in *Democracy in America* (Tocqueville 1968),[9] written in the 1830s. He saw a future in which aristocrats such as himself, imbued with a strongly hierarchical honour code, would have to take a back seat, if they survived at all, in democracies that emphasized equality and aspired to universal citizenship. Towards the end of the nineteenth century, Friedrich Nietzsche reacted strongly against what he called 'slave morality' and called for a return to the aristocratic values of the honour code, by which he meant accepting the strength, pride and creativity of outstanding individuals prepared to seize what they want and become the people they choose to be.

Both codes of modernity are focused on three things: social competition; provision of care and protection; and control of access to life-enhancing socio-cultural benefits. In handling these, the honour code values strength: the capacity to maximize your stake in the world and to destroy your enemies. It is particularistic: 'I look after mine; we look after ours.' By contrast, the human rights code respects needs and makes the demand that all human beings should be given access to the means of enjoying a decent life. It is universalistic: 'My needs will be recognized; we look after all.'

Both codes are 'modern'. This is a factual, not an evaluative statement. Neither is innately 'programmed' to disappear. The two codes are now strongly present and closely intertwined in most societies. This situation has historical roots:

1   The human rights code made a decisive advance with the spread of modern nation-states modelled on the constitutional examples set by the American Republic (after 1776) and France (after 1789). Sovereign democratic states were powerful defenders of this code.
2   However, globalization since the 1980s has seriously undermined the strength and sovereignty of these nation-states. This threatens the advance of the human rights code by weakening its main protector.
3   Meanwhile, the honour code remains strong at both the national and global levels.

In practice, most societies operate with a pragmatic mix of the two codes. The important questions are: what kind of mix will prevail and which code will be dominant? The crucial scene of action is the city. Global society is urbanizing very rapidly. What do their inhabitants want? What are they likely to get? How will they react?

Process three: dynamics of humiliation

An important spring of action is the experience of being humiliated. Not that globalization always humiliates. Nor, of course, is all humiliation, or even most of it, directly related to globalization.[10] However, the logic of the market, the imperial impulse and the cosmopolitan condition are powerful generators of humiliation, outrage and resentment among many of those at the receiving end.

Being humiliated means being forced to undergo an experience of displacement or exclusion from where you think you should be. It means being denied the recognition, security, freedom and power to act on your own behalf that you are used to having or think you should rightfully have.

There are three main types of humiliation. There is *conquest humiliation*, which removes your previous freedom and forces you into subordination. There is *relegation humiliation*, which forces you downwards within a hierarchy. There is also *exclusion humiliation*, which denies you membership of the group, hierarchy or network to which you feel you rightfully belong.

The initial reaction to humiliation is normally resentful and half-hearted acquiescence in something one cannot prevent. However, following the initial shock three other responses are possible: *escape*, *acceptance* and *rejection*. Each of these responses may, in certain circumstances, trigger further episodes of humiliation. As I argue below, escape frequently leads to *fear cycles*, acceptance to *victimization cycles* and rejection to *revenge cycles*.

Three drivers

To summarize, the future of global society in the twenty-first century is being shaped by relationships among three powerful drivers. These are located within *globalization*, as shaped by the imperial impulse, the logic of the market and the cosmopolitan condition; *the dynamics of humiliation*, i.e. conquest, relegation and exclusion leading to the responses of escape, acceptance and rejection, potentially triggering cycles of fear, victimization and revenge; and *the regulation of modernity*, through the honour code, the human rights code or a mixture of the two. Within each of these three socio-historical processes we can see certain 'stories' unfolding.

Globalization

The relative significance of the logic of the market has increased during the past half century, especially since 1989. During the past century, the advance of the human rights code has seriously undermined the imperial impulse. However, it is fighting a rearguard action. It does not want to die.

Meanwhile, the unsettling cosmopolitan condition has been gathering strength since the sixteenth century. It was initially fostered by the anxieties of urban existence. It is now reinforced by the decreasing capacity of the nation-state to contain and structure our lives as influence shifts upwards towards the global level.

Dynamics of humiliation

There have been two long-term shifts. The spread of human rights thinking with its universalistic and egalitarian tendencies ('we are fundamentally all the same') means that there has been an increase in sensitivity to exclusion humiliation, especially in the form of denial of rights. Nations, groups or individuals who are the victims of acts of conquest and relegation are more likely than before to make complaints to third parties (e.g. the United Nations, law courts or employment tribunals) about being wrongfully 'excluded' from the enjoyment of rights that should be respected.

The second long-term shift is that the escape response to humiliation has become less available. This is an old story, now being repeated at a higher societal level. In early modern Europe, peasants who ran away from servitude on the land to 'freedom' in the city typically found themselves subject to new forms of regulation, frequently oppressive, enforced by urban authorities. Property owners in town had a deep fear that violence, crime and disease would be inflicted upon them by idlers, beggars, vagrants and the multitude of wandering souls pouring through the city gates. A huge effort to discipline the urban population was under way by the late sixteenth century, involving, for example, the enforcement of curfews, vagrancy orders, forced labour and deportations, as well as committals to the work house, prison, house of correction and plague house. In some states, the enforcement of compulsory schooling strengthened the foundations of social and political discipline.[11]

More recently, descendants of migrants and settlers who left their old homes and went abroad to build new lives in various 'promised lands' in overseas colonies in America, Africa and elsewhere, have had a nasty surprise. The 'old world' their ancestors left behind has transformed itself and 'followed' them, pulling them back into its entangling grip. These would-be escapees have been drawn back into the bonds of global interdependence. Globalization does not like those who try to 'opt out'.

With escape increasingly ruled out, the fundamental choices confronting those for whom globalization means humiliation are either to accept or reject their oppressors and/or the structures that oppress them. Most people do not want to make these choices. In fact, many people find themselves falling into bemused and resentful acquiescence, a 'holding' pattern that is neither active acceptance nor active rejection. This in-between response is widespread.

Regulation of modernity

Over the past two hundred years there has been a steady advance of the influence of the human rights code, which has undermined the plausibility and coherence of empires. In 1989 the European imperial order finally collapsed. Elsewhere, the Chinese empire survived only by transforming itself into a nation dominated by the Han, a unique achievement.

The guardians of the human rights code have been national states. Their governments have had the authority and organizational capacity to implement it through their legal systems. The European Union has inherited this role although it largely depends on the constituent national governments acting as 'enforcer'.

The influence of the human rights code is now under threat. The reason is that both the sovereignty and the practical influence of national governments have been undermined by globalization during the past half century. If national states are not available to enforce human rights as strongly as before, who will?

Now that their old protector, the national state, has been weakened, groups who feel belittled or left out by others are liable to 'take the law into their own hands'. In other words, they are tempted to use force to advance their interests at the expense of others. This represents a shift back towards the honour code and its core exhortation: humiliate or be humiliated. If global-regional or global governance does not become strong enough to protect and enforce the human rights code, it is likely that the honour code will gain further ground.

In any case, it does not seem that Tocqueville's vision in *Democracy in America* (1968) of the human rights code completely displacing the honour code will come to pass. The question is: what kind of amalgam between the two codes would be most likely to help bring about a world order in which most people could live decent lives in decent societies?

Trends and circles

There are two kinds of analysis in this book. One is concerned with long-term social processes such as the following:

- the increased influence of the logic of the market;
- the growing pervasiveness of the cosmopolitan condition;
- the incongruous, uncomfortable survival of the imperial impulse;
- the increased popular awareness of exclusion humiliation;
- the reduced availability of the escape response to humiliation;
- the rise of the human rights code followed by renewed strengthening of the honour code;
- the shift from a uni-polar world dominated by the United States towards a multi-polar world in which China and the EU have greater influence; and
- the movement away from a world in which most people live in rural areas to one in which the majority of the population live in cities.

The other analytical focus is the question of how the social mechanisms within each of the strands of the triple helix actually 'work' and interrelate and how they intertwine with each other. These mechanisms will be investigated through a technique reminiscent in some respects of the hermeneutic circle.[12] Basically, this means shifting back and forth between the parts and the whole of a complex object in order to clarify its meaning or to find out 'how it works'.

At the crossroads

For the next two or three decades, but no longer, the West will hold, unchallenged, the reins of the runaway world. If, during this time, the West gives liberated capitalism its head, protected by the domineering US state, the West will suffer for it later.

As America's grip on events loosens, as global power redistributes to multiple centres, as Asia becomes resurgent, as Latin America becomes even more independent, and as Europe finally steers its own course, the politics of the big city will come to the fore on every continent. That is the politics of the frustrated high-school graduate, the frightened nearly-poor, and the revenge-seeking slum-dweller.

Business elites in these countries have been taught by the United States that capitalism 'means freedom' but what will that phrase signify when Washington's hand is no longer on their shoulders? More importantly, those that throng the city streets have learned from America that a powerful and determined government can use its military force and police powers to look after any interests it chooses to protect. It can demonize and persecute anyone who stands in its way. On present form, that will be the dominant theme of domestic and international politics for the first half of the twenty-first century. Not the peaceful perfection of global capitalism but the violent destruction of enemies in pursuit of increasingly scarce resources. There will be no long-term winners, certainly not the 'old oppressor', the West.

Another, better, scenario is possible, based on decent democracy. This incorporates the practical wisdom acquired by the Western rich in the nineteenth and twentieth centuries when dealing with their domestic urban-industrial populations. The rich learned the hard way, through two world wars, that the urban masses are dangerous unless they are fed, educated, cared for and respected. This was done, or at least partly done, through national welfare systems. Now something similar must be done globally, through increased international cooperation and strengthened global governance. Let us not learn the hard way again. The West should take the lead.

Some people find the very idea of spending their taxes on the world's people completely unthinkable and unacceptable. How thinkable and acceptable do they find the likely alternative, which is global war, disease, starvation and chaos, all posing a mortal threat to life, liberty and the pursuit of happiness?

The organization of the book

Following this introduction, the three strands of the triple helix are examined in successive chapters, moving from the codes of modernity, i.e. the honour code and the human rights code (in chapter 2) to the modes of humiliation (chapter 3) and then on to the frames of globalization (chapter 4), intermittently stepping back to remind ourselves of the larger context, the whole of which they are parts. This will give us a good working understanding of the societal processes in which globalization is embedded and what is at stake for states and citizens. The rest of the book renews the exploration of the triple helix, this time in greater depth and reversing the order.

In the next three chapters, attention is paid to the three global generators of humiliation already mentioned: the imperial impulse (chapter 5), the logic of the market (chapter 6) and the cosmopolitan condition (chapter 7). Then three ways of responding to humiliation are considered, in turn: escape (chapter 8), acceptance (chapter 9) and rejection (chapter 10).

In other words, in chapters 5 to 10 we look at key socio-historical mechanisms *within* globalization, and *within* processes of humiliation, now and then stepping back to see how these mechanisms contribute to the bigger picture. In the concluding chapter, we look *within* the dynamic interaction between honour and human rights, the two codes of modernity. This chapter draws the argument together and considers the implications of the book's analysis for globalization's hidden agenda.

2

Codes of Modernity

In the next three chapters, we make a journey around the three strands of the triple helix, visiting in turn the codes of modernity, the modes of humiliation and the frames of globalization. The journey enables us to build up an increasingly complex picture in three stages. We begin by anatomizing and comparing the honour code and the human rights code in this chapter, then explain how these codes enter into the experience of humiliation and responses to it (chapter 3), and finally explore, briefly, how humiliation is built into the experience of globalization (chapter 4).

As we now turn first to the codes of modernity, the summary contained in box 2.1 provides a reminder of the other two strands of the triple helix with which these codes are closely associated.

Act of revenge

In fact, before we get to the codes of modernity, we need to make a brief detour through globalization and humiliation. We need to discuss 9/11.

The twin towers of the World Trade Center in New York celebrated Washington's conception of business globalization backed by American political and military power. The attack on 11 September 2001 was the deliberate desecration of an American temple. It began at 8.45 a.m. local time when the first aeroplane, piloted by Mohamed Atta, hit the north tower. It was completed at 10.29 a.m., when the

Box 2.1 What are globalization and humiliation?	
Globalization	*Humiliation*
Globalization is the large-scale, long-term process of: • making links between groups and societies, links that tend to become increasingly dense, extensive, complex and dynamic; • struggling to gain advantages, avoid costs and impose order within those relationships; and • coming to terms with the fact that influence and initiative within social networks and hierarchies has tended, over the long term, to shift upwards towards the global-regional and global levels.	Humiliation occurs when: • people are subjected to the experience of undergoing an outrageous forced displacement and/or exclusion; • this displacement and/or exclusion is from a position they feel is rightfully 'theirs' within a group, network or hierarchy* to which they feel they rightfully 'belong'; and • this process is perceived by those who suffer it as a painful and destructive attack on their identity and interests, which they cannot prevent or ignore.

* The term 'hierarchy' is intended to cover not only organizational 'command structures' but also class structures, forms of state domination, and systems of status ranking. These tend to overlap but not always and not completely.

second tower collapsed. It took over half a decade to put up the World Trade Center.[1] It took little more than a hundred minutes to knock it down again.[2]

The attack on 9/11 was intended to humiliate the United States. We do not have to guess about that. We have the statement of Osama bin Laden,[3] broadcast by Al-Jazeera television on 7 October 2001:

> God Almighty hit the United States at its most vulnerable spot. He destroyed its greatest buildings. Praise be to God. Here is the United States. It was filled with terror from its north to its south and from its east to its west. Praise be to God. What the United States tastes today is a very small thing compared to what we have tasted for tens of years.

Our nation has been tasting this humiliation and contempt for more than 80 years. Its sons are being killed, its blood is being shed, its holy places are being attacked, and it is not being ruled according to what God has decreed. Despite this, nobody cares . . .

One million Iraqi children have thus far died in Iraq although they did not do anything wrong. Despite this, *we heard no denunciation* by anyone in the world or a fatwa by the rulers' ulema [body of Muslim scholars]. Israeli tanks and tracked vehicles also enter to wreak havoc in Palestine, in Jenin, Ramallah, Rafah, Beit Jala, and other Islamic areas and we hear no voices raised or moves made.

But if *the sword falls on the United States after 80 years*, hypocrisy raises its head lamenting the deaths of these killers who tampered with the blood, honour, and holy places of the Muslims. The least that one can describe these people is that they are morally depraved. They champion falsehood, support the butcher against the victim, the oppressor against the innocent child. *May God mete them the punishment they deserve.*[4]

Bin Laden referred to 'eighty years' of oppression because in World War I followers of Islam lost their Colossus, their great protector, the Ottoman Empire ruled by Turkey. The Western 'crusaders' conquered this empire, which by that time had existed for over six centuries. At its height, the Ottoman Empire had been able to stand up to major Christian powers such as Spain. For four centuries until the early 1920s the reigning Turkish sultan had also been Caliph of Islam, leader of the *Ummah*, the world community of believers.[5]

After World War I, the Ottoman Empire was broken up by Western governments keen to control key trade routes and defend resources such as the oil discovered not long before in Persia (Iran). Bin Laden was speaking for people who felt as if the roof and doors of their dwelling place had been ripped off, letting intruders burst in, hold them captive and tamper with their possessions.

From Bin Laden's point of view, 9/11 did three things:

1 It drew attention to the unacceptability of the humiliated condition of Muslims, especially in Palestine, Iraq and Saudi Arabia.
2 It took revenge against the West, especially the United States, making the score even by attacking the symbols of American civilization, desecrating its 'holy places', and giving Americans a taste of the terror to which Muslims in the Middle East had been subjected for a long time.
3 It punished the West, on behalf of God and wronged Muslims everywhere.

History and humiliation

According to Al-Qaeda, the United States is heir to a long 'crusader' tradition dedicated to the ambition of dominating and destroying Islam. How could they come to such a conclusion? What is the relevance of the crusaders?

Crusading was a core legitimating activity of Christendom's feudal aristocrats in the medieval period. The argument for having an aristocracy went as follows: Christian holy places in Palestine have to be saved from Islamic 'infidels'. Christians in Europe have to be defended against aggressive Turks. Therefore, a full-time warrior class, the aristocracy, has to be supported by servile peasants who should be very grateful for their protection.[6]

Crusading was a way to enhance the honour of a knight's family. Honour was won by demonstrating a capacity to humiliate others while avoiding being humiliated oneself. Appropriate acts included: taking others captive and either ransoming them, torturing them to death or enslaving them; seizing their land, women and slaves; taking their treasure and precious things; destroying their sacred objects; and insulting them in all possible ways. This honour code was common in many societies at that time, including Islamic ones, and had been so for several centuries. It was not exclusive to the Crusades, or to Christian knights.

Apart from aggressive religiosity and honour-seeking, a third aspect of the Crusades was the pursuit of commercial opportunities, a practice in which the Venetians specialized.[7]

This crusading tradition survived in strength right up to the Spanish conquests in Latin America and continued throughout the Reformation and Counter-Reformation in sixteenth- and seventeenth-century Europe. At that time, Catholic and Protestant Christians turned on each other with the same ferocity that their forefathers had used against the Turks.[8]

Bin Laden's use of the term 'crusaders' with reference to the United States is deceptively plausible in at least three ways:

1 American political life is full of aggressive, or at least highly assertive, religiosity, fully represented in the case of George W. Bush and his cabinet.
2 The carefully staged toppling of Saddam Hussein's statue on 9 April 2003, the public displays of the captured Iraqi president and the dead bodies of his sons, and the degrading behaviour of the American military at Abu Ghraib prison, proudly performed on

film, are all examples of inflicting humiliation following the ancient honour code: 'See how we bring the mighty low.'
3   The tightly controlled auction of investment and trading contracts in Iraq is well documented.

But this is only half the story.

Honour and human rights

In practice, the only two foreign policies an American president can sell to the American public are: the defence of the homeland (a very clear first); and the promotion of democracy abroad, as long as this can be presented as either having few costs to Americans and/or being very important for the defence of the homeland.

Traditionally, America's civilizing mission is not, primarily, to go out and improve the outside world. It is to attract people from that outside world to the United States where they will, if they have got what it takes, improve themselves. This was, after all, how America began, according to the official myth: as a destination for people determined to escape the corruption of the old world and to make a pure and prosperous life for themselves across the Atlantic. In other words, America performs its duty to the rest of the world simply by existing as 'a city on a hill', an example to all of how good a democratic, law-abiding and God-fearing society can be.

For all its religiosity, stemming from sixteenth- and seventeenth-century roots, the United States is the heir to the Enlightenment as well as the Reformation. In other words, it is a society officially hostile to the principles of aristocracy and absolutism. It is also committed to the idea of rational individuals enjoying the free use of that rationality in the market place and government. In 1776 the leaders of the American Revolution based their right to govern themselves on two ideas. One was that that empires, the grandest expression of the honour code, were illegitimate: therefore, George III had no right to tax them without asking their permission. The other was that political society should be founded on the idea of universal rights: therefore, the American Republic would be an association of free citizens.

For a century and a half, from the time of the American Civil War, the federal government in Washington has justified its major wars by saying it is fighting for the liberty of citizens against the agents of oppression. Most of its soldiers and voters have been ready to accept this explanation. After all, their forebears migrated to the United States attracted by the idea of being free from the tyrannical landlords and closed political regimes that they were leaving behind on more corrupt, backward and wicked continents.

Bin Laden assumes that the sole motivation of the United States is the pursuit of imperialist domination and a wish to impose humiliation on others as a sign of its own national honour. These tendencies are present in American political life but they face two very powerful contrary forces: a commitment to the idea of human rights (to which, incidentally, Bin Laden also objects); and a desire to escape from the 'corrupt' old world rather than to become entangled with it.

However, Bin Laden did succeed in making the US government act according to the stereotype he constructed. He made the Americans play his game. In the aftermath of 9/11, George W. Bush, like Osama bin Laden, poured threats upon any government that did not support him in his fight against the other side. The two opponents declared that this would be a battle without third parties. There were just two sides: the right side, God's side, the good side; and the wrong side, the Devil's side, the evil side. Bin Laden called down God's wrath upon morally depraved 'hypocrites' who tried to stay neutral. Bush told the world: 'Every nation, in every region, now has a decision to make. Either you are with us, or you are with the terrorists.'[9]

In the aftermath of 9/11 Bin Laden and Bush both said: 'We run this neighbourhood. Do what we want or it will be the worse for you. Join our gang or we will make you suffer.' This is the language of the Chicago mobs in the 1920s. It renewed the spirit of the feudal system in medieval Europe when peasants, urban traders and landless knights found the best way to survive was to accept the 'protection' of the nearest regional tyrant.

Two codes

The shock of 9/11 drove the White House to adopt very openly the rhetoric and mind-set of the honour code, an ancient way of thinking that emerged, historically, long before talk of human rights, one that says: humiliate or be humiliated (see box 2.2).

The honour code says: 'Because I am powerful, I can and I will, if I wish . . .'

The human rights code says: 'Because I am human, I need and I must have . . .'

Box 2.2 Codes of modernity: honour and human rights

The honour code recognizes as 'honourable' an individual or group's:	The human rights code recognizes an individual or group's claim to possess:
Capacity to enter, survive and achieve success in the social struggle, e.g.:	*Rights to enter, and be fairly treated in, the social competition, e.g.:*
(i) the capacity to humiliate others by inflicting damage on them, either disabling or destroying them; (ii) the capacity to humiliate others by making them bow down in subservience; and (iii) the capacity to defend themselves against being humiliated by others.	(i) the right to be admitted to the social competition and treated fairly in the context of universal legal and political citizenship (*legal and political rights*); and (ii) the right to be empowered within that struggle through universal social citizenship, such as health care and education (*enabling social rights*).
Capacities with respect to provision, or withholding, of care and protection, e.g.:	*Rights with respect to provision of care and protection, e.g.:*
the capacity to protect or, if they choose, abandon and/or replace, 'their' things and people, including wives, children, subjects and slaves.	ensuring a minimum standard of decency is achieved by all by enforcing the duty of care (i) on all employers and service providers; (ii) especially with respect to those incapacitated and/or disadvantaged (temporarily or permanently) and, as a result, unable to participate effectively within that struggle (*protective social rights; duty of care*).

Capacity to provide or withhold life-enhancing benefits, e.g.:	Rights with respect to life-enhancing benefits, e.g.:
the capacity to bestow individual and collective benefits upon subjects, slaves, captives and victims, or not to do so, according to the free choice of the 'honourable' individual or group.	the right of every person to be enabled to develop as a fully rounded human being participating creatively in as many aspects of a civilized society as they can or wish to (right of self-development).

The honour code is, historically, associated with dynastic and tribal societies, in other words societies where different family group-ings or lineages are in competition with each other. It is the code that fuels the spirit of feuding and duelling. It is most strongly associated with tribes and aristocracies but its influence is powerful and perva-sive in many walks of modern life.

The human rights code has a complex historical genealogy. In part, its origins may be found in universalistic and monotheistic religions, which preach the equality of all souls before the omnipotence of God. Another factor is the rise of a particular combination of social forces:

- a bureaucratic central state, freed from aristocratic control;
- an active commercial and manufacturing class;
- a large urban working class constantly being reinforced by migrants from the countryside; and
- professional practitioners (such as doctors, lawyers, engineers, surveyors, architects and so on), with occupational ident-ities focused on effective performance oriented to 'making things work'.

Central rulers tried to disarm and pacify the warrior nobility with its violent habits. The state claimed a monopoly over the right to use force. When they made this claim stick, they were able to outlaw armed conflict between their subjects. Duelling, for example, was typ-ically made illegal. The state made itself the one and only legitimate engine for humbling others in society, imposing punishment on those who broke the government's laws or displeased the ruler.

As society became urban and industrial, urban workers learned how to bargain with their employers and political masters. After some bloody struggles, deals were made and became enshrined in law.

In return for their cooperation the people got rights: legal, political and social. They became citizens and the content of citizenship gradually increased.

Rights had to be administered and monitored. New institutions like schools, hospitals, planning departments, parliaments and law courts had to be built, managed and expanded. This meant more employment and influence for professional people who acquired a strong vested interest in citizenship and the human rights code that went with it.

When governments in urbanizing, industrializing societies found themselves fighting wars against other societies of a similar kind, they needed very large numbers of fit, educated, disciplined and motivated soldiers, mainly drawn from the poor. Getting their cooperation often meant promising a further expansion of citizenship and fuller implementation of human rights.[10]

The honour code and the human rights code cover similar themes (see box 2.2):

- the struggle or competition for survival and advantage in society;
- the provision of care and protection; and
- access to life-enhancing benefits (such as high culture, travel, leisure and entertainment).

The honour code treats these themes in terms of the capacity of a powerful group or individual (typically male) to win his fights, humiliate those he defeats, protect or discard the possessions he has won as he pleases, and to cultivate himself and his possessions if he so chooses.

By contrast, the human rights code focuses on the right of all human beings to take part in the social competition on fair terms. This means that everyone has a right to be empowered by appropriate training and support according to his or her particular circumstances. Everyone, but especially people unable to participate or chronically disadvantaged within society, should benefit from a duty of care exercised by employers and service providers, including the state, and have access to benefits enabling him or her to engage in self-development.[11]

Imagine how the human rights code might look to a dyed-in-the-wool knightly product of the honour code: 'What a system! Everyone, however lowly, is treated as if he were a knight who has won his spurs and earned the privilege of being regarded as an equal by other independent members of society. Then all these upstarts get special training (at our expense, no doubt), supposedly to make them fit for battle. If they fail, they still get looked after like the lady in my castle, whom I like to keep well dressed, well fed, well schooled and well entertained. And they expect all this as a right!' These thoughts, expressed in various updated terms, can be heard in any modern tavern or café.

* * *

In this chapter we have: analysed 9/11 as an act of revenge for a previous humiliation; seen how the American response was framed in terms of the honour code; compared and contrasted the human rights code and honour code as alternative ways of handling social competition, providing care and protection as well as controlling access to life-enhancing benefits; and noticed that both codes are in evidence in American political life.

3

Modes of Humiliation

Now we turn to the second strand of the triple helix and will be able to see how profoundly the experience of humiliation is shaped by the code of modernity in terms of which it is framed.

What is humiliation?

Humiliation happens when an individual, group or society is forcibly displaced or excluded from where they think they should be in the order of things. This process is experienced as painful, outrageous and even crushing. To put it slightly differently, people feel humiliated when they are forced or kept away from a position they perceive as being 'rightfully theirs' within a group, network or hierarchy to which they feel they 'rightfully belong'.

Displacement or exclusion may be violent and cause bodily injury. However, the pain of humiliation is not physical. It comes from those at the receiving end being acutely aware of the difference between how they think they deserve to be treated in terms of consideration and respect and how they are actually being treated.

This is a distinctively 'modern' understanding of humiliation. If we go far enough back in history we encounter another meaning. In this older sense, humiliation does not just mean forced displacement or exclusion, it also means becoming humble. In other words, one might choose to come down from 'on high' to share the situation of those 'at the bottom' (like a king moving among his people in the clothes of a pauper in old folk tales, or like the descent of Christ among humankind in the Christian myth); or one might deliberately induce a humble attitude in oneself by (for example) reminding oneself that all human beings are small before the majesty of Nature, God or Society.

In its ancient usage, the term 'humiliation' carries the following message: 'Who do you think you are? You are less important than you think. You need to be brought down and put in your proper place.' The response of those at the receiving end might be either outraged resentment or humble gratitude. In other words, the term 'humiliation' includes both acceptance and rejection, by those due for humbling, of the 'message' that a process of humbling is necessary. The individual, group or society may, indeed, deliver the 'message' to itself; for example, following a process of religious conversion.

By contrast, in its modern usage, 'humiliation' means forced displacement or exclusion accompanied by outraged resentment but not humble gratitude. The rise of the modern, narrower meaning of the term 'humiliation' is closely related to the spread of the human rights code. This code emphasizes the norm of equality and is unsympathetic to the idea that 'lowliness', implying subordination, might be a good thing. However, feelings of equality among citizens might still coexist with feelings of humility before God. So, for example, we find the old use of humiliation still alive and well in 1863 in the United States.

In the middle of the American Civil War, President Abraham Lincoln declared a 'day of national humiliation, fasting and prayer'. His proclamation included the thought that since 'nations, like individuals, are subjected to punishments and chastisements in this world, may we not justly fear that the awful calamity of civil war, which now desolates the land, may be but a punishment inflicted upon us for our presumptuous sins, to the needful end of our national reformation as a whole People?' He added that Americans, 'Intoxicated with unbroken success', had 'become too self-sufficient to feel the necessity of redeeming and preserving grace, too proud to pray to the God that made us! It behooves us, then to humble ourselves before the offended Power, to confess our national sins, and to pray for clemency and forgiveness.'[1]

The modern meaning of 'humiliation' is much narrower. You can see this when you consider China's 'day of national humiliation', designated in 2005 as 18 September, the anniversary of the Japanese invasion of Manchuria in 1931.[2] In this case, national humiliation refers not to a period of humble collective self-examination but to an unacceptable and violent infringement of rights by another country.

From now on in this book the word 'humiliation' is used mainly in its modern sense.

What humiliates us?

We are susceptible to humiliation because we can be deprived of things we regard as essential to our being, things we find it unacceptable to be without. Having these things depends to a great extent on the complicity of other people, and that complicity can be withdrawn against our will. Of course, we are also vulnerable to our own bodily weaknesses and our exposure to the work of natural forces. However, the main point is we depend on people, things or processes outside or beyond our own desires and intentions. When those dependency relationships fail to provide support or confirmation of our basic sense of who we are and how we fit into society, the likely result is our humiliation.

The lack of one or more of the following characteristics is a powerful indicator that you are in a condition of humiliation:

Freedom The absence of intolerable or unreasonable constraints upon the exercise of agency; being able to do what you want the way you want to.

Agency The capacity to exercise one's will through action (including speech); making choices and putting them into effect.

Security Protection against the potentially humiliating consequences of circumstances that limit or reduce your capacity to exercise agency effectively enough to fulfil one's needs and wants.

Recognition Having your capacities, needs and wants, acknowledged and taken seriously by others who feel a desire and/or obligation to respond in a way that respects your identity and interests.

Lack of freedom

Amartya Sen shows that to overcome deprivation, destitution and oppression, a society must undergo development, strengthening its economy, political foundations and civil society in ways that make life more pleasant and satisfying for all. If a society is to develop, its people must acquire freedom. This is an instrumental necessity, not just a moral preference, a means as well as an end of development. The 'capabilities' of people to develop themselves and their societies are greatly enhanced when they acquire five things: '(1) political freedoms, (2) economic facilities, (3) social opportunities, (4) transparency guarantees and (5) protective security' (Sen 1999, 10). This approach is very influential in the Human Development Reports published by the United Nations.

Martha Nussbaum has developed her own list of necessary 'central human functional capabilities' based on cross-cultural comparative research. It includes being able to live a life of normal length; to have bodily health; to enjoy bodily integrity; to use the senses, imagination and thought; to develop a full range of emotions; to engage in practical reason; to develop affiliations with others under conditions of self-respect without humiliation; to show concern for other species and for the world of nature; to play; and to have control over one's environment, both politically and materially (Nussbaum 2000; Nussbaum 2001; Nussbaum 2006).

Sen and Nussbaum specify the 'contours' of freedom by indicating what people must be free to do and what rules and resources are needed to help them do it. In a similar spirit, David Held has produced a blueprint for 'cosmopolitan governance' within a democratic global order, identifying seven key 'sites of power', viz. the body, welfare, culture, civic associations, the economy, organized violence and legal institutions (Held 1995).[3] The capability approach identifies the roads that must be travelled but where is the dynamic human energy needed for those journeys going to come from?

Lack of agency

Michel Foucault exemplifies the energy required for effective agency. He wants to act as well as understand. However, his work expresses utter suspicion of all modern institutions. Their discursive practices are, he believes, intrinsically humiliating and cannot be significantly 'improved' (Foucault 1967; Foucault 1973; Foucault 1978; Smith 2001, 93–113).[4] The only creative action is to escape from them or reject them. In a more optimistic programme of agency, Mary Kaldor has outlined five versions of civil society, including their global implications, arguing that global civil society is properly concerned with ' "civilizing" or democratizing globalization, about the process through which groups, movements and individuals can demand a global rule of law, global justice and global empowerment' (Kaldor 2003, 12).[5]

For her part, Hannah Arendt finds that most modern human beings are quite unfit for life in a non-humiliating world. They are used to being told what to do and think. She reckons that Thomas Hobbes correctly predicted this situation in the mid-seventeenth century. Hobbes was able to outline the main psychological traits of the new type of inactive person who would fit well into modern society with its tyrannical body politic; that is, a 'poor meek fellow who has not even the right to rise against tyranny and who, far from striving for power, submits to any existing government and does not stir even when his best friend falls an innocent victim to an incomprehensible *raison d'état*' (Arendt 1976, 146).

Arendt is more optimistic than Foucault about the possibility of improving matters. She puts her faith in revolutionary moments of 'natality' during times of social breakdown. During such moments, some human beings are able to experience the excitement and utility of cooperating with each other in a spirit of solidarity and open dialogue, creating the germ of a better type of society.[6] For a while, Zygmunt Bauman had similar hopes, believing that the spirit Arendt looked for could be cultivated in the public sphere under the leadership of enlightened intellectuals. More recently, he has looked for flickering signs of a more basic human solidarity between the 'I' and the 'other'. In other words, pockets of non-humiliating human interaction may be created. One possible outcome is that in time they may expand and link up with each other.

Lack of security

Peter Singer locates the key locations of agency much higher up in the socio-political order than the individual citizen. He looks towards the future creation of an effective form of world government. He conceives global society as potentially 'a world community with its own directly elected legislature, perhaps slowly evolving along the lines of the European Union' (Singer 2004, 199).

Singer elaborates some ethical principles that should guide our actions in a globalized world. For example, we should not use more than our strictly calculated per capita share of the atmosphere's limited capacity to absorb our pollution.[7] A major element of his approach is the need to provide security for the weak, vulnerable and marginalized. Singer refers to the Canadian government's commission of intervention and state sovereignty whose report of 2001 was entitled *The Responsibility to Protect*.[8] He looks forward to a time when the United Nations is provided with the means to act as the ' "protector" of last resort' (149).

The work of Barrington Moore adds strength to this general position with his principle, set out in *Injustice* (1978), that members of a polity have a legitimate expectation that the government will exercise 'rational authority', meaning that it can be convincingly shown that decisions are based on the most effective use of available means to optimize the welfare of those citizens who are affected by those decisions.[9]

Lack of recognition

Barrington Moore is, along with Edward Thompson,[10] one of the more empirical scholars cited by Axel Honneth in his work on recognition (Honneth 1996). Drawing on Hegel, Mead, Winnicot and others, Honneth explores the interplay between what people need if they are to realize their potential as human beings and the way relations of mutual recognition develop within societies. He distinguishes between primary relationships,[11] legal relationships and relationships within the 'community of value': primary relationships (e.g. within the family) generate friendship and love which nurture *self-confidence*; legal relationships (e.g. within the polity) generate rights which sustain *self-respect*; and relationships within the 'community of value' (e.g. within the national or global society) generate 'solidarity' which supports the *self-esteem* associated with occupying a particular social position.

Honneth is right to emphasize the social and relational character of self-confidence, self-respect and self-esteem.[12] He is not alone in his focus on recognition.[13] Avishai Margalit (1996) argues that the institutions of a decent society should reject no-one from the human commonwealth: no members of society should have their humanity denied, their control over their own lives diminished, their cultural identity demeaned or their dignity, which is the external sign of their inner self-respect, undermined. In other words, societies should not humiliate their members.[14]

Jonathan Glover looks for ways to build an acceptable morality based on the actual psychological make-up of human beings as they are and, realistically, could be. Like Bauman, he is aware that the human capacity to empathize with others and to recognize their moral identity may be eroded under certain conditions. Bauman focuses on bureaucracy,[15] Glover more specifically on military combat and the tug of 'tribalism' (Glover 2001, 133) with its taste for revenge. His message is that we should use intellect and imagination to avoid being trapped by false beliefs and a climate of fear.

Richard Sennett develops related themes, arguing that 'inequalities of class and race clearly make it difficult for people to treat one another with respect'. He looks at how 'the strength of self... diminishes others, the ill fit between self-confidence and the regard of others' and the way 'social forces shape such personal experiences' (Sennett 2004, 46–7).

Ambiguities, conflicts, deceptions

This list contains ambiguities and potential inner conflicts. It also allows for some ideological sleight of hand. It is worth noting that:

- people who enjoy a state of *freedom* do not necessarily possess the resources, skills and knowledge needed to exercise *agency* in ways that advance their interests or sustain a satisfying sense of identity – free people may lack what they need to escape poverty, for example;
- it is difficult to combine high degrees of *security* with high degrees of *freedom*, especially when security is enacted through extensive surveillance, regulation and control – more security may mean less freedom, more freedom may mean less security; and
- those who seek *recognition* for themselves may be keen to deny it to others.

Those ambiguities, conflicts and potential deceptions can be confronted as long as they are recognized. They emerge in different forms in the honour code and the human rights code as described in the previous chapter.

Those who are successful in terms of the honour code demonstrate their own capacity to exercise agency, enjoy freedom, demand recognition from others and forcefully protect their own interests. They do this by *weakening the capacity of others* (their enemies and victims) to do the same. The honourable victors, the glorious 'top dogs' may use their discretion to recognize the interests of some of those they have defeated, whether by giving some of them freedom or by investing them with the resources (such as money, land and weapons) that are needed to exercise a limited amount of agency. They may decide to give special protection to those they favour. They may, however, choose not to do these things.

The lurking shadow of the honour code in the midst of human-rights societies helps to explain, for example:

- how the strength of self may diminish others (Sennett 1999);
- how the force of tribalism raises its head in battle situations (Glover 2001);
- how the urge to humiliate may persist in the would-be decent society (Margalit 1996); and
- how societies which develop legal rights fostering universal self-respect may have socio-political orders within which specific groups, roles or occupations are systematically demeaned in the mass media and popular culture (Honneth 1996).

Experiencing the unacceptable

As we have seen, humiliation happens when human essentials such as agency, freedom, security and recognition are wrenched away. Those at the receiving end find themselves rudely displaced from where they think they ought to be. They are brutally shown, by words, actions or events, that they cannot be who they think they are. Humiliation is the experience of being unfairly, unreasonably and unwillingly pushed down, held down, held back or pushed out.[16] This forced displacement or exclusion is normally followed by anger or resentment on the part of the victim, which needs to be contained, defused, released or recycled in some way. That resentment provides a deep reservoir of energy which political and military leaders may try to use for their purposes. That is what makes 'humiliation' much more explosive than 'mere' exploitation, domination or alienation.

But, first, what is 'experiencing' humiliation? By 'experiencing' I mean interpreting perceptions that occur within social relationships. This process is influenced by particular ways of understanding and reflection built into specific cultures and languages.[17] Since cultures differ, so do the particular ways in which the experience of humiliation is triggered, recognized and undergone. However, in every case, those who suffer humiliation have their own sense, albeit complex and often ambiguous, of the following:

- who they are;
- what is happening to them;
- who or what is debasing them; and
- how this affects their own or their group's or society's capacity to live their lives in the way they are used to, the way they desire, value and expect.

Humiliation is a process that occurs within social relationships, not simply a 'feeling' that 'happens' within the body and mind. On the one hand, an act or event is humiliating insofar as it is perceived and interpreted as such by specific persons or groups. On the other, this experience of humiliation is an event and a condition within a network of social relationships and affects how those relationships develop.

A common reaction to humiliation, from the victim's point of view, or that of sympathetic onlookers, is to make comments such as 'that's outrageous', 'we can't stand for that', 'how impossible' or 'that is going too far'. The message is basically that the thing being done is 'unacceptable'. In practice, people often have to acquiesce in the unacceptable but their intense unwillingness to do so is a powerful indicator that something humiliating has occurred.

'Unacceptable' here means more than one thing. First, an act may be regarded as unacceptable if those judging it believe that it infringes the society's code of justice. For example, it may be regarded as a denial of citizenship or universal human rights. However, what are the implications if neither those who perform the act, nor those who endure it, nor, indeed, those who witness it believe in citizenship or universal human rights? Suppose the act occurs in a place where there is no shared code of law or justice to which anyone can appeal with the confidence that others will understand or recognize it?

In these circumstances, an act can still be experienced as humiliating by the victims, a fact that can be understood by anyone able to empathize with their perspective. The act is humiliating if it forcefully overrides and contradicts the claim that particular individuals, groups or societies are making about who they are and where and how they fit in. For example, it is humiliating when a powerful incoming group forcefully dismisses the assumption of an indigenous people that it rightfully occupies a certain position, (such as a tribal existence on the North American plains), which gives it a particular identity and specific interests.

In this situation, it is impossible for those concerned (the 'victims') both to accept the viewpoint of those wishing to sweep them aside and, at the same time, to retain their existing identity, enmeshed as it is with a specific way of life. So, 'unacceptable' has two possible meanings:

- impossible to reconcile with whatever overarching code governs the social relationships within which the humiliating act or event occurs; and/or
- impossible to reconcile with the humiliated party's own sense of their identity, interests and worth.

Matters become especially complicated when the overarching code in a society or global region is focused on citizenship and human rights but specific groups have their own version of the honour code which conflicts with this in important respects. In such cases, it is both necessary – and imaginatively difficult – for those adhering to the overarching code to recognize that they may be dealing with a group that is not only, as they see it, 'in the wrong' but also feeling humiliated by the efforts of 'outsiders' to override their particular approach. However, it is rarely a straightforward case of, for example, the honour code versus the human rights code. Most communities work with a mixture of both. The very claim to have your particular version of the honour code respected by others is an appeal to the universalistic human rights code.

Conquest, relegation, exclusion

We can distinguish between three types of humiliation (see box 3.1). One is conquest humiliation. This happens when a person, group, institution or society, having been used to a high degree of relative autonomy (in ordinary language, freedom), is overwhelmed by another person, group, institution or society. The conquered party is forced into subordination. It is, so to speak, held down. A hierarchy is formed with the conqueror at the top. This happens when, for example, a military invasion is successful, when a feudal lord makes those he defeats into his vassals, or when captives are turned into slaves.[18]

It is exceedingly unpleasant to be on the receiving end of such treatment. According to Elias Canetti, each command a ruler gives is bound to cause deep resentment: 'Every command leaves a painful sting in the person who is forced to carry it out' (Canetti 1973, 67). This becomes 'a hard crystal of resentment' (360) that can be

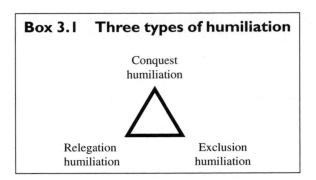

overcome only by reversing the power situation. In other words, the urge to revolt, to resist humiliation, is endemic within all hierarchies.[19] Humiliation is, in fact, a profound source of social energy: 'What spurs men on to achievement is the deep urge to be rid of the commands one laid upon them' (355).

Another variant of conquest humiliation is the conquest of the individual by the group. For example, in many societies new recruits into the armed services and the police are put through humiliating experiences, often ritualized, which tell the newcomer: 'You will learn to think our way, you will identify strongly with this group, or you will suffer for it.'

The anthropologist Victor Turner describes tribal societies in which, every now and again, the sense of hierarchy is temporarily weakened so that the feeling of belonging to a united group can be strengthened (Turner 1969). When the 'grid' of high and low statuses is relaxed, it allows all members of the tribe to feel totally immersed in the encompassing group and to share a sense of solidarity with all other members of the community. These are moments of liminality[20] during which, for example, rites of passage take place, notably the preparation for office of a new chief. During these rituals, the chief-to-be (shrewdly) adopts an attitude of great humility while being subjected to intense criticism and even abuse.[21]

A second type is relegation humiliation. This happens when an individual, group, institution or society is forced into a lower position within an existing hierarchy against their will and in a way that conflicts with their own perception of their social identity and interests. It is intrinsic to the experience of humiliation that the relegation should be perceived as 'unacceptable' although in some cases the 'victims' may eventually find themselves accepting, or at least, acquiescing, in it. Perhaps the most recent geo-politically significant example of relegation humiliation has been the toppling of the European empires, whose old rulers have been forced to accept the global lordship of the United States. At their height, these empires were themselves responsible for imposing relegation humiliation on kings, princes and chiefs throughout the world. Like conquest humiliation, relegation humiliation produces intense resentment.[22]

A third type is exclusion humiliation.[23] In this case, those at the receiving end are forcefully excluded or ejected from membership within the specific groups, hierarchies or networks to which they believed they had a right to belong. Examples include the excommunication of heretics by the Church; the ejection of religious and ethnic minority groups from specific territories; the expulsion from a foreign embassy of a diplomat suspected of espionage and declared 'persona non grata'; and campaigns to exclude or eliminate pariah groups such as German Jews (under Hitler) and the Russian kulaks or rich peasants (under Stalin).

The experience of being made an excluded outsider may, ironically, be a majority experience. According to Mary Douglas in *Natural Symbols* (1970), this condition is especially likely to arise in situations of strong grid but weak group. This category includes not only 'Big Man' societies in Melanesia[24] but also modern urban-industrial societies in which 'men see the world as a morally neutral, technical system which is lying there for themselves to exploit with their special gifts' (160).[25] In this modern, highly competitive world, the winner takes all. Losers get very little. As Douglas puts it, the 'sense of being excluded, disregarded, of being made to feel of no value is a regular experience in the system of strong grid' (166).[26]

Finally, there is reinforcement humiliation. This is a kind of shadow of the three types of humiliation just described. Reinforcement humiliation occurs when insulting behaviour is enacted towards those who have been humiliated, reminding them of their degraded status in the eyes of others. This might include the use of demeaning stereotypical terms to describe particular races, nations or religions or in relation to such groups as women or the elderly. Other examples include the delivery of kicks and blows to those in inferior positions such as slaves and servants; the deliberate management of body language to convey disgust towards those held to be inferior or untouchable; and the wilful transgression of personal space as an expression of blatant disrespect for those who are 'below' or 'outside'.

Escape, acceptance and rejection

Humiliation may totally destroy those who experience it. However, normally it does not completely eliminate agency, the capacity to respond. But what response is best?

One of the most famous depictions of exclusion humiliation occurs in John Milton's epic poem *Paradise Lost*, first published in 1667 with a revised edition following in 1674 (Milton 2004). The story begins with the forced removal of Satan and his followers from Heaven. After describing this spectacular event, Milton takes us into Pandemonium, the fallen angels' debating chamber, where the Devil and his lieutenants are discussing what to do following their recent humiliation at the hands of the Almighty. In the second book, Moloch recommends that the fallen angels *reject* their fate and fight back because he thinks that nothing could be worse than staying in Hell, condemned to anguish after their blissful existence in Heaven. Belial takes the opposite point of view. Fighting back will indeed make things worse. Far better to *accept* the way things are since their fate has been determined. He is an optimist and hopes that in time God may become less angry, lose interest in them and stop punishing them. Beelzebub offers another response. In effect, he says: don't bother either accepting or rejecting the humiliating circumstances into which God has thrown us; instead, we should make an *escape* from Hell and find a new empire to conquer, not back in Heaven but on the still unspoiled territory of Earth where a new species called 'Man' has been installed.

So, here are three potential responses to the challenge of humiliation: rejection (Moloch), acceptance (Belial) and escape (Beelzebub). Just for the record, Satan backed the strategy of escape.[27]

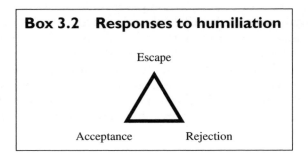

Box 3.2 Responses to humiliation

Escape

Acceptance   Rejection

Escape

The first possible response is *attempted escape* from the humiliating situation. Escapees may experience a feeling of *rebirth* in the process but at the same time they are likely to feel *wounded* and *fearful* as a result of the humiliation they have suffered in the past. The attempt to escape, and its aftermath, may be successful in some cases. In other words, the wounded but 'reborn' victims of humiliation may succeed in establishing a protected special place of their own. Having done this, they may succeed in building trust within the relationships upon which they depend for a secure, peaceful, non-humiliated and non-humiliating existence. But that is a very difficult challenge.

The danger is that the wounded but reborn victims of humiliation, having made their escape, will continue to have high levels of fear. They may be inclined to exaggerate the dangers lurking in their environment, becoming very 'jumpy' and looking for excuses to take aggressive action against the objects of their fear. They may even make pre-emptive attacks to remove the perceived danger. The problem is that the victims of these attacks are likely to complain and strike back. In fact, aggressive action of this kind typically leads to embarrassing entanglements. If the aggressors manage to extricate themselves, they may withdraw once more into their protected special place until rising fear levels stimulate another round of this *fear cycle* during which those who are trying to escape humiliation impose it on others.

Acceptance

The second possible response is *attempted acceptance* of the humiliating acts within the relationship while trying to interpret them as non-humiliating. A common way to do this is by identifying with the values of the humiliating party. For example, by adopting the role of *shamed penitent* the role of *victim* might be avoided. In such a case, penitents try to turn humiliation into shame by acknowledging responsibility for what has happened to them. They say, in effect: 'We got above ourselves and deserved to be taught a lesson, but now please accept us once more, even though we realize our status is bound to be a diminished one from now on.' In this case the preferred outcome, as far as the victims of the humiliation are concerned, is reintegration into the group or hierarchy. They also want those who were responsible for their humiliation to give them support in improving their behaviour, attitudes and understanding.

However, suppose the tormentors think their victims are intrinsically degraded? In such a case the victims' continuing submissiveness and self-blame will simply confirm the abusers' perception of the victims' unworthiness. The latter's claim to humane treatment will be ignored. The likely result is a *victimization cycle* perpetuating humiliation.

Rejection

The third possible response is *attempted rejection* of the humiliating acts and, possibly, also of the person, group, institution or society that has carried them out. The object in this case is to diminish the impact of the humiliation on the intended victims. Rejection may take the form of passive or active *resistance* and/or the search for a satisfying *revenge*. A successful strategy of resistance would be one in which the humiliated party deploys its resources as effectively as possible in a carefully directed and controlled effort to do two things. The first is to limit the destruction produced by humiliation. The second is to conserve and nurture its capacity to act in an autonomous and effective way in pursuit of its objectives.

In the case of the rejection response to humiliation, a revenge cycle might be stimulated. Such cycles are perpetuated when at least one party to the humiliating relationship rejects the other's worthiness, their right to occupy the place they do and even, in some cases, their right to exist. Acts of retaliation continue because each side believes their own attacks are justified while those of the other side are outrageous and unjustified.

The changing standards of humiliation

In 1550, as for centuries before, successful rulers were feared, recognized and admired for their capacity to humiliate those around them, at home and abroad. This capacity was exercised in various ways, for example through regular public executions. These signs of greatness were expected and relished. At a lower social level, honourable masters beat their servants and inflicted verbal insults upon them as a matter of course.

Tribal societies, 'divinely appointed' monarchies, absolutist empires and arrogant aristocracies all developed strong codes of honour. Honour in such contexts means independence, mastery[28] and successful performance, all of which should command recognition, respect and approval on the part of superiors, equals and subordinates alike. The honourable person, family or group is able to fill their proper place in society with style, employing their own resources. They renew and expand these resources through their confidence, strength, initiative and courage. These qualities are proven in action by victory and conquest in conflict, especially in battle.[29]

The basic honour code is centuries old and is still widespread, though with local variations. It justifies slavery, massacre, forced marriage and domestic servitude for women. The prizes and conquests most valued within this code are other people and their possessions, including their land, residences and livestock. Honour is enhanced in several ways: by destroying other people and their possessions, or by taking those possessions and making their previous owners bow down to you, by making others suffer pain and degradation, or by making them flee from you in terror.

Virtuoso performances in the field of honour, for example in feuds, duels and military campaigns, are almost certainly going to bring humiliation for the losers. Consider, for example, how the Ottoman army treated Marcantonio Bragadino, Governor of Famagusta in Cyprus when this city fell after a long siege in 1571:

> 'Bragadino's officers and staff were beheaded in front of him, so that a rivulet of blood flowed across the hard dry ground and washed over his feet. Then he was ceremonially disfigured, with his nose and ears hacked off like a common criminal . . . After prayers on Friday 17 August the Ottoman army gathered on the siege works that surrounded the city. Bragadino was brought before them . . . forced to his hands and knees, and a mule's harness was put on his back, with a bridle and bit in his mouth. Two heavy baskets filled with earth were loaded on to the harness, so that he bent under their weight . . . Throughout the morning he was led back and forth in front of the troops, in and out among the tents, whipped forward and abused by the mass of the soldiers. Each time he passed the Ottoman commander's tent, he was forced to prostrate himself and eat a handful of the dusty soil . . . [Later, he] was hauled to the topmast of a galley, in front of all his former troops, now galley slaves . . . [and then] taken to the marketplace and tied to a whipping frame where all the people of Famagusta could witness his humiliation.

Let us skip the gory details of his skin being hacked off while he was still alive. The skin was later stuffed with straw, paraded on

Bragadino's horse through Famagusta, left hanging on the yardarm for several weeks, and finally put on show in the galley slaves' prison in Constantinople 'as a mute warning to any who thought to resist or rebel' (Wheatcroft 2004, 22).

The audience of galley slaves, Bragadino's former soldiers, had all suffered the common fate of war captives in honour societies: this was to be consigned to a lesser category of subjugated humanity, forced into back-breaking labour. Miguel Cervantes, author of *Don Quixote* (1605), who fought on the winning side at the Battle of Lepanto soon after the ending of the siege of Famagusta, had personal experience of being a galley slave. Following the Christian success at Lepanto, sweet revenge for Bragadino's humiliation, equally gruesome and dramatic, was taken upon the unfortunate losers.[30]

The status of humiliation has changed profoundly since those days. A new standard has arisen centred on the ideas of human rights and universal citizenship, given wide publicity by the American Revolution of 1776 and the French Revolution of 1789. Cruel and aggressive acts that used to be seen as 'honourable' are now widely seen as 'abusive'. By 1950 many national governments were providing their people with the benefits of the welfare state. In other words, they were setting themselves the task of guaranteeing all their citizens legal, political and social rights intended to *prevent* them suffering a wide range of humiliating circumstances caused by poverty and ignorance.

According to this new standard, the humbling of others, bringing them back to a 'proper' view of themselves, is permitted in appropriate circumstances using appropriate methods, but not humiliation, which involves a degradation of humanity. This represents a radical change in relation to the honour code. Honour culture thinks vertically. It 'wants' hierarchy. When tribes or dynasties are locked in feuds, each of them is struggling to be top dog and push rivals down. If a king emerges and forces his old 'peers' to accept subordinate positions, members of the 'pacified' aristocracy still hanker for the field of honour. They battle with each other constantly, in jousts and duels, each aiming to put themselves higher up the pecking order and to force their opponents down or even out.[31]

By contrast, the human rights code thinks horizontally. It 'wants' equality. It assumes that *every* competent and rational human being equally deserves to belong to a society organized in such a way that they are all able to exhibit independence, competence and successful performance. That means making sure all such citizens get the knowledge, skills and material resources they need. It also means having a powerful agency such as the state to ensure that each citizen is treated equally in these matters, that each is accorded equal respect.

The honour code is alive and well

On the face of it, the spread of the human rights code and citizenship culture seems like an effective way of abolishing humiliation. But the strong residual influence of honour culture has, historically, in real political situations, been the force dictating 'common sense' answers to the question of who is 'competent and rational' and therefore entitled to full citizenship in practice.

What about women? What about slaves and ex-slaves? What about people without any property to speak of, men and women routinely described as 'losers' in the West? What about colonial subjects? What about those on the losing side in political or military conflicts? In other words, what about members of those categories that are traditionally the victims of humiliation in honour societies?

When the introduction and expansion of citizenship enters the political agenda, it is tempting for those with vested interests in the old honour system to treat groups that have been systematically humiliated in the 'old days' as inadequate, inferior, degraded, and, therefore, unfit for citizenship. So, in many cases, women, slaves or ex-slaves, people without property, and colonial subjects and ex-colonial subjects are given inferior versions of citizenship or denied any substantial rights. Furthermore, the idea of an 'official parliamentary opposition' is slow to develop in many 'democratic' one-party states with strong traditions of tribal, ethnic or dynastic honour. After all, why give rewards (in other words, political 'rights') to humiliated losers?

What happens when those who control the state in societies with a strong tradition of honour decide to introduce citizenship or broaden its scope? There is intense opposition, as happened, for example, in the national states of Europe, North America and Latin America during the nineteenth century, and in many parts of the world during the twentieth century. Major internal conflicts developed on these issues. The American Civil War was a major example. These conflicts continue and affect many people's lives today.

The promise of human rights very often travels faster and further than the actual implementation of citizenship. This has a paradoxical consequence. As people within an honour society hear about the promise of potential emancipation, this has the effect of intensifying their experience of humiliation. The blows do not become harder, but they do become less acceptable.

However, in the first few years of the twenty-first century, the new standard has not wiped away the old. They live together, side by side: the old honour code, which recognizes the validity of humiliating others as a way of establishing personal, social and political credibility, and the new human rights code, which teaches that all people should expect to be able to live a decent life and not become victims of events and circumstances that can be avoided or alleviated.

The most dramatic recent example of the rough cohabitation between the two codes is that of Iraq after the American invasion in 2003. On the one hand, there were many speeches about freedom and the liberating impact of the free market, as well as frantic efforts to establish a new constitution based on the principles of parliamentary democracy. On the other, local tribal, ethnic and religious groups engaged in bloody duels with each other according to the age-old practices of the honour code.

Iraq is far from alone in this intertwining of the two codes. Almost any western or, indeed, non-Western, society will illustrate the case. Consider the following:

1 The tabloid media often belittle well-known personalities in politics, sport and entertainment. Teachers, social workers and members of other professions can be berated for 'getting above themselves'. Hostility can be fomented against various groups depicted as 'outsiders' such as 'asylum seekers'. All these are forms of inflicting humiliation according to the customs of the honour code.

2 The rhetoric of sport encourages supporters to take delight in 'slaughtering' their rivals.

3 Some religious creeds have popular leaders who emphasize the 'wrath of God' and encourage their followers to bring their enemies low on God's behalf.

4 Capital punishment has been retained in the United States, sometimes taking the form of semi-public execution when interested guests (such as relatives of murder victims) are allowed to sit in an adjacent room and watch.

5 States continue to treat 'enemies' in a way that bears comparison with how the Ottoman army dealt with Bragadino. It is true that they no longer turn them into straw-stuffed dummies. However, instead they create insulting stereotypes of their opponents in the popular press.

To sum up, the honour code and the human rights code are the two main frameworks that people use to make sense of what life does to them. At present the two codes are both vigorous and coexist in various forms of pragmatic compromise. The kind of compromise that we make between them will be crucial for whether or not the world is worth living in during the twenty-first century.

*   *   *

In this chapter, we have: distinguished between the ancient and modern meanings of humiliation; investigated the part played by the lack of freedom, agency, security and recognition; considered how humiliation is experienced by its victims; contrasted three forms of humiliation (conquest, relegation and exclusion); looked at three forms of response (escape, acceptance and rejection); and seen the implications of the honour and human rights codes for our understanding of humiliation.

4

Frames of Globalization

Now we come to the third strand in the triple helix. This is where we begin to explore how globalization can produce intense feelings of being humiliated.

Globalization as empire, market and cosmopolis

Over the past four centuries there have been profound changes within the process of globalization.[1] By 1550 European imperialism was well established and vigorously expanding. The Spanish and Portuguese empires were not 'mere' commercial enterprises. Imperial possessions were gorgeous trophies, visibly demonstrating the might and honour of the monarchs in whose names they were carried out. They also glorified the generals who did the bloody work of seizing new territories and defending those already acquired. Such men, if not already noble, were in search of titles and estates.

The European empires soon stretched across Asia, America and Africa, as well as across Europe itself. They were run in an absolutist manner, just as aristocracies managed their landed estates at home. The imperial masters asserted complete control over lands and resources, including indigenous populations whom they considered so inferior that they were barely regarded as human. As the cliché has it, trade followed the flag. By the eighteenth century large businesses such as the East India Company had gained enormous influence.[2] However, the market had to operate within the strict boundaries set by rigid social hierarchies and dictatorial political authority.

By 1950 several of the empires had collapsed and others were on their last legs. In the end, the empires could not contain conflicts between two opposing principles: the absolutism of the landed ruling class, including the monarchy and military leadership; and the ideas of citizenship and people's rights. By the early twentieth century, the latter were becoming increasingly influential in the 'headquarter societies' of the empires – in France, Britain, Austria, Russia, Turkey and so on.

These 'modern' ideas made ordinary soldiers in the imperialist armies increasingly discontented with their own officers. Meanwhile, subject peoples began to organize defence of their own rights as 'imprisoned' or 'unborn' nations. They began to feel not just 'put down', the common experience of losers in the battle for precedence under the old honour regime, but also wrongly 'excluded' from full membership of the human race. They wanted to be liberated and emancipated.

For these reasons, *imperialism was the first great global generator of humiliation*. The internal coherence of the empires was weakened by the political fall-out from such feelings, deliberately heightened by 'consciousness-raising' political orators who called for protests, revolts and boycotts. The empires were left weakened, much less able to resist the external pressures imposed by war.

As European imperialism declined in strength during the second half of the twentieth century, the market values expressed in the World Trade Center were asserted more aggressively. This coincided with the global rise of the United States. *The global marketplace became the second great generator of humiliation.* Critics have targeted international big business and the 'Washington Consensus' as a cause of victimization and belittlement for national governments, workers and consumers throughout the world. The accusation is that the big multinational corporations dictate their own terms to local 'partners' in resource-rich but credit-poor countries in Asia, Africa and Latin America. Critics assert that business takes what it wants, accepts little responsibility for the long-term social effects of its intrusion, and threatens to leave if there is any trouble.

Not everyone agrees with this assessment. International business and finance are defended strongly, as was imperialism in the days of the British Raj. Advocates of an ever-expanding global market praise it as the primary agent of liberation. To parody the 'official' view: freedom and openness bring the market and the market brings yet more freedom and openness. Here, for example, is Mike Moore,[3] speaking as Director-General of the World Trade Organization:

Globalization isn't a new concept. It's been around since before Britain ruled the waves and waived the rules. What is new is the extent to which information flows have exploded. You all know this, because you now have to deal with the consequences for your businesses not just quarterly or annually, but daily, hourly and sometimes by the minute. The world is a much smaller, and vastly more transparent and democratic place, than when Tulip futures peaked in Amsterdam in the 17th century.[4]

However, freedom is more complicated than that. It is not just a question of switching from colonial subjection to consumer sovereignty. This takes us to *the third global generator of humiliation: the human costs of living with the uncertainties and ambiguities imposed by the 'in between' cosmopolitan condition.* By 'cosmopolitan,' I mean a situation in which many different cultures, religions, ethnicities or nationalities share the same social space without any settled hierarchy or set of boundaries between them. None of them is clearly 'best' or rules the others.

Freedom from colonial subjection imposed a heavy emotional and psychological price upon those who were freed. In the 'old days' of imperial rule, when the indigenous population faced repression on a daily basis at the hands of uniformed officers representing the colonial powers, life had a refreshing clarity: the colonial subjects were oppressed and they demanded their freedom. Everybody knew who they were and what they wanted.

As more people were freed from imperialist oppression they came to experience with much greater intensity the tensions and difficulties of a 'liberated' cosmopolitan existence in which values and identities are often contradictory and ambiguous. More specifically, they found that in the course of the long struggle against their oppressor, 'modern' ideas and practices had infiltrated into the colonized society, challenging the old ways.

Once they had got rid of their imperialist oppressor, the liberators turned round to discover that their old way of life had also gone. When both the oppressor and the object you were defending have been lost, it is difficult for people to achieve a coherent sense of self or to live in a morally satisfying way. This situation may be experienced as a humiliating displacement.[5]

This discussion has an interesting twist. *Imperialism has made a comeback*, although its latest beneficiaries, the Americans, are ambivalent about it. The United States has a strong anti-imperialist heritage: having played a major part in preventing Britain and France from re-establishing their empires after 1945, the leaders of the

United States also attacked and ridiculed the Suez invasion in 1956. However, their successors in the White House and the Pentagon went on to use the military methods of the old imperialists, for example during the late 1960s and early 1970s in Vietnam, the former stamping ground of the French colonial masters, and, more recently, twice, in Iraq, where the British flag used to fly. The essence of imperialism is the systematic use of force to make others do want you want them to do. You end up treating those you push around as inferior, whatever your ideological excuses or moral motivations.

The US-Israel alliance and two wars in Iraq have been precious gifts to the desperate elements among intellectually and morally tormented cosmopolitans, especially in the Middle East.[6] These examples of 'imperialism' have allowed those attacking the West to activate hostilities cultivated since World War I and before. The return to tradition has given humiliated cosmopolitans a way of restoring their fractured sense of self. Extremist forms of fanatical religion have provided ideological and emotional encouragement, which has persuaded some to follow the road to a violent end.

*   *   *

In this chapter, we have: identified three frames of globalization – the imperial impulse, the logic of the market and the cosmopolitan condition; and noticed that although the relegation of Europe in global politics seemed to be the end of empires, imperialism made a comeback during and after the Cold War, providing new political opportunities for victims of the cosmopolitan condition.

The next part of the book explores this chapter's themes in much greater depth. We are at a point of transition in the argument. So far we have travelled around the triple helix in one direction: *codes of modernity (honour/human rights) → modes of humiliation → frames of globalization*. During the rest of the book the same journey is repeated in reverse: *frames of globalization → modes of humiliation → codes of modernity (honour/human rights)*. We begin with an investigation of the propensity of globalization to generate humiliating situations and experiences.

5

The Imperial Impulse

The imperial impulse means being determined to be top dog and exercise absolute command and control from the top of a socio-political hierarchy. It means making it clear to everybody that you intend to get your way. It means being prepared to humiliate others and having the capacity to do so.

President Bush and King Hammurabi

President George W. Bush addressed the American nation and the world shortly before the invasion of Iraq in March 2003:[1]

> [The] only way to reduce the harm and duration of war is to apply the full force and might of our military, and we are prepared to do so. If Saddam Hussein attempts to cling to power, he will remain a deadly foe until the end. . . . Should enemies strike our country, they would be attempting to shift our attention with panic and weaken our morale with fear. In this, they would fail. No act of theirs can alter the course or shake the resolve of this country. We are a peaceful people – yet we're not a fragile people, and we will not be intimidated by thugs and killers. If our enemies dare to strike us, they and all who have aided them, will face fearful consequences . . .
>
> As we enforce the just demands of the world, we will also honor the deepest commitments of our country. Unlike Saddam Hussein, we believe the Iraqi people are deserving and capable of human liberty, and when the dictator has departed, they can set an example to all the

Middle East of a vital and peaceful and self-governing nation . . . Good night, and may God continue to bless America.

President Bush is saying to his enemies: I can humiliate you. He is standing in a long tradition. Since we are speaking of Iraq (ancient Mesopotamia), let us also listen to the words of Hammurabi, who once ruled most of Mesopotamia. These words were written approximately four thousand years ago, around 1770 BCE:

Hammurabi, the protecting king am I . . .
With the mighty weapons which Zamama and Ishtar entrusted to me,
with the keen vision with which Ea endowed me,
with the wisdom that Marduk gave me,
I have uprooted the enemy above and below,
subdued the earth,
brought prosperity to the land,
guaranteed security to the inhabitants in their homes;
a disturber was not permitted.

The great gods have called me,
I am the salvation-bearing shepherd, whose staff is straight,
the good shadow that is spread over my city;
on my breast I cherish the inhabitants of the land of Sumer and Akkad;
in my shelter I have let them repose in peace;
in my deep wisdom have enclosed them.
That the strong might not injure the weak, in order to protect the widows and orphans.

Hammurabi anchors himself between Heaven and Earth. He borrows god-like power and authority from above, from such figures as Marduk, the great Babylonian divinity. At the same time, he reminds his people that he, Hammurabi, makes their lives more peaceful and secure. The ruler's message is:

• the gods have endowed me with benefits;
• I, in turn, endow the Babylonian people;
• I am and should be your ruler;
• you shall and should obey me.

Compare Hammurabi and Bush. The first claims to express the strength and wisdom of the god Marduk, who has chosen Hammurabi to represent his will. The second claims (in using the word 'we') to express the strength and wisdom of the American people, who have chosen the president to represent their will.

At the heart of Bush's speech is Hammurabi's own assertive message:

- I can kill you but I will protect you if you obey my rules and commands;
- I am wise, omnipotent and all-seeing;
- I shall bring justice to those who deserve it and punish evil enemies.

In the United States, the part played by the god Marduk has been taken over by another god, Demos – in other words, by the American people. When God blesses America, he is asking and allowing the American people to do his work in the wider world through their agent, the American state.

The American public judges its politicians and, if they do not pass the test, it throws them out. In fact, it is more complicated than that because the mass media play a huge role in shaping public opinion. This is a crucial function. In ancient Mesopotamia, the priests of Marduk interpret the god's will. In modern America, the servants of Murdoch interpret the will of Demos.[2] In Hammurabi's time, a king who stayed close to the priesthood, satisfying its wishes or dominating it by charisma, bribery or fear, could hope to have great influence on the voice of the god, making it say the right thing. In modern times, the dynamics of the relationship between the state and the 'priesthood', in other words the mass media, remain crucial.

Terror and care

The image of the shepherd used by Hammurabi is significant. Empires were often made or conquered by leaders of nomadic tribes.[3] These typically bred horses or camels and herded sheep or goats. It was shepherds within such a tribe who supposedly brought up the legendary figures of Romulus and Remus, mythical founders of Rome.

Like the state, shepherds administered both care and terror: while looking after their flocks, they could repel potential aggressors. Herdsmen were armed and war-like, ready to defend their animals and themselves against potential predators. The New Testament angel who disturbed the shepherds watching their flocks by night was lucky not to have his wings torn off.

Long before the invention (or 'discovery') of human rights, rulers boasted about their capacity to humiliate others, including their subjects, and about their capacity to protect themselves and their subjects from humiliation. In the first respect, the state is like Leviathan, the monstrous sea-beast in the Old Testament, 'king of all the children of pride' (Job 41: 34; see also Hobbes 1996, 284). Prouder and more powerful than any of its subjects, the state inspires terror in the human beings it controls. In the second, the state applies the practical lesson that populations are easier to manage if the humiliations they impose are balanced by tangible benefits. Not just peace and order but also some opportunity to fulfil normal human desires such as the wish for material comfort. Hammarabi reminded his subjects that he had not just 'guaranteed security to the inhabitants in their homes', but also 'brought prosperity to the land'.

Hierarchy and humiliation

There was a time when the question of how rulers and subjects should deal with each other was not on anybody's agenda. For over 90 per cent of human history, men and women lived in scattered hunter-gatherer bands. Every adult in such a band depended on all the others. There were no rulers except insofar as the whole group ruled all its members.[4]

In such societies, humiliation was something groups sometimes imposed on individuals, perhaps by killing or excluding them. It may have been, so to speak, a 'nuclear' option, deployed only when routine shaming of 'offensive' people failed to bring them back into line.[5] However, as more powerful technologies developed, based on the use of irrigation, digging sticks, ploughs, wheels and draught animals, human groups began to produce a material surplus. This increased the possibilities for specialization, trade between groups and the development of socio-political hierarchies.

Societies gradually became fixed in specific territories and families found themselves tied to particular plots of land and, in many cases, to particular masters. Farming meant a loss of freedom. Then humiliation became routine, as normal as stormy weather. Some hunter-gathering bands turned into nomadic tribes. These continued a wandering life with vast herds of animals. Farming and herding increased the amount of food that a given number of people could grow and rear. Two things changed: the surplus, the amount left over when everyone had been fed enough to survive, increased;[6] and this surplus could be stored more easily, for example as grain in store-houses or on the hoof as herds of livestock.

A surplus could be fought over. In tribal societies, this took the form of stealing animals. As a result there was continual feuding, each revenge attack leading to another in the opposite direction, with no single tribe or dynasty being left permanently better off or in charge. However, when producers were shackled to the soil, unable to run away easily, ambitious power-mongers started to get substantial results. They could get control of the surplus, use it to build up their own strength, and use that strength to get their own way within society.

Farming brought with it social hierarchy, through which the rich and powerful dominated the poor and weak. Hierarchy, in turn, helped to spread agriculture, forcing many reluctant hunter-gatherers or nomadic tribespeople to take part, often as serfs or slaves. Who would volunteer to fill the lowest places within such unequal regimes? Social hierarchies often had to be imposed by force.

Humiliation and hierarchy are closely linked. The historian and philosopher Ibn Khaldūn[7] criticized the humiliation that hierarchy brings into societies where everyone had previously enjoyed the solidarity of tribal brothers sharing equal conditions. Writing in the fourteenth century, Ibn Khaldūn cited many instances of how the strong group feeling that holds together a dynasty and its tribal followers gradually collapses as the central power gets more luxurious, arrogant and corrupt. For example:

> When the natural luxury of royal authority makes its appearance, and when the people who share in the group feeling of the dynasty are humiliated, the first to be humiliated are the members of the ruler's family and his relatives who share with him in the royal name. They are much more humiliated than anyone else. . . . They become sick at heart when they see the ruler firmly established in royal authority. His envy of them changes to fear for his royal authority. Therefore he starts to kill and humiliate them and to deprive them of the prosperity and luxury to which they had in large measure become accustomed. (Khaldūn 1969, 246)

In Ibn Khaldūn's view, the end result is the weakening of the unifying factor of group feeling and, eventually, the disintegration of the dynasty. Present-day Iraq, before, during and after the regime of President Saddam Hussein, provides many examples of Ibn Khaldūn's insights into the relations between the tribe, whose members stress the equality and unity of the group in conflict with other tribes, and the ruling dynasty, hungering for hierarchy and fearing rivals.

Obedience and resistance to the secular hierarchies of government were central themes of Thomas Hobbes's *Leviathan* and John Milton's *Paradise Lost*. Hobbes and Milton were on opposite sides in the English Civil War. Hobbes was on the royalist side. Milton was on the side of Oliver Cromwell and the parliamentary forces. At the time they wrote their works, each was on the losing side.[8] They were both concerned about how thinking people with lives to preserve (Hobbes) or souls to save (Milton) could navigate their way through a world in which anarchy and tyranny competed as the most frightening prospects. How much humiliation could be stomached in return for the benefits brought by political hierarchy? Not much, says Milton. Quite a lot, says Hobbes.

For Milton, to have an ungodly and wasteful king with a vicious royal court in charge of society was a fate to be avoided. Milton was a republican, a 'masterless man'.[9] He sympathized with just the kind of rebellious person that Hobbes wanted to keep under control. Milton's Satan, the glamorous rebel who swashbuckles his way through *Paradise Lost*, has the very characteristics that Hobbes saw as causing perpetual violence in the state of nature before Leviathan is established. Satan wants to be admired, praised and revered – he is greedy; he is aggressive; and he tries to get his own way by force and fraud in turn.[10]

For Milton, human beings should assent to a hierarchy of the following kind:

- at the top is Christ the liberator who personifies all humankind by descending to Earth and accepting humiliation on everybody's behalf;
- the earthly realm has at its head the most virtuous and talented people in the country who act in the best interests of all; and
- the structure of political power is as decentralized as possible.

Hierarchy without humiliation of the people would be the result.

Hobbes had different priorities and envisaged a different kind of hierarchy:

- at the top is a ruler who has the capacity to impose humiliation on everyone below him, thus forcing all subjects to behave peacefully;
- the ruler personifies all his subjects in the sense that they have assented to his acting on behalf of them all, even when he is humiliating them; and
- the ruler should, as a matter of rational prudence, enforce natural law, allowing subjects to organize their lives in ways that aid their comfort and material happiness, bearing in mind that subjects who are denied this will be liable to rebel, returning society to a war-like state of nature.

According to Hobbes, subjects should be prepared to acquiesce in humiliation by the ruler in return for peace and the possibility of comfort and prosperity.

By contrast, over two centuries later, in the 1880s, Friedrich Nietzsche argued that in past times aristocrats, the masters of society, took guilt-free pleasure from humiliating others. It was the essence of high culture: 'Not so long ago', he wrote, 'a royal wedding or great public celebration would have been incomplete without executions, tortures, *autos da fé*. . . . To behold suffering gives pleasure, but to cause another to suffer affords an even greater pleasure' (Nietzsche 1956, 198).

The aristocracy assumed that whatever they did, however cruel, was 'noble' (and therefore 'good') simply because they did it.[11] Nietzsche observed, with some regret, that democracy was levelling society: 'The lords are a thing of the past, and the ethics of the common man is completely triumphant' (169). One result was a 'slave revolt in morals' (168) driven by the resentment of the common people against their noble masters.[12] This slave morality preached equality and peace.[13]

Elias Canetti concluded from his own study of the deep structure of human groups, first published in German in 1960, that: 'Anyone who wants to rule men first tries to humiliate them, to trick them out of their rights and their capacity for resistance, until they are as powerless before him as animals' (Canetti 1973, 245). Such a ruler may enjoy to the full the pleasure we all take 'in relegating something to an inferior group, while presupposing a higher group to which we ourselves belong' (346).[14]

The theatre of empire

At the top of imperial hierarchies one can relish the exercise of 'empire'. At the emotional heart of this term is the pleasure of making conquests, issuing commands to the vanquished and disposing of them as one decides, in other words, the pleasure of showing that one is capable of achieving and exercising total dominion. In his *Theory of the Leisure Class* (1899) Thorstein Veblen caught this feeling of joy in conquest and mastery, putting it at the heart of modern capitalism, linking it to the spirit of the medieval knight lusting for battle (Veblen 1970).[15]

In ancient Rome, the title *imperator* or emperor was given to rulers whose generals were victorious in battle. By the time of Emperor

Vespasian (69–79 CE) it was the normal title of the Roman Empire's first citizen.[16] As is well known, prominent captives from battle were brought back to Rome to be put on display in public recognition of the successful general's triumph. Triumph for the general meant humiliation for the captives, many of whom were slaughtered in various 'entertaining' ways. The others were turned into slaves.

Seen from this viewpoint, imperialism is a theatrical stage on which rulers and generals show what they are capable of. Empire-builders humiliate others, sometimes through *force majeure*, sometimes through seduction, as a way to magnify themselves. Absolutist hierarchies are created by making conquests, imposing one's will on others in spite of their resistance, issuing commands to the vanquished, disposing of them as one decides, and putting them where you want them, not where they think they should be.

The 'theatre of empire' is mainly concerned with displaying the grandeur, high status and honourable superiority of the lord, leader, people, nation or 'race' concerned. It has existed for millennia, reaching back to the time of Hammurabi and before. The theatricality of the Nazi regime was a latter-day expression of this form.[17]

Fighters, traders, settlers and citizens

The imperial impulse took more than one form. For example, there were dynastic empires, settler societies and two kinds of nation-state empire, the European and the global.

Dynastic empires

If empire is, originally at least, about the *éclat* of conquest, then imperial Rome represents one version of its pristine form. In this case, military expansion was a proving ground for ambitious military cliques linked to rich and powerful families. The great exploits of individual commanders strengthened the social and political position of the dynasties they served, their own and the emperor's. In fact, many successful generals were themselves ambitious to be Roman emperor.

Dynastic empires expressed the dynastic interest's 'outward reach'. its capacity to project its dominant influence outwards from within an impregnable and well-established homeland. The main agent of this 'outreach', the one that delivered the punch then opened the fist to grasp the prize, was the military 'man on horseback' or in his chariot.

In practice, the warrior made room for other interests besides his own. Take the case of Spanish dynastic imperialism in America during the sixteenth century. The Church was hungry for new souls and quick to hitch a ride across the Atlantic. Franciscan friars were in Mexico City a mere five years after Hernán Cortés began his conquest of the Aztec empire in 1519. Religious interests continued to weave themselves into Europe's imperial fabric during the following few centuries.[18]

Many of the original Spanish *conquistadors* were *hidalgos*,[19] minor nobles or gentlemen keen to put their fighting skills to use in getting rich enough to get feudal estates of their own. They had aristocratic pretensions. What they needed was an aristocratic income. Using slave labour to dig gold and silver directly out of the earth was the most direct route to great wealth. Later, ranching or establishing a plantation of some kind was another way of turning seized territory into personal riches. This meant staying in the colony to supervise the enterprise, especially if it was the main source of income. When that happened on a large scale, another kind of imperial project came into play.

Settler societies

Unlike dynastic empires, which projected power capacity outwards from an existing homeland, settler societies founded *new* homelands abroad. The Boer settlers in South Africa fall into this category. So do the Protestant settlers in Northern Ireland, the English settlers in North America and the Jewish settlers who established Israel.

This is a very interesting category.[20] Founding a new homeland is a daunting and dangerous exercise. The pioneers may often find themselves 'on their own', with little external economic and political support for their intentions and considerable local resistance to them. Why would anyone undertake such projects? One possible reason is desperation, the desire to escape unacceptable conditions. Another is a strong desire to make a society that reflects the settlers' view of how the world should be and how they should fit into it. In other words, settlers want a world that they can shape and dominate. Many other reasons, motives and causes are involved but these two, the wish to escape and the desire to dominate, are especially relevant, as I argue below. However, there are two other types of imperial project to consider.

European nation-state-empires

By the late nineteenth century, all the major class interests had a stake of some kind in Europe's imperial enterprises. The way the empires were managed reflected the particular social and political power balances in their 'headquarter' societies. All these societies were affected by the technological and organizational revolutions brought by modern industry and the growth of large cities, pulling peasants away from the countryside. All of them had to cope with the turbulent consequences of the democratic and nationalist ways of thinking that had spread across Europe, and deep into other continents, following the American and French revolutions.

Within each of the headquarter societies, rising urban-industrial and declining agrarian interests battled for influence. Empires played their part in these struggles. For example, imperial possessions bolstered the prestige and authority of aristocratic and court circles. This was a significant factor in societies where peasants supplied the main body of army recruits and where the officer class was largely drawn from noble or genteel families, or at least shaped in that tradition.

Propertied families in city and countryside poured funds into imperial ventures. There were enormous, if risky, profits to be made by exploiting 'inferior' races, especially if military force could be called upon when 'inferior' peoples began to protest and get out of hand. Back home in the headquarter society, conflicts between capital and labour in the manufacturing cities could be alleviated by banging the patriotic drum, emphasizing the loyalty of both workers and employers to the national flag proudly flying over the nation's imperial possessions.

The European empires were based on compromises between the ambitions and obsessions of landed, trading and working-class interests (see box 5.1). Beneath these compromises lurked a contradiction. It was, in the end, practically impossible to combine imperialism with democratic citizenship. European governments were gradually forced to concede civil, political and social rights to their citizens. As a result, the old dynastic-cum-trading empires were turned into 'European

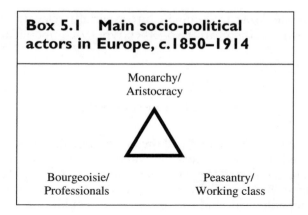

Box 5.1   Main socio-political actors in Europe, c.1850–1914

Monarchy/
Aristocracy

Bourgeoisie/   Peasantry/
Professionals   Working class

nation-state-empires'. In other words, the headquarter societies, Britain, France, Germany and so on, gradually increased the range of citizenship rights given to their national citizens while trying to retain absolutist systems of rule as far as possible in the colonial dependencies.

Nation-state-empires were built on a contradiction. The idea of empire is absolutist. In other words, it 'wants' complete domination, absolute difference between superiors and subordinates and an unbridgeable gap between them. By contrast, nation-states typically incorporate the idea of citizenship. Citizenship 'wants' equality. A citizen is someone with universal rights, held by all, that the state must recognize and fulfil. A subject within an empire is someone whose task is to serve, demonstrating absolute subservience and giving complete obedience. A proper citizen could not also be a proper subject. Whose claims should take priority? This matter had been argued out violently during the American and French revolutions.

It was difficult for the citizen of a nation-state or the would-be citizen of a would-be nation-state to be at the same time the subject of an imperial dynasty. There were activists around ready to point out the contradictions and remind people of the humiliation they were confronting: Gandhi, for example, in India, and Michael Collins in Ireland.[21] In practice, these irrational arrangements survived for a while, in India, Ireland and elsewhere, lasting half a century or so, but they led to bloody conflict in the end.

The nation-state-empire was a kind of political 'mule'. In other words, it was a hybrid with a reasonable life expectancy that could not reproduce itself. It was, so to speak, time limited, even though the 'use by' date was obscure. The modern European nation-state empires were destined to disappear from the moment they were invented. This fate was metaphorically in their genes. Disappear they did, gradually, after World War I, but then they were resurrected in an even stranger form.

Global nation-state-empires

After 1945 the Cold War pitted two world empires against each other. Moscow took over, in large measure, the old continental empires that had collapsed in 1918. Stalin's regime not only reclaimed much of the previous Russian Empire in Eastern Europe but also imposed its influence over European territory previously held by the German, Austro-Hungarian and Ottoman empires, all, like the Russian Empire, shattered by World War I. For a while, it seemed to have great influence over Asia's greatest empire, China, an empire that had made great progress in transforming itself into a nation-state.

Meanwhile Washington settled into nests vacated by the old European sea-borne empires. The US government had already, early in the nineteenth century, asserted that Latin America, once under Spanish and Portuguese imperial control, was its own exclusive sphere of influence. After 1945 it moved into world regions that the British, French, Dutch and Belgians used to think of as their own, such as Africa, the Middle East and Indo-China.[22]

The global nation-state-empires differed from their European predecessors in three ways:

1 Most of the countries belonging to each empire, and not just the 'headquarter' nations, were officially described as democracies with citizenship rights or 'protectorates' of various kinds en route for democracy; in other words, they were empires constructed from nation-states.
2 The centre of gravity shifted away from Western Europe towards the East (Moscow) and West (Washington).
3 Instead of one very big empire (the British) alongside a number of medium-sized and smaller ones, now there were two very large empires (American and Russian).

How modern empires pass away

To summarize, imperialism in the form of nation-state-empires has passed through European and world history over the past century in two large waves:

- the first wave of European nation-state-empires, which hit its peak in the late nineteenth century before crashing down during and after World War I; and
- the second wave of global nation-state-empires, which hit its peak in the mid-1960s before losing its force during the 1990s and the first few years of the twenty-first century.

After they had passed their peak, these waves each went through three phases: intensification of competition between empires; partial system collapse; and succession contest. Let us start with the European nation-state-empires.

Phase one: intensification of competition between empires (1898–1917)

In 1898 European imperialism suffered a severe blow to its prestige when the Americans destroyed the Spanish fleet. This was echoed seven years later, when the Japanese defeated the Russian navy at Port Arthur (Korea). By that time, military competition between the stronger imperial powers, especially Germany and Britain, was intensifying. Meanwhile, there was growing insubordination within the British Empire, especially in South Africa, Ireland and India. The British establishment suffered a number of humiliating setbacks, notably the disastrous Gallipoli landing in 1915.[23]

Phase two: partial system collapse (1917–c.1931)

By the end of World War I the great empires of continental Europe, with capitals in Moscow, Berlin, Vienna and Constantinople, were all in smithereens. The British Empire, left standing, seemed larger by contrast. In fact, it grew bigger by picking up remnants of the Ottoman Empire, including Mesopotamia (Iraq).[24] During the

1920s the British Empire had never looked larger or less troubled by rivals. It governed one fifth of the world, roughly the same proportion as the Chinese government in the early twenty-first century.

The Treaty of Versailles (1919) after World War I apparently left the British Empire in a commanding position. Where were its competitors?

1 The German Empire was in ruins.
2 The Russian Empire was torn by revolution and civil war.
3 The Ottoman Empire was gone.
4 The United States was much less hostile than it had been forty years before, and was in any case mainly preoccupied with its own internal affairs.

Despite its lonely global pre-eminence, the British Empire still had to cope with insubordination. There was resistance to its rule in Ireland, Iraq and India and increasing restlessness in the 'white dominions'. Canada, New Zealand, Australia, the Union of South Africa and the Irish Free State all got their formal 'independence' in 1931.[25]

These internal difficulties did not prevent the British Empire from putting up a good front. During the 1920s Edward, Prince of Wales (later, briefly, Edward VIII), was arguably the most famous man in the world. He circled the world repeatedly in highly publicized royal visits to the West Indies, New Zealand, Australia, India, the Gambia, the Gold Coast, Nigeria, South Africa, Kenya, Uganda and so on. These visits were all designed to maintain enthusiasm, loyalty and respect for the imperial idea and the Crown, within both the British Empire and the dominions.

Phase three: succession contest (c.1931–c.1965)

By the mid-1930s both Germany and Russia were rapidly getting stronger, and within twenty years the British Empire was caught up in a bitter fight for its very existence. World War II left the United Kingdom impoverished and exhausted, unable to resist the demands of its colonies for independence. During the two decades after the victory of 1945, India won its freedom, the African colonies were liberated, the British Empire broke apart and Britain's global position was thoroughly undermined. The victory and prizes won in 1918–19

Box 5.2   Phases of imperial decline

	Phase 1	*Phase 2*	*Phase 3*
Main characteristics of the phase:	Intensification of competition *between* empires Insubordination *within* empires	Partial collapse of the imperial structure One survivor empire remains prominent although insubordination persists within the empire	Competition and/or negotiation about the successor global order This occurs within the global framework that the survivor empire's continued existence provides
European nation-state-empires:	1898–1917	1917–*c.*1931	*c.*1931–*c.*1965
Global nation-state-empires:	*c.*1965–89	1989–2001	2001–35?

and the apparently unchallenged supremacy enjoyed during the 1920s had all been thoroughly deceptive.

Biting back

During the middle third of the twentieth century the British Empire provided a convenient global framework and a stable reference point while a ferocious battle went on between its would-be successors in Germany, Russia and the United States.[26]

In each case those contending for global leadership tried to make their potential supporters feel:

- that they had been subjected to humiliation by their old masters;
- that they should revolt and strike back violently; and
- that if they were to do so a brighter future would be available to them.

The Nazis in Germany drew deeply on the ideas of Gobineau and Nietzsche, who combined deeply reactionary approaches to race with profound regret about the decline of Europe's aristocracy. Nazi ideology combined the two themes in its glorification of the Aryans as a master race. World War I had been a humiliation for the German aristocracy, which, along with the Kaiser, had been forced to leave political life. From one point of view, this lifted a tremendous burden off the backs of ordinary Germans. Hitler took another approach. He taught the German people that the surrender in 1918 and the Versailles peace settlement of the following year were an insufferable humiliation, not just for the aristocracy but for all true Germans.[27]

Hitler 'dignified' and 'raised up' his audience by telling them that they, the ordinary German people, were important enough within the German nation to be able to share in its humiliation. Furthermore, they had a right to revenge. They were not underlings of little account. On the contrary, they were a 'master race', absolutely superior to all others. They were to be, so to speak, a global aristocracy.

Meanwhile, in Russia, Lenin and the Bolsheviks looked forward to bringing about the 'dictatorship of the proletariat', uniting urban workers and peasants under the banner of state socialism. They would march towards true communism under the leadership of the party. Once in power, Lenin repeatedly reminded Russians of 'the oppression, humiliation and the incredible torments of penal servitude' that they had suffered under the tsarist regime.[28] Many of his party looked to a utopian future when the working class would take possession of the whole world.

Finally, in the United States, the capitalist market was glorified.[29] Here the central figures in the socio-political drama were business leaders, those who succeeded in building up massive private fortunes and large corporations.

During the 1930s and 1940s two changes occurred, bringing the American experiment into line with the Soviet and Nazi experiments. First, the state was brought into action through the New Deal. Tax income was used to protect the existing business order against the market itself by making sure that there was work for the people and money in consumers' pockets. Second, during and after World War II, capitalist democracy, the American system of business and government, began to take up a global role and viewpoint. The delivery of Marshall Aid to Europe and the forced restructuring of Japan began the work of reshaping the world so that it was safe for international business and finance.

There is another way in which American leaders adopted tactics similar to those of their counterparts in Germany and Russia. Like them, politicians in the United States encouraged others to realize how deeply they were being humiliated and to seek a brighter future by following a better way that was on offer. In fact, the Americans had been using this strategy for a long time. Since 1886 the Statue of Liberty had made its direct appeal to the world's 'wretched refuse', the 'huddled masses, yearning to breathe free'. America told the world's people that the 'Mother of Exiles'[30] offered liberation and succour for down-and-outs everywhere.

A quarter of a century earlier, the proclamation emancipating American slaves in 1861 had been, in part at least, a calculated attempt by the North to stir discontent within the South and undermine its ability to resist the North during the American Civil War.[31] The United States adopted the same strategy in Europe by issuing what were, in effect, international versions of the Emancipation Proclamation, respectively Woodrow Wilson's 'Fourteen Points' speech in 1918 and Franklin Roosevelt's declaration about the 'Four Freedoms' made in 1941. For his part, Wilson was cultivating the discontents of the colonized peoples of Europe by his rhetoric about freedom and justice. Roosevelt 'globalized' the same message. His call for liberation from tyranny was directed against the Germans and Japanese but it was also a shot across the bows of the old imperialist enemy in Western Europe. The message was calculated to appeal to the millions of colonial subjects who felt humiliated.[32]

Cold War and after

By 1945, the contest for the succession to European imperialism had narrowed down to two contenders. Moscow and Washington both proclaimed egalitarian ideologies and declared that they were hostile to imperialism. When Britain and France, in secret league with Israel, invaded Egypt in 1956, hoping to overthrow President Nasser and regain control of the Suez Canal, the United States made sure that the European imperialists were severely reprimanded in the United Nations. The Russian invasion of Hungary in the same year gave the

United States another opportunity to present itself as the proud and righteous spokesperson for humiliated satellites, colonies and ex-colonies everywhere. At that time the Americans could look around them with a degree of satisfaction no less than, say, the British in the 1880s.

But the Cold War brought a second wave of empire-building.[33] The 'free world' and the 'communist bloc', to use phrases common in the West at that time, were global (not merely European) empires. This raises an obvious question: is this second wave passing through the same three phases as the first? There is some evidence that it is (see box 5.2).

Phase one: intensification of competition between empires (c.1965–89)

By the 1960s the Soviet Union had achieved a rough parity with the United States in some aspects of its military capability.[34] From the late 1960s onwards, there was intensified competition between the two sides, roughly similar to that between the British and Germans before World War I. Both the Americans and the Russians played a humiliation game, trying to make the other side look inadequate, incompetent and cruel. The deep embarrassments of the Vietnam War, fought against allies of China and Russia, were paid back by deliberately drawing Moscow into a hopeless invasion of Afghanistan.[35]

Meanwhile, like the European nation-state-empires before World War I, both the Soviet Bloc and the American empire faced insubordination within their own ranks. In the West, colonial liberation movements in Africa coincided with protests by African Americans against segregation. They were soon followed by student militancy against the Vietnam War, the rise of feminism and the harsh blow of oil price rises imposed by OPEC, the non-Western cartel of producers. Religion played a key role in mobilizing resistance to the Soviet Union, not just by Islamist warriors in Afghanistan but by shipyard workers in the Polish Solidarity movement.

Phase two: partial system collapse (1989–2001)

The collapse of the Berlin Wall and the break-up of the Soviet Union were not unequivocally 'caused' by the West. The demise of the Soviet

Union was at least as unexpected as the sudden German surrender in 1918 had been.[36] Its causes are complex and still not understood. However, whatever the causes, the United States was the beneficiary of the ending of the Cold War, rather as the British had benefited in 1918 when the remnants of the German fleet sailed into British waters in the Firth of Forth.[37]

As the British Empire had done in the 1920s, during the 1990s the United States stood alone, prominent on the skyline. Where were its competitors?

1 The Soviet Union was in ruins.
2 Japan was tearing itself apart with political infighting and was no longer the economic threat that it had seemed to be in the 1970s and for most of the 1980s.
3 The European Union was proving incapable of coping with a dangerous civil war in ex-Yugoslavia on its south-eastern borders and had to rely on American help.
4 China was much less hostile than it had been forty years before, and was in any case mainly preoccupied with its own internal affairs.

The US government carried out the first Iraq invasion (1991) and the Kosovo War (1999) almost as if they were playing exhibition matches. The American soldiers with their superb military equipment were like the Harlem Globetrotters on a world tour, showing off their abilities to admiring foreigners.

However, like Britain between the wars, the United States after 1989 had to cope with the problem of 'subordinate' nations within its empire. At the start of the 1990s, the Maastricht Treaty signalled that Europe's leaders wanted a European Union that was strong, state-like and independent, eventually capable of counter-balancing America.[38] The disagreements some leading European states had with US foreign policy were laid bare when France and Germany both opposed America's planned invasion of Iraq.

This European spirit of independence was an ironic consequence of the fact that for over four decades after 1945, the United States had been a firm but benevolent emperor within the 'free world'. In this role it had sent Marshall Aid to Western Europe and forced the main Western European powers into economic cooperation. Washington kick-started the movement that led to the European Union. The Americans also restructured Japanese economic and political life so that Japan became a thriving modern capitalist democracy.

Box 5.3 The decline of imperial systems: succession contest

Phase 3	c.1931–c.1965	2001–35?
Imperial system in decline:	European nation-state-empires	Global nation-state-empires
Remaining imperial power:	Britain	United States
Would-be successors:	United States, Germany, Russia, Japan	China, European Union, Japan, India
Struggling giant:	China	Russia

This was not simply altruism. The American economy had avoided a painful post-war downturn by strengthening its overseas business in terms of trade and investment. It wanted those investments to be safe. It wanted its businesspeople to be working in friendly environments.

After 1945 the United States 'Americanized' much of the world. Business increased in social status, becoming highly respectable and professionalized. American-style business schools grew up everywhere. Trading partners and governments in both Europe and Asia learned quickly and well from the Americans, helped by the rising tide of prosperity running through the 1950s and 1960s. Their economies grew and their governments became more powerful.

Phase three: succession contest (2001–35?)

The EU and Japan are now playing in the same league as China. India is coming up fast. The result is that the United States no longer has economic preponderance in the world.

The United States can still have a profound effect on the global economy and the fate of particular national economies. For example, it has claimed the leading voice and a powerful veto in those global institutions it has shaped, such as the IMF, the World Bank, WTO and the UN. However, this influence is not so easily asserted in such important bodies as the EU, ASEAN and OPEC.[39] The gradual loosening of institutional control is matched by the rising influence of non-American transnational corporations. The top one hundred transnationals owned $2,453 billion in foreign assets in 2000. Only 28 per cent of those assets were in American hands.[40]

The United States became militarily strong because it was both rich enough to pay for the technology and skills needed and sufficiently worried about its own security to wish to acquire them. Other large states are now moving into the same situation. The European Union, China, Japan and India are all much richer than they were in 1945. Russia is benefiting from the income provided by its abundant supplies of gas and oil. These countries are also beginning to feel much more insecure. Until 1989 global security was provided by the Cold War nuclear stalemate.[41] Now, over a decade and a half after the end of the Cold War, the climate of international relations is strongly affected by:

- increasing fear of terrorism;
- the spread of nuclear weapons;
- the destabilizing consequences throughout Eurasia of the collapse of the Soviet Union;
- the divisions between leading Western powers over the Iraq War of 2003 and its aftermath; and
- concerns about the increasing strength and assertiveness of China.

If these anxieties deepen, and if inter-state relations become increasingly uncertain and unpredictable, then it is feasible that the world's leading economic powers will build up their military strength. This could happen very quickly, especially if citizens are sufficiently frightened to accept tax increases. If, or more likely when, that happens, the world will cease to be uni-polar, as it was for a while after 1989. Instead, it will be multi-polar in both economic and military terms.

When the configuration of global forces in the first third of the twenty-first century comes to be seen in retrospect, they will probably bear an uncanny resemblance to the second third of the twentieth century. In other words:

- a half-collapsed imperial system, with the dominant empire still standing though increasingly troubled by internal dissent;
- a collection of increasingly powerful competitors with dissimilar ideas about how the world should be run; and

- a struggling giant that is trying to restructure itself and rebuild its strength.[42]

Meanwhile, we are in the middle of a 'war on terrorism'. A basic element in the strategy being adopted by the West is to show that it can deliver even greater humiliation against its enemies than its enemies can themselves deliver. This response betrays the anxiety of an empire that fears belittlement and sees its rivals growing more powerful.[43]

The danger is that in the decades to come those contending for global leadership may once again, as in the 1930s, try to make potential supporters feel:

- that they have been subjected to humiliation by their old masters;
- that they should revolt and strike back violently; and
- that if they do this a brighter future will be available to them.[44]

Culture of resentment

The signs are not good. Bin Laden's greatest 'success' has been to transfer the atavistic politics of the Middle East upwards to the global level. Since 2001 international relations, in other words, the politics of global society, have been increasingly framed in terms of humiliation, resentment and revenge. This is expressed by striking out against tormenters, then preparing for the answering blow. Permitting this to happen has been a bad move, one the West did not need to make. The long-term consequence of perpetuating this atmosphere is to undermine the credibility of all political authority. In fact, this process has been under way for some time. Consider how much sustained training in feelings of humiliation and resentment the fascist, communist and capitalist contenders for the global crown gave to the whole world's population during the twentieth century – not just to Muslims who felt a bitter chill after the collapse of the Ottoman Empire and the end of the caliphate after World War I, but to almost everybody.

Over the past few generations, the forces contending to succeed the old European imperialists have all promised their followers a better life. They have all said that to get this better life the people have to overthrow those who are humiliating them. Most of the twentieth century was characterized by a mixture of hope and hatred, a mixture that was fed to the people in large doses during two hot wars, one cold war and the anxious periods in between. We are now living with the consequences of this forced feeding.

In recent decades this mixture has been made even more volatile than before. During the late 1960s and early 1970s the 'student revolution' in the West coincided with the Cultural Revolution in China, and, as a consequence, young people felt free to express contempt for teachers, bureaucrats and politicians. During the late 1970s and early 1980s popular uprisings in Iran, Afghanistan and Poland boosted the prestige of religious organizations, sending the message that assertive expressions of faith were at least as meaningful and effective as voting for conventional political parties, a practice in decline throughout the West. During the 1980s and 1990s the market was heavily promoted as a supposedly superior alternative to the public sector, which was stereotyped as being corrupt and inflexible.

As a result of this century of sustained disaffection, almost all authority now seems illegitimate, a harsh and insulting imposition from above. Almost. Why was the funeral in Rome of Pope John Paul II in April 2005 such a massive media event? Why were over two hundred presidents, prime ministers and royal representatives present?[45] One motive for attending was that it gave them the chance to bathe themselves in the waves of authority surging out of the Vatican. They hoped that some of that authority would rub off on them. They wanted some of that papal aura.

Compared to religious authority, political authority has acquired a different aura, not good but very bad. It is subject to two attacks simultaneously:

- from the statist 'left', for neglecting its duty of care, its responsibility to protect the people from avoidable humiliations; and
- from the neo-liberal 'right', for imposing itself on the people, subjecting citizens to humiliation.

The central state and local government now have the kind of aura that emanates from the legendary Sheriff of Nottingham – the kind that makes you think of garlic, not incense. The Sheriff of Nottingham is of course the evil opponent of Robin Hood, that European medieval folk hero whose stories have been passed from generation to generation in countless versions, ranging from ballads, folk tales and poems to Walt Disney's films.

In fact, two medieval legends epitomize the conflicts and dilemmas at the centre of globalization. One is the tale of Robin Hood and the Sheriff of Nottingham. The other is the story of the Pied Piper who played his magic pipe to rid Hamelin of its plague of rats; when the citizens refused to pay him, he lured the town's children away.

In the Robin Hood legend, the Sheriff of Nottingham is an unwelcome despot imposing himself on the local people. His power in Nottingham derives from the Norman kings, French invaders who placed their yoke upon the English at the time of William the Conqueror. Like his French masters, the Sheriff of Nottingham has imposed himself from above without being invited. He is not the 'good' sheriff of classical Wild West mythology, one who supposedly looks after everybody's interests. On the contrary, he is a 'bad' sheriff: a greedy tax-collector, a ruthless enforcer, a corrupt official acting for a despotic government that does not care about the people.

For many decades now the world's population has been taught to feel frustration and resentment. Who are they to blame for their condition? Contemporary political rhetoric offers up two main candidates, two damning stereotypes:

- *big business*, which supposedly resembles the Pied Piper, who gets his victims under his control, exploits them, steals their most valuable possessions, ruins their communities, leaves, and takes no responsibility for the destruction he causes; and
- *big government*, which supposedly resembles the Sheriff of Nottingham, brutally imposing the will of an unloved and unwanted evil empire, taking as much as he can, giving back as little as he can.

In the days of the Cold War, the following dialogue could be regularly heard, here transmuted in terms of the Pied Piper and the Sheriff of Nottingham:

> *Washington to Moscow*: You are an evil empire, imposing your tyrannical will on others, sending your wicked Sheriffs of Nottingham with armed guards to inflict terror on people wherever you can, forcing them to pay tribute.
> *Moscow to Washington*: Rubbish. In fact, you are a global conspirator, sending out Pied Pipers with conjuring tricks to seduce and trick people wherever you can, using them for your own exploitative purposes.
> *Washington to Moscow*: Rubbish. You are an evil empire . . . (etc.).

The force behind the accusations – 'you are the exploitative Pied Piper', 'you are the wicked Sheriff of Nottingham' – was much diminished when it came to meet its counter-accusation. The two opposing winds blew each other out, greatly reducing their effectiveness. Since 1989, both winds have begun to blow in the same direction. They are both directed against the United States, which is now seen as an amalgam of the Pied Piper, whose symbolic base is (or was) the World Trade Center, and the Sheriff of Nottingham, resident in the Pentagon. The attackers on 9/11 scored a direct hit on them both.

The United States, now the one and only global Sheriff of Nottingham, has brought into existence a global Robin Hood whose name is Osama bin Laden. Al-Qaeda is not an accidental creation either. During Russia's Afghanistan war, the CIA armed the Islamic resistance fighters. In doing so, they were giving strength to people such as Osama bin Laden and Mohammed Omar who would later form the kernel of Al-Qaeda and the Taliban regime. The US government evidently did not anticipate that this fanatical force might be directed against themselves in the future.

From the point of view of the Sheriff of Nottingham and those who shelter behind his castle walls, Robin Hood is a terrorist. However, Robin Hood receives protection from the crowd beyond the walls. The crowd is deeply suspicious of Pied Pipers who try to hypnotize it. But a Robin Hood that enacts the crowd's own secret fantasies is a very different matter.

*   *   *

In this chapter we have: considered the parts played by terror and care in the working of the state, ancient and modern; noted the interplay between ruler and priesthood (or mass media); considered the relationship between humiliation and hierarchy (with reference to Ibn Khaldūn, Milton, Hobbes, Nietzsche and Canetti); acknowledged the theatricality of empire; distinguished between dynastic empires, settler societies, European nation-state-empires, and global nation-state-empires; discovered a common pattern in the decline and fall of the two forms of nation-state-empire; recognized that a culture of resentment against political authority has developed in the twentieth century; and seen that this was part of a wider pattern of hostility to big government (the Sheriff of Nottingham) and big business (the Pied Piper).

Where have we arrived in our development of the book's argument? We are making our second circuit of the triple helix, this time in reverse order, more slowly, and in greater depth. We have completed our examination of the imperial impulse and we are about to investigate the second generator of humiliation driven by the dynamics of globalization: the logic of the market.

6

The Logic of the Market

High Noon

The idea of the United States as the Sheriff of Nottingham does not please everybody. On the contrary, according to Robert Kagan in *Paradise and Power* (Kagan 2003), the United States is, in a very responsible and self-sacrificing way, taking on the tough task of policing a disorderly world so as to enable decent people to live decent lives. Kagan has in mind a very different kind of sheriff, rather like the one in *High Noon* (1952), Fred Zinnemann's film starring Gary Cooper and Grace Kelly. Will Kane (played by Cooper) wants to give up his job as a lawman and live peacefully. But the Miller gang, the town hooligans, are a-coming, and they are gunning for the sheriff. Instead of running, the sheriff stands up to the Miller gang. He knows this is the only way to make a lasting peace so that citizens can have the chance to live in a democratic atmosphere of mutual respect.

Sadly, no-one in the town gives him serious help. They would rather tolerate the Miller gang's predations and put up with having their lives ruined. Only the sheriff is prepared to get his hands dirty and take on the gory task of slaughtering the terrorizing gang. Having done the job, like every true cowboy hero, he rides off into the sunset. Kagan sees America as the sheriff, Islamic terrorists as the Miller gang and the world as the threatened town. Europe plays two roles: that of Amy, the sheriff's Quaker wife who hates violence at all costs, and the bar tender in the town saloon who serves drinks to all comers, good or evil, then hides beneath the counter when the bullets fly.

This analogy seems quite plausible – until you think about it. Kagan gets the film's message completely wrong. The message is not that most people are either impractical idealists or compromising cowards who need a special breed of hero to protect them, following his own gut instinct and noble ideals. No, the message is that *the whole community has a duty of care to all its members* and when this is neglected the result is violence and injustice. The sheriff's behaviour was part of the problem, not part of the solution:

- Why did the sheriff stay to face the Miller gang? To defend his personal honour.
- How did he deal with the situation? Violently.
- What did he do when the killing was over? He left.
- What difference did he make to the fundamental problem of creating a peaceful community in which the human rights of everyone were respected? Absolutely none.

Even if you were persuaded by the Kagan version of America as a noble and self-sacrificing 'global sheriff', the American occupation of Iraq has surely cast doubt on the sheriff's capacity to get his way.

But what *are* the would-be global sheriff's intentions? According to one well-placed source (Thomas Barnett, who works at the US Naval War College), the overall strategic goal is to make sure that 'labour, energy, money and security all . . . flow as freely as possible from those places in the world where they are plentiful to those regions where they are scarce' (Barnett 2004, 198). To give an example, if you invest manpower, capital and weaponry in 'exporting security' to Iraq, you can improve your access to its oil.

The global sheriff is the fixer, someone who does the job that is needed, then goes. In Iraq, for example, the 'best-case scenario' will be in place 'when America internationalizes the occupation force . . . and successfully "indigenizes" the apparatus of political control. . . . Then you work to attract foreign direct investment and let Iraq's more than adequately educated masses do the rest' (291–2). In other words, get in, fix security – that is, guarantee business and property rights so the market is safe and investment can flow – then get out.

Barnett is expressing a central assertion of the US administration installed in 2000, which is that the market provides the golden road to freedom. When a society is free (i.e. where the market is dominant), its people have the basic ingredient needed to enjoy human rights.

But, assuming that human rights are worth having, what are the *specific* advantages of having them? One answer is that they justify and embody the expectation that human beings should be enabled to live decent lives. In other words:

- unacceptable and routinely avoidable suffering and humiliation should be excluded; and
- protection and support should be available from others at times when the means of decent existence for an individual, community or society are threatened or destroyed.

Let us proceed on the basis that the criteria just set out are reasonable. Is it also reasonable to suggest that by enforcing a universal human right to engage in market transactions and to hold private property you are making it possible for all members of a society to live decent lives and have them protected?

This proposition received a relevant test when Hurricane Katrina arrived on the south-east coast of the United States on Monday 29 August 2005, bringing another airborne disaster, nearly four years after 9/11.

Hurricane Katrina

The 9/11 hijackers hit the most prominent symbol of American wealth and power, towering above New York. By contrast, Hurricane Katrina struck at the districts occupied by poor people of the Old South living below sea level in New Orleans. Several thousand people did not get out of New Orleans in time. Some took shelter in the Superdome, a huge sports stadium in the middle of the city. Many others were left in their homes. On Tuesday 30 August the 17th Street Canal levée broke, sending a flood wave through the city. Very soon 80 per cent of the city was under water. The world's media quickly arrived. This spectacular disaster had been predicted for some time.[1]

By Wednesday 31 August there were about 25,000 people in the Superdome without food, water or facilities. There was violence and intimidation. Many thousands more were scattered through the flooded city without policing or support. Shops were raided for consumer goods and basic supplies. There was shooting. On Thursday a shot was fired when a helicopter tried to take people from the Superdome to safety. Rescue efforts were halted.

On 30 August the New Orleans disaster became headline news throughout the world. The enormous scale of the crisis was clear to all for three whole days before government agencies got their act together. The levée system failed on that Tuesday. The help New Orleans needed did not arrive until Friday. Only then did significant amounts of food, water, medicine, troops and police appear in New Orleans.

The commander of the Louisiana National Guard's Joint Task Force told the *Army Times* on Friday: 'This place is going to look like Little Somalia.'[2] News coverage included scenes of soldiers and police pointing rifles at the men, women and children they were rescuing from flooded houses, ordering them to put their hands in the air or to lie on the ground. In such cases, the fear, distrust and contempt on both sides were palpable.

Hurricane Katrina had repercussions on world oil prices, since the hurricane put most of the region's refining capacity out of action. The hurricane was a global event in another way also. The American response to Katrina gave the whole world a shocking exhibition of upper-class arrogance combined with uncaring incompetence. This probably caused more 'shock and awe' among global spectators than any number of spectacular smart bombs falling on Baghdad.[3]

The public display of America's 'domestic life' presented to the world in September 2005 was both unexpected and unintended. It was like a quarrelling family turning on the lights at home before closing the curtains, giving the world outside a glimpse of how they live.

The logic of the market

The aftermath of Katrina exposes a fundamental conflict between two approaches to human rights in American society. One approach may be labelled the 'duty of care'. It is the ethos that led the stranded residents of New Orleans to expect they would be helped and rescued. The other approach is the logic of the market, which should now be described in more detail.

By the logic of the market I mean the following sequence of reasoning:

- the possession of private property is the best way for people to maximize their chances for survival and comfort, enabling them to live decent lives as full human beings;
- people who do not own sufficient property to be full human beings are in a humiliating situation and it would be reasonable

to expect them to try and get out of this situation by any means open to them;

- wealth and the capacity to own property are generated through the market, which must remain open to all talents;
- the market generates wealth most efficiently when people are given the freedom to pursue their own profit-seeking plans single-mindedly and vigorously within the law;
- the law must, above all, protect the right of people who own private property to enjoy it undisturbed in ways that they choose;
- through the market, wealth flows to those who are most energetic and cunning, which is only fair since they are the ones who deserve it;
- the poor are poor because they lack sufficient energy, guile and forethought to equip themselves to be effective players in the market;
- it is a proper task of government to prevent discontented poor people from organizing to undermine market institutions or steal the wealth of those who have earned it, deservedly, through the market;
- private wealth in homes and businesses should be protected through tough policing and efficient prisons; and
- efforts should be made to undermine by any legitimate means the credibility and effectiveness of 'socialistic' enterprises, including expensive welfare programmes which interfere with the market by creating the wrong attitudes and giving people habits of dependence.

In terms of the interplay between *freedom, agency, security and recognition* discussed in chapter 3, the logic of the market does two things:

1 It places much more emphasis on providing everyone with the *freedom* of the market (the right to buy if they have the money) than on giving the poor and weak *security* (the right to support and protection if they do not have the money to use their market freedom).
2 It defines the socio-political order as a set of mechanisms for encouraging *agency* (especially business entrepreneurship) by private individuals and companies rather than a way of giving effective *recognition* to the social rights of those who are marginalized.

This pattern of thinking means that the poor are both pitied and feared. In the South, where Katrina struck, the historical effects of slavery intensify the situation. Its main legacy is the deeply embedded stereotype of African Americans as being less 'human' than whites: human enough to be resentful and dangerous, but not human enough to be accepted as equals. There is an equally virulent, and equally inaccurate, counter-stereotype of whites as being cold and cruel.

New Orleans belonged to the Old South and most of its population were African American.[4] Many survivors of the hurricane were evacuated to cities such as Houston in Texas, part of the more prosperous and modern New South and, incidentally, home of the elder Bush and his wife, Barbara. The Old South and the New South are different in some ways but similar in others. When slavery was abolished, it left behind a deep-ingrained racism that was the basis of a rigid caste system in the cotton states. Its memory remains strong even though racial segregation was officially abolished half a century ago. Slavery was one manifestation of the honour code whose other forms included the predeliction for duelling and 'manliness' still associated with Texas and the New South.[5]

Wherever news arrived in neighbouring cities that evacuees from New Orleans were coming, gun sales increased. The middling rich were quietly terrified. The super-rich behaved a little like courtiers at Versailles in the late eighteenth century, talking in a half-amused, half-frightened way about the degraded condition of the provincial peasantry. One well-known resident of Houston unintentionally played the role of Marie Antoinette.[6]

New Orleans, a poor, mainly black city that traditionally returned Democrats to Congress was not automatically at the top of the agenda for a federal administration primarily concerned with the interests of rich, mainly white people who voted Republican. In any case, the logic of the market, reinforced by racism, provided an explanation for why the people of New Orleans were in trouble and why they were having difficulties getting out of it: they were 'evidently' inadequate.

The logic of the market dictated that the main initial task of the police in New Orleans when the hurricane struck was to protect businesses from theft, whether motivated by starvation or greed. It absolved the rich from any blame for the humiliation and suffering that occurred. The disaster simply did not seem to be their fault or responsibility.

Many people in New Orleans had a different viewpoint. There was a strong feeling that the duty of care was being neglected. Aaron Broussard, president of Jefferson Parish, said the aftermath of the hurricane was 'one of the worst abandonments of Americans on American soil ever in US history'.[7]

In an open letter to President Bush on Sunday 4 September the editor of the New Orleans *Times-Picayune* angrily complained that the government had seriously neglected the city's needs. The people of New Orleans had deserved rescuing but many who could have been were not. That was to the government's shame.[8]

On the same day the paper reported New Orleans City Council President Oliver Thomas as berating neighbouring cities such as Baton Rouge for refusing to take in evacuees from New Orleans. Meanwhile, the mayor of New Orleans, Ray Nagin, criticized nearby Jefferson Parish for refusing entry to people trying to escape from New Orleans crossing the bridge to the higher ground in the mainly white suburbs. He said they had been met at the parish line by people with dogs and guns who said they intended to preserve their assets. Nagin's comment was: ' "Some people value homes, cars and jewelry more than human life." '[9]

A few statistics will help explain the mayor's resentment at this apparent example of racial and class exclusion inflicted on poor blacks by more comfortably-off whites at a time of life-or-death crisis. The populations of the Orleans Parish (including much of down-town New Orleans) and Jefferson Parish (part of the New Orleans suburban area) are approximately the same, each containing about half a million people. However, Jefferson is 70 per cent white with a home ownership rate of over 60 per cent. By contrast, Orleans Parish is over 70 per cent black with a home ownership rate of under 50 per cent. In Jefferson, 13.7 per cent of the population lives in poverty. In Orleans Parish the figure is 27.9 per cent.[10]

Between honour and human rights

The conflict between the duty of care and the logic of the market is not exclusive to the United States. It can be found in many other places throughout the world. However, it takes a particular form in America because of two things:

- the special cultural and political position given to the market within that society; and
- the residual strength of the racist form of honour code inherited from the days of American slavery.

To make sense of the way the logic of the market works, not just in the United States but elsewhere, we have to start by recalling that there are two general approaches to humiliation (see box 6.1).

One approach is to accept humiliation in all its many forms as a fact of life. That is the way of the honour code. Within this framework, the world tends to get ruled by those who humiliate others while those at the bottom experience little other than being humiliated. The people in the middle of the social order have to suffer humiliation imposed by those above them but are able to humiliate those below themselves. This was the code of the racist Old South where those 'in the middle' were the poor whites.

The honour code also applies in tribal societies such as Iraq, where the ruling tribes, mainly Sunni Muslim during the time of Saddam's presidency, try as far as possible to relegate or exclude members of rival tribes (mainly Shia or Kurdish). Meanwhile, alongside this 'vertical' or top-down humiliation, there is a constant undercurrent of 'horizontal' humiliation and counter-humiliation between rivals within the main religious or ethnic groups.

The other general approach to humiliation is to 'outlaw' it and take all feasible action to eliminate it. That is the way of the human rights code, which in its fully fledged form includes a general 'duty of care' by society for all its members. By *duty of care* I mean the idea that a society has a responsibility to do everything possible to reduce, alleviate or eliminate social deprivation. By *social deprivation*

Box 6.1   The logic of the market: between honour and human rights

The logic
of the market
(mixture of the honour code
and the human rights code)

The honour code
(Humiliate or
be humiliated)

The human rights code
(Duty of care: eliminate
all avoidable humiliation)

I mean circumstances that lead to individuals or groups within that society being denied or deprived of the means of having a decent existence. A *decent existence* is one in which each individual is treated in a respectful way and given substantial opportunities to acquire a reasonable and satisfying education, job and income. If they are unable, through no fault of their own, to participate in society in this way, they should still be protected from hardship. To deny or deprive someone of those means and opportunities, to which they have a right, either as a deliberate policy or by wilful or ignorant neglect, is to impose humiliation upon them.

In many societies throughout the world at present, one or other of these two general approaches is dominant, although the other usually maintains a powerful presence. In the European Union, for example, the fully fledged human rights code has held sway for many years. In much of Asia, the honour code has a much stronger presence, closely related to the residual strength of the extended family and the importance of ethnic and religious affiliations.

All these countries have been under siege during the past two decades from the United States and multilateral organizations pursuing the 'Washington Consensus'. They have been told to implement a third approach, the logic of the market, in the name of globalization.

As we have seen, the logic of the market is neither fish nor fowl. It does not fall exclusively in either the human rights or the honour code camp. In fact, the logic of the market has characteristics derived from both codes:

- like the honour code, it accepts humiliation as a fact of life;
- like the human rights approach, it says everyone has the right to aspire to a decent life and should be free;
- like the honour code, it sees life as a struggle in which the winners are those people who know how to look after themselves;[11] and,
- like the human rights code, it wants to eliminate violence from human relationships as much as possible.

In practice, the logic of the market sometimes veers more closely to the honour code than this summary might suggest. In other words, private property may use its power to imprison trouble-makers on a large scale, deliberately subjecting them to humiliating conditions. Also, a degree of violence or the threat of violence may be tolerated in the name of protecting private property.[12] In its extreme manifestations, the logic of the market sometimes appears to be an honour code masquerading as a code of human rights.[13]

The peculiar aspect of the United States in the early years of the twenty-first century is that, unlike other societies, the logic of the market has 'swallowed' both the human rights tradition and the honour tradition. This has happened during the last quarter of a century. The overt racism of the Old South has gone underground. So has the duty of care embodied in the New Deal tradition. Both the Republican and the Democrat parties are targeting the mainly white suburbs and broadly agree on the need to keep taxes low, business happy and government small. The logic of the market no longer has any competitors. The United States has painted itself into a corner, for the moment at least.[14]

Inside the Lexus

Standing in that corner is Thomas Friedman. For readers of the *New York Times* he is America's window on the world. He sees that world, figuratively speaking, through the window of a Lexus, symbol of all that is global and modern. The car speeds past olive groves, symbol of all that is local and traditional, groves that Friedman expects to see uprooted, taken over by multinational companies, or turned into 'Olives Я Us' theme parks.

In *The Lexus and the Olive Tree* (2000) Friedman contrasts the dynamism of societies such as the United States – which, he asserts, is thoroughly committed to globalization and the logic of the market – with the inertia and resistance found in nations that prefer their own local ways and want olives from their own trees. Friedman thinks globalization is an irresistible force that imposes a harsh but ultimately benevolent discipline on every society. In his view, the United States is showing the way: its assets are a diverse population, efficient capital markets, transparent business regulation, democracy, flexible labour markets, cultural tolerance, a positive attitude towards risk-taking and innovation, and a willingness to think big.

Friedman believes that the rest of the world is bound to want to follow the pathway of American success. To do so, he advises, all countries should adapt to rapid decision-making and change, accept the market and new technology as forces of creative destruction, harvest all the available knowledge, maintain a clear brand image as a country, and be open and transparent in all their dealings. Then they will fit more easily into a globalized world in which the spirit of connectedness and connectivity will tear down all walls and barriers. Globalization turns enemies into competitors, forces businesses to decentralize, and democratically welcomes anyone with enough information, finance and basic technology.

Friedman's account of the logic of the market links economic deregulation with political democratization, and relates both to rationalization in the spheres of science, technology and government. We will return to his work below. For the moment, let us notice that he is part of a small flotilla of analysts sailing in broadly the same optimistic direction.[15]

Francis Fukuyama arrives at conclusions broadly compatible with Friedman's but by a more complex intellectual route. In *The End of History and The Last Man* (1992), Fukuyama gives a special place to science and technology which confer military advantages on the most highly developed states, permit the accumulation of wealth and allow an ever-increasing set of human desires to be satisfied. Because all countries that modernize want these advantages, they are bound to develop the rational and efficient institutions that produce them. They are, therefore, also bound to become more alike: urban, industrial, scientific and capitalist.

Science leads to capitalism, according to Fukuyama, but 'there is no economically necessary reason why advanced industrialization should produce political liberty' (Fukuyama 1992, xv). To explain why it does he turns to Hegel, who follows Plato's belief that human beings have a strong 'desire for recognition' (xvi).[16] If this is denied they feel angry. If they fail to live up to their own standards they feel shame. According to Hegel such desires and emotions 'are what drives the historical process' (xvii).[17] Here Fukuyama's argument overlaps with the case made, in different ways, by Honneth, Margalit and Sennett (see chapter 3). However, Fukuyama's analysis is more optimistic than theirs.

Fukuyama follows Hegel's account of history as a battle for prestige which initially divided society into masters and slaves but then led to dissatisfaction. Slaves did not want their servitude; masters did not want to depend on the worthless recognition provided by abject slaves, in other words, imperfect human beings. The French and American revolutions resolved this contradiction.

The solution was for the state to grant rights to all members of the society: in other words, democracy. In the international arena this lead to the break-up of empires and recognition of the rights of national states. This process was completed with the break-up of the Soviet Union. So, argues Fukuyama, since the force that drives history has been largely satisfied, our 'truly global culture' (126) has arrived at the end of history.[18] Liberation has displaced humiliation.[19]

Bitter olives

Many analysts disagree with both Friedman and Fukuyama. They are not convinced that the logic of the market drives clearly and straightforwardly towards prosperity, rationality and liberation. Nor do they think the game is over or its rules settled.[20]

No, they say, the world is becoming more insecure and risky. The labour force is undergoing 'Brazilianization' (Beck 1999a, 161), losing its job rights.[21] The old contract between employers and employees is breaking down. Loyalty and hard work no longer bring security and a good life. Ordinary people don't feel so insulated from the inherent riskiness of science, technology, business and government. People increasingly see themselves as potential victims. Humiliation is a more prominent feature on their horizon than liberation.

Box 6.2   Some possible costs and benefits of the global logic of the market

	Political	*POSSIBLE COSTS*	Economic	
For rulers/ leaders	*Humiliating loss of face*		*Corruption*	For rulers/ leaders
		POSSIBLE BENEFITS		
		new technology new jobs flexible labour market efficient capital market transparent business regulation democracy innovation rapid social change liberation		
For ordinary people	*Resentment Desire for revenge*		*Loss of job rights Increased risk*	For ordinary people
	Political		Economic	

How do you balance gains in economic productivity against the costs of losing political face? In the words of Josef Joffe[22]:

> whether among men or nations, the most intractable conflicts are those that centre on pride, prestige and position. Russia has lost an empire; democratic or not, it may want it back. . . . China remembers itself as the 'Middle Kingdom', one that was humiliated first by western, then by Japanese imperialism . . . Japan modernized without Westernizing . . . pride and resentment might come to weigh more heavily on the Japanese soul than the memory of utter devastation between 1941 and 1945. . . . The Islamic world . . . is the most combustible segment of the international system . . . [with] regimes incapable of granting either democracy or prosperity to their populations, ineradicable memories of lost glory and humiliation by the West, an ideology that refuses to distinguish between mosque and *majlis* [parliament], simmering conflicts within and between states, and, above all, the temptation to close the power gap between itself and the West with the short cut of nuclear weapons. (Joffe 1998, 48–9)

In his *Global Disorder* (2003) Robert Harvey has his own list of threats to global stability: not just the nuclear proliferation crisis,[23] but also disintegrating states such as Yugoslavia, Afghanistan, Yemen, Sudan, Somalia, Chechnya, Congo and Columbia; he further notes poverty, mass migration, hunger, disease, debt, the globalization of crime (including drugs trafficking) and the absence of enforceable human rights in many parts of the world.[24]

Harvey, a former Conservative MP and assistant editor of *The Economist*, does not share Alan Shipman's confidence in large business corporations. Harvey recalls the capitalist free-for-all that incubated communism, and warns that 'global capitalism is reaching a critical mass of irresponsibility and remoteness that could incubate another horrific anti-capitalist changeling early in the millennium' (269).

Robert Kaplan surveyed this unstable world at ground level for his book *The Ends of the Earth* (1996). He travelled, mainly by bus and car, from West Africa, through Egypt, Turkey, Iran, Central Asia and India to Southeast Asia. Appropriately, one of his first ports of call was Adjamé-Bramakote in the Ivory Coast: Bramakote means 'no choice' (Kaplan 1996, 15). Kaplan thinks he has seen our global future in the scenes of hopelessness he found in rapidly growing cities where disease, disorder and despair were getting beyond the control of government. In most places nobody was in control of the situation, although some people were profiting from it.

Only occasionally, as in the Rishi Valley in India, did Kaplan find a local population that was successfully regenerating its environment and securing its livelihood without outside help.[25] Sri Naidu, the Rishi Valley estate manager, told Kaplan: 'A society has to self-discover things, even if it is already known to outsiders. That way it will stick through experience and become ingrained in the local mentality' (Kaplan 1996, 367).

Contrast this case with the story Kaplan heard in Sierra Leone, where a member of the government told him that his country was suffering 'the revenge of the poor, of the social failures, of the people least able to bring up children in a modern society. The boys who took power in Sierra Leone [in 1992] came from houses like this', he said, jabbing his finger at a corrugated metal shack a few feet away, teeming with children. 'On Wednesday they took over, on Friday they robbed the central bank. In their first three months in office, these boys confiscated all the official Mercedes, Volvos and BMWs and wilfully wrecked them on the road.' The minister mentioned one coup leader who shot the people who paid for his schooling, 'in order to erase the humiliation and mitigate the power his middle-class sponsors held over him' (Kaplan 1996, 32–3).[26]

Such feelings are not confined to Africa. The revenge of the poor may also take place in New Orleans or Watts or in any big city anywhere in the world. Perhaps it has hardly begun. If and when it happens it will probably take many people by surprise. This is because for decades the voice of the poor has been drowned out by the voice of big business.

Marketing the market

The one thing that most people 'know' about globalization is that big business is now a large part of it. One reason they 'know' this is that big business tells them so, repeatedly and loudly. This is the latest episode in what has been, and continues to be, a difficult historical journey for merchants and traders.

During the twentieth century business had to demonstrate considerable flexibility in its pursuit of profit. Market operators had to be prepared to ride in whatever socio-political vehicle was going, persuading those in the driving seat to let them come along. The political and moral climate has changed quite radically, in more than one direction, in the space of a few decades, even if we leave aside the challenges of trading in or with fascist or communist regimes. By 1900 Western business entrepreneurs had become well adapted to European imperialism: drilling for oil here, mining for gold there, and sending their agents north, east, south and west to make sure that whiskey, tobacco, marmalade and other home comforts graced expatriate kitchens and verandas from Mombasa to Mandalay.

By 1950 the world had changed. European imperialism was politically incorrect, and social democratic governments were setting a new tone. The Keynesian welfare state was in full spate and national planning was the vogue. Business needed to hitch another ride. It made itself part of the planning process, tying itself to the state and its social purposes, winning prestige by doing this.

Fast forward another half century: the game had changed profoundly once again. By 2000 the Keynesian welfare state had gone out of fashion in the United States and much of Europe. One reason is that a large part of the generation born in the 1940s, the main beneficiaries of the welfare state, got themselves good jobs, felt more secure, bought their own homes, and began to think of themselves as property owners who could look after their own interests without government interference. They started to object loudly about paying taxes to support people who had not been so successful. They wanted to pull the ladder up and leave the stragglers down below.

Governments that took a 'profligate' 'tax-and-spend' approach were voted out. One result was a fashion for the privatization of many government functions, from air traffic control to prisons. Government sold off as many assets and functions as they dared. For a few years this squared the circle, bringing in extra income while allowing well-publicized tax cuts to take place.

This new climate evolved in the 1970s, especially in Britain and the United States, where central government's authority had been significantly weakened by that time. The root cause was a successful revolt by nationalist and tribal movements in many parts of the world against Western imperialism. This new refusal to kow-tow led to a chain of humiliations for the West in Asia, Africa and the Middle East during the 1960s and 1970s, culminating in the oil crisis, the US withdrawal from Saigon, the devaluation of the dollar and the US embassy siege in Tehran. It was a dramatic payback for two centuries of Western imperial rule.

The overall result at first seemed disastrous for business and the market. While the colonial empires and later the Keynesian welfare state had given them political and ideological cover in the past, in the late twentieth century this was lost. Imperialism and social democracy had provided larger frameworks around which business and the market could entwine themselves. In those days, big business could justify itself on patriotic grounds. It had been able to infiltrate its own private interests into these grand enterprises with their great public purposes. By the 1980s, however, these hosts were dying off. It became much more difficult to suggest that profits made by business were won in the service of a larger public interest. Instead, multinationals began to seem like modern Vikings, scouring the oceans and continents for attractive targets. It became much easier to say that business was too powerful, too greedy and too irresponsible.

In other words, after a century of borrowing other people's imperialist and national rhetoric, business and the market found they needed an ideology of their own. It was easier to dust off an old god rather than invent a completely new one. So Adam Smith, whose *Wealth of Nations* appeared in 1776, was resurrected (Smith 1979). Market fundamentalists[27] made selfishness respectable by claiming it had a public purpose. In Margaret Thatcher and Ronald Reagan they found leaders who were happy to carry the message to a wider political public. Spokespeople for business and the market turned their potentially humiliating loss of face, their exposure as being selfish and irresponsible, into a propaganda triumph.

Market fundamentalists marketed the market. They re-branded it as an engine of human liberation. Their story was that supporters of the market had seen through the false claims of the modern state which over-regulated citizens. They knew, they said, that behind the 'emancipated' social hierarchy running the welfare state were the same old absolutist pretensions. In their view the state was intrinsically rigid, unjust, anti-enterprise and hostile to the broadening of opportunity. It would be best to keep it weak and small, best to leave the work of society as far as possible to good citizens in groups and networks such as those forming naturally within the marketplace.

In practice, this approach has had major consequences at both the national and global levels. Within national societies, the activities of private investors and private consumers have been promoted as the key expression of democratic citizenship. Private market decisions have moved into space previously given over to public debate. The idea that the people as a whole should have the most powerful say in how their social, economic and cultural environment develops, and that this voice should be expressed and enforced through democratic government, has been allowed to wither.[28]

How the market can humiliate

If you have enough money or credit to get what you need for a decent life, then the market is not a matter of life and death. Instead, it is a serious game, sometimes stressful, sometimes entertaining. At the very most this applies to 20 per cent of the world's population. For the other 80 per cent, the market generates repeated humiliation. This has relatively little effect on local markets, where people deal on familiar terms with each other, buying and selling the goods and services they need. In such cases, the local crowd provides a moral pressure that keeps the game relatively fair according to the norms prevailing in the community. In other words, the law of supply and demand is interwoven with a complex structure of social obligations to do with family, religion, custom, tribal or ethnic sensitivities and the prevailing view of 'how we do things round here'.

Markets of this kind, however, are marginalized when outsiders with a new range of goods and services and powerful backing move into the local area. This has occurred many times over the centuries as regional, national and international market networks have pene-trated into previously sheltered enclaves. It may be that fears engen-dered by this disturbing process lie behind the enduring popularity of medieval folk tales such as the Pied Piper of Hamelin and Robin Hood.

The outsiders bring new values, a new set of cultural attitudes embodied in their goods. With their deep pockets, they undercut local prices and overbid local competitors for facilities. Once installed locally, they use their links with wider networks to offer new oppor-tunities for talented and cooperative locals, especially the young, some of whom move out into these wider networks. If too many local people prove too troublesome, the powerful outsiders withdraw their investments and move on to another locality.

Market transactions become disengaged from their previous inti-mate involvement with the do's and don'ts of the local culture. The local pecking order is disrupted. Some families and groups that did badly under the previous regime do much better in the new condi-tions. The old community leaders have their noses put out of joint. At the same time many people discover that:

- the skills, beliefs and assets they possess have little worth within the big new marketplace;
- the cost of acquiring marketable assets such as a more 'modern' education is much too high to meet;

- the place they were brought up to think of as home is now like a prison;
- they are becoming dependent on technologies brought by 'outsiders' over which they have no control and little understanding; and
- many of the younger, more adaptable people are being lost to the community as they leave their parental homes and discover the big, wide world.

These painful discoveries have been made repeatedly over many generations and centuries: in smaller towns and villages during the weaving together of national markets; and, more recently, in larger cities as multinational corporations have McDonaldized, Disneyized, Wal-Marted, Hondarized, Toshibarized and Nokiarized the whole world.

Two sides of the story

It is fairly easy to see how the local audience perceives the difficulties just described. Powerful and glamorous strangers come into town and tell everyone about the good life available to emancipated citizen-consumers. They are as alluring as the Pied Piper of Hamelin. At the same time they use their influence, directly and through bodies such as WTO and IMF, to make sure local business taxes are not raised to pay for a decent local infrastructure (health care, schooling, housing, pensions and so on). In other words, they get people excited about the good future they could and should have, then stop them getting it.

The other side of this story, however, is an important one. Suppose you are an ambitious, intelligent person in a non-Western country appalled by the poverty and ignorance all around you. Suppose you want to make a significant contribution to raising standards of all kinds in your country. What do you do? You may be very reluctant to enter the passionate and ruthless worlds of politics and religion, whose practitioners often 'play the humiliation game'. To do well there you probably need to have great wealth or many family connections. If you don't, you must become the servant of someone who has those things. Suppose you do not wish to play it that way.

Another possibility is to join the military or to enter big business. In both cases, there are strong links to Western organizations, channels along which new technology, fresh investment capital and the latest organizational techniques can flow to your country. You can be part of this process, especially if you get yourself to a good business school or military academy.[29]

The key test is performance. If you conduct successful operations you get noticed, get promoted and can rise to the top. That is good for you. Perhaps you can also do good things for your society, or at least for your own children and grandchildren since you may want to give them the chance to live in a stable, prosperous country, without having to emigrate. If you acquire sufficient influence as a corporate executive or a military officer you can make a contribution to the mission implied by box 6.2, which outlines possible costs and benefits of the global logic of the market. The possible benefits of the global logic of the market appear as a kind of forest clearing surrounded on all sides by possible costs. How do you get your country into that clearing without its people being devoured by the beasts lurking within the surrounding forest?

Seen from this vantage point, the mission of the military and big business, working together, is to engineer stability within the political framework of the society and to maintain it for a period long enough to:

- prevent the costs of business globalization (the global logic of the market) from getting out of hand; while also
- enabling substantial new resources (capital, skills, knowledge, organizational techniques and modern attitudes) to enter your country and become deeply embedded, not just at the top of society, but also in the urban neighbourhoods and rural villages.

There is a trade-off. You are liable to be accused of being a servant of Western interests, especially by Western 'radicals' or, more seriously, by many political or religious leaders in your own country. However, like the home-grown but 'Romanized' provincial establishments of the Roman Empire in its latter days you are quietly building up the strength of your own society for the days when the Roman legions withdraw and leave your country to fight its own fights and make its own way in the world.

*   *   *

In this chapter we have: discovered that the logic of the market excludes or minimizes the duty of care and is an amalgam of the honour and human rights codes; reviewed arguments about the benefits and costs of the logic of the market; carried out a historical survey of the shifting relationship between business and globalization; analysed how the market can bring humiliation in certain circumstances; and seen how the market can, if skilfully managed, bring benefits to developing societies.

7

The Cosmopolitan Condition

Discussions of the imperial impulse and the logic of the market both evoke sharp-edged images of 'perpetrators' (wicked sheriffs, heartless traders) and 'victims' (defenceless subjects and workers). The third global generator of humiliation is less easy to characterize. Why do some people experiencing the cosmopolitan condition identify themselves as 'victims' while others do not? How do they decide who is to 'blame' for their feelings of displacement and belittlement?

Cosmopolitan conspirators

The conspirators who flew the two hijacked aeroplanes into the twin towers on 9/11 were not poor. Nor were they scarred by a childhood and adolescence lived in the prison-like conditions of the Gaza Strip. They were thoroughly middle class. It would be difficult to make the case that they were humiliated by a denial of freedom, opportunity or the means to live a comfortable modern life as that is generally understood.

To understand them we should turn neither to Robin Hood nor to the Pied Piper, but to Guy Fawkes, one of thirteen men involved in the Gunpowder Plot, an attempt to blow up the English Houses of Parliament on 5 November 1605.

The leading 9/11 hijackers were urbane religious zealots: well-educated, well-heeled, well-travelled and well-connected. They were global citizens or, more accurately, global denizens.[1] Consider some of their backgrounds:

- Mohamed Atta, who lived in Germany, was an urban planner, the son of an Egyptian attorney;
- Ziad al-Jarrah, born in Lebanon, also came from an affluent family and, like Atta, was pursuing higher education in Germany; and
- Marwan al-Shehhi, Atta's cousin, remembered as being 'convivial' and 'a regular guy', wore Western clothes and occasionally rented cars for trips to Berlin, France and the Netherlands.[2]

If we want to make sense of what they did, to know why they carried out such a desperate and deadly act, we should go back four centuries, not to the Middle East but to Europe in the early modern period, the period of the Reformation and the Counter-Reformation, the time in the sixteenth and early seventeenth centuries when men and women killed each other in very large numbers in the name of religion.[3]

Let us compare the conspirators who carried out the 9/11 attacks in the United States with the gunpowder plotters of 1605, Guy Fawkes and the rest, all devoted Roman Catholics, all determined to detonate a huge explosion beneath the English ruling class at the opening of parliament.[4] These men were also urbane religious zealots: well-educated, well-heeled, well-travelled and well-connected. They were men about town:

- Robert Catesby was prosperous, from a very good family, known in court circles, and much travelled on the continent of Europe;[5]
- Everard Digby was also a courtier, well regarded;
- Robert Wintour, rich from the salt trade, married the daughter of an aristocrat;
- Christopher Wright, old schoolfriend of Guy Fawkes, owned property at Lambeth in London and spent much of his time there;
- Thomas Percy was related to the Earl of Northumberland.

Why, in 1605 or 2001, were a number of relatively affluent, educated men, apparently with so much to live for, willing to get involved in extreme actions that carried the certainty or, at least, a very high risk of death?

That question is worth asking, and the parallel worth drawing because Europe in the sixteenth century and the early seventeenth had many striking similarities to the world in which we live today. History can teach us something about what is happening now.

The half-built upper storey

A metaphor may help. Suppose you and your neighbours live in a row of houses. You begin to notice that builders' scaffolding is being assembled around all the houses and a new platform is being created at roof height over the whole row. You protest but the work goes on. You cannot prevent it. More and more material gets shifted up onto the overhead platform. Machinery springs into life, loudspeakers blare, and you can see walls being built up there and doors and windows being installed. Some of your children and hired help start to clamber up the scaffolding to have a look. Many of them stay there and don't come back down. The next indignity occurs when pile drivers burst through your roof and force steel girders down through your living space to ground level. Life gets very difficult and you cannot rely on anything any more.

By now you are busy consulting your neighbours, sending delegations upstairs to the new upper storey that is being constructed over all your heads, and thinking of moving up there yourself, not because you particularly want to, but because it seems the only way to survive.

That is a picture of early modern Europe at the time of Guy Fawkes (see box 7.1). It is also a picture of the late modern world four centuries later (see box 7.3).

Early modern Europe

By the sixteenth century European feudalism was falling apart. It was eventually replaced by national states operating at a higher societal level. Feudal lords fought against this without success. Some went down fighting but others had to adapt to a new socio-political regime, eventually dominated by glorious monarchs buttressed by glamorous royal courts, imposing judicial systems, well-equipped armies and loyal bureaucrats. By the late seventeenth century the regime of Louis XIV of France was the supreme example of this new order.

A new breed of monarchs emerged, building their power base outside the feudal bonds of loyalty between lords and vassals. For a

---

Box 7.1 Building a new upper storey: before and after in early modern Europe

BEFORE	▯ ▯ ▯ ▯ ▯ ▯ ▯ ▯	▯ ▯ ▯ represent feudal landed estates, local dynastic lords, and petty princedoms in *medieval* Europe until about 1500
AFTER	New 'upper storey' ▯ ▯ ▯ ▯ ▯ ▯ ▯ ▯	▯ ▯ ▯ represent feudal landed estates, local dynastic lords and petty princedoms in *early modern* Europe, i.e. *c.*1500–1650 Represents the new 'upper storey' appearing above ▯ ▯ ▯ as stronger dynastic (national) monarchies develop, exploiting resources from rural society and the cities (after *c.*1500)

---

long time these monarchs were as insecure as they were glorious. However, their campaigns to impose conquest humiliation on the old, localized feudal order of lords and peasants was helped by another process that was simultaneously undermining that order: the drift of people from the countryside to the cities. This diminished the authority and resource base of the seignorial lord on his local landed estate (see box 7.2).

The towns, especially ports and capital cities, had grown in size during the two hundred years since the Black Death in the mid-fourteenth century.[6] The invention of printing helped to make more people aware of the excitements of city life and strengthened their magnetic pull. The towns offered an exciting alternative to the boredom and oppression of life in the village. Town life was risky and dangerous. You might, for example, catch a nasty disease, get mugged, lose all your savings, get injured trying new kinds of work, be lynched by an angry crowd or suffer abuse from an employer who felt no sense of responsibility towards you. Despite these dangers, the towns were pulling many energetic, ambitious and

Box 7.2   The drift of power and influence away from feudal landed estates in early modern Europe, c.1500–1650

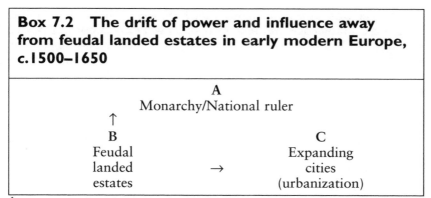

↑ → = shift of power and influence.

Box 7.3   Building a new upper storey: before and after in the late modern world

BEFORE	⬜ ⬜ ⬜ ⬜ ⬜ ⬜ ⬜ ⬜	⬜ ⬜ ⬜ represent sovereign national states in the *early and mid- 20th century*
AFTER	New 'upper storey' ⬜ ⬜ ⬜ ⬜ ⬜ ⬜ ⬜ ⬜	⬜ ⬜ ⬜ represent sovereign national states in *late 20th and early 21st centuries* Represents the new 'upper storey' appearing above ⬜ ⬜ ⬜ as multinational corporations, multilateral organizations (e.g. EU, WTO, IMF) and a new 'global monarchy' (US) assert their influence

skilled workers away from the countryside and out of the lord's influence. This fluid, expanding, social arena in the cities was vigorously and effectively challenging the control that feudal powers in the countryside had over the European population. In town, the role of the market was clear, and highly mobile assets such as cash, credit, specialized knowledge and technical skills were an important power resource. In these new market-driven arenas people could make their own way in the world, become 'masterless'[7] men and women, lapse into anonymity, and undergo profound changes in their approach to life. All these things were much less likely in small rural communities where everybody knew everybody else. They threatened the old feudal order.

During the sixteenth century and the early seventeenth, European dynasties such as the Tudors, Stuarts, Valois, Bourbons and Hapsburgs put on a grand show of propaganda, employing quite effective torturers and spy systems.[8] But seen from below, from the viewpoint of those fellow dynasts left behind by the royal families when they seized the crown, it was evident that the national rulers did not have the sort of day-to-day control over the urban population that the rural aristocrats and their fathers and grandfathers had enjoyed over the locals in the countryside.

The growing cities were dangerous and violent places, harbouring fanatics and visionaries. They were the seedbeds for the Protestant Reformation and the resultant Catholic Counter-Reformation. These movements brought fundamentalism, crowd violence, rebellion and war to Europe for much of the sixteenth century and well into the seventeenth.

In large part, the story of globalization in our present cosmopolitan era is a larger, louder, version of the urbanization story. The challenge of finding modes of communication and coexistence between different cultures was being confronted in microcosm in Europe over three centuries ago.[9] When emigrants from the little local worlds of early modern Europe moved to settle in the big city, the resulting clash of cultures was considerable. In spite of the best efforts of the Church to impose uniformity, people in adjacent valleys often had quite different traditions and quite distinctive dialects.

The late modern world

Now, four centuries later, the story is being repeated at a higher societal level. But in addition to urbanization, which continues in strength throughout the world, the part played by globalization has become more prominent.[10] This process is enabling many more people to live much of their lives shifting from one society to the next, occupying the social spaces above and between them. This provides both a challenge to, and an escape from, the pressures of life in specific national societies.

The global arena is a fluid, amorphous zone of ramifying networks and rapidly shifting people and capital. In this arena global finance, global business, global crime, global migration, global NGOs and global diplomats operate and exercise influence in several ways: through the internet, along airline routes joining major cities, within networks linking expatriate communities across national borders, and in shopping and entertainment spaces in almost every locality. The global arena, with its crowds of economic migrants and global investors and its complex intertwining networks, is a far cry from the old national state, characterized by a sturdy hierarchical structure integrating groups that 'know their place'.[11]

In our late modern world, in a similar way to sixteenth-century Europe but at a higher societal level, there is a shift in power balances away from the old territorial powers. This shift is happening in two directions (see box 7.4): towards the winners in the contest for domination among national states, although the main winner for the moment (i.e. the United States) has not securely or fully institutionalized and legitimized its rule; and towards a new, fluid, expanding, social arena where the market is of great importance, where highly mobile, non-fixed assets (as distinct from the fixed asset of land or territory) are the main power resources – in other words, towards the increasingly urbanized arena of globalization.[12]

Like the feudal landed estates in Europe centuries before, national states throughout the world are finding that power resources and authority are drifting away from them. In the old days, when they

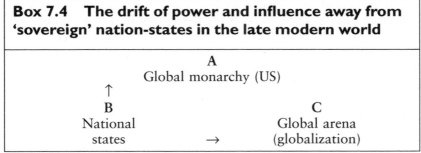

Box 7.4   The drift of power and influence away from 'sovereign' nation-states in the late modern world

A
Global monarchy (US)

↑	
B	C
National	Global arena
states →	(globalization)

↑ → = shift of power and influence.

looked upwards, the old feudal lords saw the royal insignia of an upstart Bourbon, Stuart or Hohenzollern ('who do they think they are?') at whose court they were commanded to attend.[13]

These days, a similar experience is being imposed on many national leaders. When they look upwards they see the Stars and Stripes. For the moment at least, the new global monarch and royal palace ('who do they think they are?') are in Washington. These days, the equivalent of being presented at the royal court is being admitted to the World Trade Organization.

It is easy to understand that these changes produce widespread feelings of being displaced, undervalued or left out. These experiences are deeply unsettling for everybody. They are unsettling for the new and insecure global monarchy, the United States, which, like the new monarchies in Europe centuries ago, is making up its new role as it goes along and is highly sensitive to criticism. They are unsettling for the 'old feudal barons', in other words, the leaders of the other nations, now forced to bow down before a state their predecessors had treated as culturally inferior. They are unsettling for ordinary people, many of whom either enjoy or would like to enjoy the high-tech wizardry associated with American life but who do not want to be ruled by a foreign government that they cannot think of as 'their own'.

Displacement and revenge

In early modern Europe, some people hated the new upper storey being built above their heads, especially if they lived in a country where the ideological cement of the new national monarchy was a religion they could not accept. Men such as Fawkes, Catesby and the others belonged to a long-established religion that had lost its political protection. The old rules no longer applied and the roof beneath which they had sheltered was being destroyed. In the 'good old days' Henry VIII had been pleased to receive the title 'Defender of the Faith' from the pope. But his eventual successor, James I, showed every sign of becoming a persecutor of the Roman Catholic religion when he assumed power in 1603.

Over eighty years before, the split in Christendom following Martin Luther's Protestant revolt in 1517 had weakened the influence of the Papacy and the Holy Roman Empire throughout Europe.[14] Extremists such as Fawkes and Catesby could neither forget nor forgive.

The similarity to Bin Laden and his adherents is striking. The caliphate was abolished in 1924. Eight decades later, Bin Laden was still lamenting the effects of this loss upon Muslims in the Middle East. There are interesting parallels between this situation and the impact of the Reformation on English Catholics. In both cases, historical events transformed a long-established overarching structure that had provided political and psychological security. In both cases, a religious group was left feeling deeply exposed to its enemies.

The main motivation for the gunpowder plotters was the fear that Catholicism was about to be criminalized.[15] England had been a Catholic country until a few decades before but those who clung to Rome became, in effect, enemies of the state. James I, imported from Scotland to succeed Elizabeth I, wanted legislation that would deprive Catholics of their civil rights, making them virtual outlaws.

The gunpowder plotters' drive to action was four-fold. First, they felt displaced: a tightly knit group that had been forced out of its rightful social position and denied what it was owed. Second, they felt crushed and conquered: any open display of faith was immediately repressed. Third, they were aggressively determined to strike back and take revenge, hurting their tormenters as much as possible. Fourth, they wanted to impose their own way upon others, with no choice except acquiescence or death.

The 9/11 hijackers had a similar four-fold drive: a sense of displacement, a feeling of being crushed and diminished, a desire to take revenge and a determination to fight for the triumph of the faith. Consider the description of Mohamed Atta given by Volker Hauth, a German urban planner who had been friendly with him.[16]

1 *Displacement.* Hauth said that Atta took an interest in the democratic practices of the West but remained somewhat detached from daily life in Germany, which to him was 'a strange world' with 'a strange language'. He maintained a strict personal life, praying daily.
2 *Diminishment.* Ideally Atta would have liked to be an urban planner in Egypt but he feared being criminalized for his religious beliefs. Instead, he had to suffer an 'inner exodus', a painful experience because it meant that he could not express his true opinions openly.
3 *Revenge.* When Hauth was asked to try and explain Atta's involvement in 9/11, he mentioned the provocation caused by Ariel Sharon's visit to the Temple Mount in Jerusalem. He assumed that Atta must have wanted to answer this by

threatening 'the holy place of the western world' – in other words, the World Trade Center.

4 *Determination to fight*. When Hauth first met Atta in 1993, he did not wear a beard, but he acquired one in late 1994. This, he had declared, was a sign of his solidarity with the religious people in Egypt who had been criminalized. He had decided that he no longer wished to hide his opinions but to express them freely.

Humiliated liberation

The conspiratorial networks of the gunpowder plotters and the 9/11 hijackers were embedded within much larger networks of cosmopolitan men and women who became vulnerable to a paradoxical condition: feeling liberated and humiliated at the same time. The reason is that urban immigrants in the sixteenth and early seventeenth centuries discovered, as new global denizens are now discovering, that the arenas of social existence to which they now belonged, or half belonged, were full of new conflicts and anxieties.

Most men and women living urban lives, cosmopolitan people, find that they have more freedom to think and feel for themselves. In fact, they are obliged to think and feel for themselves, however inadequate they find the results. There is no alternative. Unquestionable sources of authority are very difficult to find. For example, in this new world, those who wield most power resources worry constantly about their legitimacy. Their right to rule is frequently contested, sometimes violently.

In early modern Europe, people from rural villages, where neighbours, priests, teachers, aunts and uncles and so on had kept an eye on them, must have felt a distinct change of climate when they moved to the towns, a barometric shift as pressure to 'do the right thing' decreased. Such newcomers would have found opportunities to please themselves without someone reporting back to their family or their employer. Where was the strong voice of authority, the clear guidance about how to behave? Town-dwellers were caught between feudal lords busily protecting their own dynastic interests, monarchs who were as insecure as they were glorious, and a Church that had lost much of its credibility. Surrounded by evidence of society's instability and life's uncertainty, how could they chart a passage through their mortal existence towards the hereafter?

Now, as then, cosmopolitans receive mixed messages. The primordial socio-political orders, the village or city 'back home' from which they have half escaped and to which they still half belong, are being transformed by the pressure of competition from the dynamic new world taking shape outside and above. The town imposes its influence upon rural society, just as, later, globalization penetrates the boundaries of national states and transforms the life within.

The new urban or global arenas in which they find themselves and to which they also only half belong do not provide strong, clear, coherent and morally satisfying rules and structures. There are many new opportunities for advancement or failure, and a high degree of freedom from moral surveillance. This is liberating. However, urbanization and globalization also impose humiliation. In the new sociopolitical arena, the level of social support for the cosmopolitan's distinctive primordial identity, the one inherited from the old society, is greatly reduced. Meanwhile, the old society seems as if it is being washed away by tides of commerce and bureaucracy driven by outside interests in league with local collaborators.

Cosmopolitan wanderers are caught between the devil and the deep blue sea. They lose their old position within the local communities they have left behind. The longer they are away, the more likely it is that when they return 'home' they are half-strangers. It is a strain trying to avoid embarrassing your relatives with your much greater knowledge of the wider world while concealing your amusement at their old-fashioned ways. Meanwhile, you see the old place changing, becoming more 'modern', less authentic. After a while, it hurts to be there too long. You get bored and angry.

Back in the big wide world, where has the cosmopolitan 'arrived'? Life is a disorderly jungle of people getting by, getting high, getting on – and going where? There are too many confusing answers on offer and too many people satisfied with no answer at all. What does one do, surrounded by slick salesmen and turned-off cynics? Cosmopolis – the big city, the global arena – does not provide a simple, straightforward, supportive and reassuring source of authority that tells you who you are, how you should live and what you should be satisfied with.[17]

This analysis of the cosmopolitan condition accounts for two of the elements identified in the make-up of the potential religious zealot: a sense of displacement, and a feeling of being crushed or diminished. These are both aspects of humiliation. However, most cosmopolitans do not become religious zealots, even if they may be openly or secretly sympathetic to some of their actions, and even if they sometimes take part in crowd actions led by such zealots. The other two elements, the desire for revenge and the determination to resist by fighting to the death, are both ways of responding to humiliation. Why some people choose these potentially lethal responses is a matter requiring more detailed investigation of particular communities, cultures, social networks and personalities.[18]

Technology, politics and religion

The part played by the cosmopolitan condition as a global generator of humiliation is clearly a complex one: long-term historical trends in the spheres of technology and politics are important, as is religion. Let us look at these factors, briefly, in turn.

Information and identity

Some aspects of our contemporary cosmopolitan condition have been well described by Manuel Castells in *The Information Age* (1997–2000). The central argument of his three volumes may be summarized in a single sentence: new technology makes possible informational capitalism, which is producing crises of identity within national states, families and communities.

Castells argues that during the 1970s cost pressures from wage increases and the rise in the price of oil drove the leaders of advanced capitalist economies to use new information technology as a tool in restructuring their organizations. This meant more flexible labour, decentralization of control, and a shift away from rigid hierarchies to open and dynamic networks that could handle great complexity and a constant traffic of information. Informational capitalism was able to integrate dynamic economic sectors worldwide into a network of networks, especially in the arena of finance.

There were two results. Financial volatility was quickly transmitted around the world, damaging vulnerable national economies. A gulf opened up between global managerial elites, living in gated communities, and their labour forces: poor, localized, individualized, atomized and trapped in their ghettos. Cities became 'spaces of flows' (Castells 2000, 407), nodes within global networks, not valued places full of meaning for their inhabitants.

Three kinds of identity crisis have developed:

1   National states become players at the global level at the cost of losing touch with their national citizens, whom they can neither serve nor control to the same extent as previously.

2 Throughout the world the patriarchal family is undermined as women are drawn into the labour force and acquire increased control over their fecundity.
3 Media screens bring new cultural forces into local communities, undermining their old sense of reality.

These identity crises may, hopes Castells, lead to proactive social movements based on 'project identities' (1997, 8) seeking to make the world more just. However, the initial response consists of challenges expressing 'resistance' identities (8), for example, fundamentalism, ethnic conflict and riots in poor neighbourhoods. These forces may be found at work in Russia, Africa, Latin America, Southeast Asia and Europe. Castells' conclusion is: 'There is nothing that cannot be changed by conscious, purposeful social action, provided with information, and supported by legitimacy' (1998, 360).

Broken bonds

Castells is a little too optimistic. A social movement seriously seeking greater justice, one with a 'project' identity (in his terminology), would need either to win control of important levers of political and economic influence or cooperate with allies who already have such control.

However, both strategies are made more difficult by the weakening of the bond between governments and citizens in recent decades. The proportion of men and women abstaining from voting increased during the 1990s throughout the world.[19] People are steering clear of formal party politics, not getting involved if they can avoid it. This represents an active refusal to participate in a political system that many ordinary people think is now failing them. It is a revolt against being taken for a ride.

In response, government has become a 'stalker', watching its estranged citizens, silently and uninvited. The state's message 'We are watching you' is a forceful reassertion of a relationship that many citizens are trying to weaken.[20]

Since 9/11 the 'war on terror' has provided an opportunity for states to become more active and forceful. The need to defend the nation against terrorism has provided a rationale for increasing the state's powers to arrest and imprison people. Some of these powers may infringe previously untouchable civil liberties and even go some way beyond what defence against terrorism strictly demands.

The current climate is very unfavourable to political initiatives arising outside the charmed circle that includes national government circles, the top level of 'official' politics and the media, mainly controlled by large business interests. When major economic and political interests are involved, it is difficult to behave like an active democratic citizen without feeling like a trouble-maker. Those who are resentfully wrestling with the indignities of the cosmopolitan condition will not find much satisfaction there.

The situation is made more difficult still by the fact that throughout the American, Eurasian and African continents a kind of reformation is occurring.[21] Like the Reformation in early modern Europe it has two elements.

On the one hand, it is a protest against 'false' intermediaries between the people and higher authority. Nowadays these intermediaries include not only party politicians but also the mass media, a modern 'priesthood' claiming to interpret the words of the great god Demos. Many people are saying to these intermediaries: do not speak and act for us; do not tell us how to feel; we will do these things for ourselves. Disillusionment with the failed promises of those holding political authority has led many to withdraw, to privatize their ambitions and hopes, to turn themselves into workers and consumers first and foremost, looking after themselves and their families.[22]

On the other hand, the new late modern global reformation is, like the early modern European one, a search for identity and meaning. The most ambitious and dedicated worker-consumers, those who want to 'get on' not just 'get by', have to impose and accept a high degree of self-discipline. They learn to control and shape their bodies, minds and emotions.[23] Such a determined regime of self-preparation is likely to lead towards two questions: what kind of person do I want to be? And are the identities on offer satisfying? A kind of filtering process may occur as summarized in box 7.5.

Cosmopolitan America

The old system of national states cannot easily contain, control and institutionalize the flows of people, capital, goods, weapons and ideas around the globe. The world has undergone political deregulation as a result of the break-up of the European empires, the collapse of the Soviet Union and the end of the Cold War. There is no global political force that is sufficiently capable and motivated to perform the task of regulation.

The United States, or the American empire, is the nearest thing there is to such a force. The US government has an unrivalled capacity to get its own way on specific matters. However, its current and, indeed, 'normal' stance is 'America first'. The US government is trying to protect its basic supply lines, guarantee its own strategic security, and advance the business plans of influential American corporations. The rest of the world is perceived as a relatively disorderly and potentially dangerous 'environment' in which the United States, the 'real' world so to speak, is located.

At the centre of the American empire is, figuratively speaking, the tightly closed circle made by a wagon-train and within this circle the Western pioneers are hunkered down, enjoying their protected camp-fires but always remaining alert, on guard, prepared for attack at any moment. The hinterland outside the wagon-train circle has to be

---

Box 7.5 The cosmopolitan filter

Some worker-consumers find the modern urban identities on offer deeply unsatisfying.

Among those, some have the mental and emotional discipline that is needed to continue searching.

Among those, some turn towards religion.

Among those, some find that that the disciplines required for surviving the cosmopolitan condition match well with a religious frame of mind teaching the need to overcome wasteful diversions from the 'true' journey of life leading towards the heavenly end-goal at journey's end.

Among those, the supportive and persuasive bonds of comradeship and discipleship forged within fundamentalist religious groups encourage a few to think of themselves as heroes and martyrs enacting God's commands and purposes on earth.

monitored regularly for useful resources,[24] and checked out for lurking threats. Life outside the wagon-train circle can be exhilarating for short spells, especially if those involved have the military means to go wherever they like whenever they like. It is pleasant to feel liberated and, to a high degree, free of practical, legal and even moral restraints. It is exciting to exercise the imperial impulse.

However, it is important for those pioneers to be able to retreat back inside the protecting wagon-train circle and warm themselves at the homely campfire. This option is a vital psychological and political safeguard. But this option is disappearing, as we might expect in the light of experiences undergone by exiled cosmopolitans everywhere. The old American haunts change. The United States stops feeling like 'home'. Recently, commentators such as Pat Buchanan, Samuel Huntington, Thomas Frank and Michael Moore have all begun to worry that America just isn't America any more. Their book titles speak volumes: *The Decline of the West* (Buchanan 2002), *Who Are We?* (Huntington 2004), *What's the Matter with America?* (Frank 2004) and *Hey Dude, Where's My Country?* (Moore 2004).

In a cosmopolitan world, Americans are experiencing the cosmopolitan condition at double strength. They do not feel as content as they used to in their own homeland, the old 'new world' they thought they knew. It is changing in ways they cannot control and do not like. Nor can they agree upon their proper place in the new 'new world' that is the global arena.

*   *   *

In this chapter we have: compared the 9/11 hijackers with the gunpowder plotters in 1605; commented on urbanization and the growth of national monarchies in sixteenth- and early seventeenth-century Europe, and half a millennium later, found similarities with globalization and the development of the American 'global monarchy' in the late twentieth century and early years of the twenty-first; analysed the cosmopolitan condition these circumstances generate leading to humiliated liberation; looked at the parts played by technology, politics and religion in mediating the cosmopolitan condition; and considered how these pressures impinge upon American society and politics.

8

Escape

Now we turn to the second strand of the triple helix shaping globalization's hidden agenda: the way people *respond* to the degradations imposed by the global generators of humiliation. We are going to begin by looking at the response of attempted escape.

Riding into the sunset

One example of the feedback mechanisms that operate within the triple helix is the escape response to humiliation, which has affected globalization in a profound way. It has shaped a whole category of 'new' societies: the settler society, the most powerful of which is the United States. America is an unusual and fascinating phenomenon. It is a settler society that has also acquired a global empire; or, as I have labelled it, a global nation-state-empire. Almost all commentators accept that there is an American empire. The main disagreement among them is whether the existence of such an empire is a good thing or a bad thing; and whether it is inclined to strength or weakness.

Ask Andrew Bacevich, a former soldier turned academic, and we hear that the US government has gladly seized the opportunity to use its military power 'to expand an American imperium' where it served US interests to do so. Its 'ultimate objective is the creation of an open and integrated international order' (Bacevich 2002, 3) based on American-style democratic capitalism. This has been going on for at least a century, he says.

Turn to Thomas Barnett from the US Naval War College and you hear basically the same story, only this time projected into the future as an expanding mission to 'export security' into disorderly regions relevant to maintaining the smooth working of the world's 'functioning core' (Barnett 2004, 125). The same historical and future landscape surveyed by Noam Chomsky is portrayed as a bid for global dominance at the expense of human rights, pushed forward through the use of force and fraud (Chomsky 2003).

Michael Ignatieff takes a third position on the global deployment of military power by the United States and its allies in battle. Wars sometimes have to be fought on behalf of human rights. These days such interventions are generally intended to put matters right quickly so those intervening can leave: this is 'empire lite' (Ignatieff 2003). Such interventions are usually relatively cost-free in terms of casualties for the US. They are also subject to diminished democratic control by a relatively uninvolved public back home. This entails much moral jeopardy and the need for careful reflection.[1]

Charles Kupchan thinks the end of the era of American hegemony is in sight (Kupchan 2002). The European Union is gaining power, and China will not be far behind. American voters in the increasingly

Box 8.1	**The state of the American empire**			
	Strong and/or Getting Stronger		*Weak and/or Getting Weaker*	
Good	Bacevich, Barnett Kissinger, Brzezinski Ikenberry, Bobbit Nye		Ferguson	*Good*
	Ignatieff		Kupchan	
			Todd	
Bad	Chomsky	Mann	Wallerstein	*Bad*
	Strong and/or Getting Stronger		*Weak and/or Getting Weaker*	

influential South and West are not internationalist in spirit and do not want to pay the costs of American global hegemony. Taking a different tack, Henry Kissinger wants the US government to 'recognize its own pre-eminence but to conduct its policy as if it were still living in a world of many centers of power' (Kissinger 2002, 288).[2]

Zbigniew Brzezinski, one-time National Security Adviser, has a slightly different approach. In deliberately provocative language, he says that 'the three grand imperatives of imperial geo-strategy are to prevent collusion and maintain security dependence among the vassals, to keep tributaries pliant and protected, and to keep the barbarians from coming together' (Brzezinski 1997, 40). However, in the longer term it needs to take the lead in creating 'a global community of shared interest' (Brzezinski 2004).

John Ikenberry sees this process as already under way due to the 'open and penetrated character of the United States and the other advanced democracies'. He describes a 'sort of layer cake of intergovernmental institutions [that] extends outward from the United States across the Atlantic and Pacific' (Ikenberry 2001 pp. 254).[3] Joseph Nye stresses the need to share responsibility with other states whenever the action shifts from the military sphere, where America is pre-eminent, to the multi-polar economic sphere and to the complex transnational realm occupied by terrorists and others (Nye 2002).

Philip Bobbitt pitches the scale of the challenge facing America at a still more daunting level (Bobbitt 2002). He gives the United States the role of taking the lead in helping the world adjust to the transformation from a system of nation-states, focused on providing welfare for citizens, to a system of market-states which will help global markets to work more efficiently. Different kinds of market-state will emerge. They need rules for peaceful cooperation but armed conflict is also likely. However, war should be recognized as 'a creative act of civilized man' (xxxi).

There are plenty of critics who do not think America is able to cope with these challenges, irrespective of whether or not they are worthy ones. Niall Ferguson, who is 'fundamentally in favour of empire' (Ferguson 2004a, 24), believes that although there is no danger of 'economic overstretch' there is a serious problem: Americans 'lack the imperial cast of mind'; they have no 'will to power' (28–9). Michael Mann sees more profound structural problems. America's power capacities are very uneven, leading to fatal incoherence in its strategic behaviour. It is a 'military giant' (Mann 2003, 18) but an 'economic backseat driver' (49) with very few powers over other major economies, a 'political schizophrenic' (80) caught between multi- and uni-lateralism, and an 'ideological phantom' (100) operating in a world where imperialism has no moral credibility (81, 120).

Immanuel Wallerstein also sees structural factors that lead towards decline, inevitably in his view. Western Europe and Japan/East Asia are already competing economically on equal terms with the United States. US military expenditure is diverting capital and innovation from productive enterprise. The widespread use of the term 'imperial' to describe the United States, however satisfying it is to elements within the American leadership, is actually a profoundly 'delegitimizing term' (Wallerstein 2003, 308).[4]

Finally, Emmanuel Todd, in a subversive and witty book, notices that 'at the very moment when the world is discovering democracy and learning to get along politically without the United States, the United States is beginning to lose its democratic characteristics and is discovering that it cannot get along without the rest of the world' (Todd 2003, 20). The US, he says, is reduced to pushing around 'minor league powers such as Iraq, Iran, North Korea, Cuba, etc' (21) and developing showy items of military technology which do not, in practice, increase its capacity to tell Russia, Europe or Japan what to do.

In Todd's view, 'the declining economic, military, and ideological power of the United States does not allow the country to master effectively a world that has become too vast, too populous, too literate and too democratic'. The world's task is to find a way of 'managing, in everybody's best interests, America's losses' (22).

However, to gain understanding of America and ourselves we must expand the frame of reference. We must return to the theme of escape, and go back half a millennium.

The curse of responsibility

If we want to understand ourselves, and if we are either European or North American or influenced by Western culture, a good place to start is the Reformation. Go back to 1517 when Martin Luther took the immense personal risk of posting his Ninety-five Theses on the door of the church in Wittenberg. Luther was not prepared to leave the fate of his soul in the hands of an authority he did not respect.

The Reformation was ultimately about people taking responsibility for their own fate, in life and after death. It made them value the right, and fear the need, to choose for themselves. It made them hate anything that stopped them choosing freely. The Reformation burned into Western consciousness two impulses: the impulse to *escape*, to liberate oneself from potentially constricting circumstances; and the equally strong impulse to *dominate* and, if necessary, destroy those who might stand in your way. Each impulse came with a partner. The desire to escape was accompanied by deep feelings of *resentment* against the oppressive conditions that made escape necessary or highly desirable. The wish to dominate bred a strong feeling of *virtuousness* that enabled one to justify the imposition of one's own wishes, needs and agenda on others, often violently and destructively.

So, the escape response to humiliation typically comes with other baggage: the desire to dominate, deep feelings of resentment, and an obsessive need to feel virtuous. This broader constellation, of which escape is a part, will help us understand some aspects of the behaviour of Western ruling establishments, especially in settler societies, in other words, societies whose leading members had escaped from an old world in order to be able to dominate a new one.

Within this category, it will be especially useful for probing some aspects of the most powerful settler society of all, the United States. In particular, this analysis will help to make sense of some of the twists and turns of the US government's behaviour in the world since Vietnam, including the global strategy implemented by the neo-conservative interest that gained increased influence after 2001.

The disappearance of God

But first, let us return to the dreadful shattering of the medieval understanding that God was not only the maker of the world to which people belonged, but also an inhabitant of that world. The Reformation finally destroyed the medieval idea that the world was a place in which men and women could look around and both believe what they saw and see what they believed.

People lost their previous confidence that a readily explicable divine purpose existed and they and their world were expressions of it. From that point on, the self and its relationship to the world became problematic. The problems were not confined to signed-up members of Protestant creeds. The Catholicism of the Counter-Reformation had a distinctly 'protestant' anxiety about the soul's health and salvation.

Every thinking person now directly confronted issues relating to identity ('Who am I?'), knowledge ('What do I know?') and ethics ('how should I treat others?'), all of which had previously been the preserve of priestly authority. These problems faced all human beings trying to find their way through the shattered universe. That journey became much more dangerous to the soul and the body. What could be done? Luther found a princely protector. Calvin became master of a fortified city. The fate of Galileo (imprisoned by the Inquisition) and Bruno (burned at the stake) was a warning about what happened to those who were bold but unprotected.[5]

Matters became urgent, since souls were at risk, when different selves resolved their confusions and uncertainties in different ways that could not be reconciled with each other. One way to escape was to dissolve the self within a greater whole. John Donne conveyed this sense of membership within a larger body in his Meditation written in 1624:

> No man is an island entire of itself; every man is a piece of the conti-
> nent, a part of the main; if a clod be washed away by the sea, Europe
> is the less, as well as if a promontory were, as well as any manner of
> thy friends or of thine own were; any man's death diminishes me,
> because I am involved in mankind. And therefore never send to know
> for whom the bell tolls; it tolls for thee.[6]

Another approach was to improve the self's capacity to resist 'alien' intrusions, to strengthen the self through self-discipline. Ignatius Loyola, author of *Spiritual Exercises*, written in 1548, made this a basic strategy of the Society of Jesus (or Jesuits) whose guiding prin-

Box 8.2	Escape and domination	
	Management of the self	*Dealing with others*
Escape	Dissolve the self within a greater whole (for example, a crowd or a congregation)	Remove the self from 'corrupting' influences (for example, by migration)
Domination	Strengthen the self's capacity to resist and overcome 'alien' intrusions and sinful thoughts, for example, by prayerful self-discipline	Eliminate all possible external threats to the integrity of the self by attacking rival creeds and destroying all sources of ungodly temptation

ciple was loyalty to the Church (Loyola 1950). Having been educated by the Jesuits, Donne later became an Anglican. René Descartes, both philosopher and mathematician, was another product of Jesuit education. Ironically, Descartes used his Jesuit training in mental discipline not to strengthen loyalty to an existing belief, the intention of Ignatius, but rather to make a new discovery, to find the indissoluble core of existence. At the end of his lonely search, using the medium of thought, Descartes discovered that indissoluble core: it was the thinking self. Unlike Donne, Descartes was convinced that his own consciousness was not part of something larger but isolated. His mind tried to penetrate the surrounding fog with beams of rational thought but it systematically doubted all reports of 'continents' in the vicinity. For Descartes, every man was, indeed, an island.

Cosmopolitans like Donne and Descartes were deeply involved through their personal lives in the intense battles going on between Catholics and Protestants.[7] For some people, these issues were psychologically intolerable. Hamlet was far from alone in contemplating suicide, a theme on which Donne wrote a learned treatise.[8] However, there were other forms of escape also.

One way of absenting oneself from an oppressive and humiliating situation was to move to an uncivilized and uncultivated wilderness, where one might even establish a colony. This way of coping with uncertainty, confusion and threat involved removing the self physically from the danger of corruption in the old world one used to inhabit, and destroying all potential threats to the new world being constructed.[9]

The unsettled settler

Settlers wanted to start afresh. Some envisaged making a new and better society in an unspoilt Eden. That is the theme placed in the foreground by the American myth of the Pilgrim Fathers. But 'the city on the hill' had some very nasty suburbs.

Establishing a new colony meant using a heavy sword with two sharp edges: escape and domination. The first was a means to achieve liberation for the self. The second led to destruction for others. During the seventeenth century, and after, settlers in Ireland, South Africa and the American colonies used both edges of the sword. They wanted to be liberated from the evils of the old world they had left behind. They wanted to transform the new world they had found into their own empire. They wanted to turn it into the kind of land they had promised themselves in their dreams.[10] That meant being brutal to those that got in their way.

Early in the seventeenth century the English crown encouraged lowland Scots to emigrate to Ulster in the northern part of Ireland. Many of the settlers came from humiliating circumstances of poverty and marginality, scratching a living on the borderlands between Scotland and England. In Ireland they were caught between the Anglo-Irish upper class that despised them, and the indigenous Catholic population whom they despised in their turn. As a consequence, the relations between Protestants and Catholics were violent and full of resentment from the very beginning.[11]

This tone was set at the very top during the 1650s by Oliver Cromwell's systematic and ruthless policy of slaughtering, enslaving or, at least, corralling the locals. He set about establishing a 'reservation' in Connaught where the dangerous 'wild Irish' who had opposed the English (as opposed to the 'civilized' ones who had not) could be physically segregated, safe beyond the River Shannon.[12] This plan was an administrative failure but it anticipated later exercises such as 'Indian reservations' in the United States and 'native reserves' in South Africa.

Meanwhile, the descendants of Dutch settlers in South Africa were imposing slavery upon local tribes people. The doctrines of the Dutch Reformed Church confirmed their own superiority as a chosen people with no obligation to labour, just as centuries later they justified apartheid. The Boers felt very little obligation to their slaves, had no peasant bond to the soil and were thoroughly unsociable. Each man, it was said, 'fled the tyranny of his neighbour's smoke',[13] preferring isolation to neighbourliness.

Rather like the descendants of the lowland Scots who emigrated to Ulster, the children of the original Dutch settlers lived a poverty-stricken existence, little better than the 'inferior natives' they exploited and abused. Treated in a humiliating way, both by those who ruled the old 'home country' and by the British, the Boers responded by glorifying their own mission while humiliating the group below them in the absolutist hierarchy.

When the British arrived in the nineteenth century, the Boers switched from domination mode to escape mode. They left behind farms they had been cultivating for many generations and trekked hundreds of miles into the wilderness to recover their isolation.[14]

Like the Boers and lowland Scots who moved to Ulster, the American colonists were Protestants with a strong sense of mission and a powerful feeling of superiority over the indigenous population. But there was a major difference in the American case. The settlers in

Ulster were dominated by, and highly dependent upon, the British establishment from the seventeenth century onward. The Boers (or Afrikaners) were under constant pressure from the British in South Africa from the early nineteenth century until the formation of the Union of South Africa in 1910.[15]

By contrast, the American colonists broke free of the British Empire well before the end of the eighteenth century, and they stayed free of the British despite the War of 1812. As a result, the Americans have had over two centuries during which the dialectic between domination/destruction and escape/liberation has been able to work itself out with little in the way of check or hindrance.

Regeneration through violence

America's chosen 'Founders' (an institution or society usually decides these things long after the event) were a group of 'separatist' Puritans. These men and women could not practise their particular religion in Europe without being treated as criminals. So they took a chance and crossed the Atlantic. What kind of culture did they create? Richard Slotkin looked at the literature they produced in the first two and a half centuries leading up to the Civil War and gave an answer to that question (Slotkin 1973).[16]

American settler culture was characterized by anxiety and fear: anxiety in the form of guilt, and perhaps a vague expectation of punishment, for having abandoned the old world in Europe; fear of the loneliness and danger facing them in their new world. Would they be caught and chastised for abandoning those who nurtured them? Would they be swallowed up by the wilderness? Would they be turned into savages? Another element in American settler society was hope, hope of spiritual and material profit won through strenuous experience and divine help.

A typical example of the many stories of settlers being captured by wild natives, then escaping through the fortunate intervention of divine providence, is Cotton Mather's account of the captivity of Hannah Dustin. Published in 1697, it has a revealing title and subtitle: *Humiliations follow'd with Deliverances. A Brief Discourse On the Matter and Method, Of that HUMILIATION which would be an Hopeful Symptom of our Deliverance from Calamity. Accompanied and Accommodated with a NARRATIVE Of a Notable Deliverance lately received by some English Captives From the Hands of the Cruel Indians and some Improvement of that Narrative.*[17]

Mather's narrative transforms degradation at the hands of 'Cruel Indians' into hope of deliverance at the hands of God. In this case, God is introduced as an 'involved third party' who monitors and evaluates how the 'English Captives' respond to forced abasement. The lesson is that if God recognizes signs of Christian humility among the captives, he may be inclined to intervene on their behalf, enabling them to escape from their unfortunate entanglement.[18] This captivity myth reinforced the original 'founding' experience of humiliation followed by escape embodied in the story of the Pilgrim Fathers' journey from Europe.

Settlers would also have to adapt themselves to the strenuous experience of hunting and killing. The hunter and the fighter merge into a single mythical figure, the 'frontier hero'. One of the most famous exemplars, Davy Crockett, who died at the Battle of the Alamo in 1836, was from a family that had emigrated from Ulster, another settler society influenced by ardent forms of Protestantism.[19]

As Vernon Parrington recorded in his study of American thought:

The real Davy [Crockett] was pretty much of a sloven. . . . [His] autobiography reveals the backwoods Anglo-Irishman as uncivilized animal . . . yet with a certain rough vigor of character. Wastefulness was in the frontier blood, and Davy was a true frontier wastrel. In the course of several removals he traversed the length of Tennessee, drinking, hunting, talking, speculating, begetting children, scratching a few acres of land to 'make his crap,' yet living for the most part off the country. . . . He was a hunter rather than a farmer, and the lust for killing was in his blood. With his pack of hounds he slaughtered with amazing efficiency. . . . His hundred and five bears in a single season, his six deer shot in one day while pursuing other game serve to explain why the rich hunting grounds of the Indians were swept so quickly bare of game by the white invaders. Davy was but one of the thousands who were wasting the resources of the Indian Empire, destroying forests, skinning the land, slaughtering the deer and bear, the swarms of pigeons, the vast buffalo herds. (Parrington 1930, 2: 178–9)[20]

The American hunter myth tells a different story. According to this myth, the hunter-fighter frontier hero is a disciplined expert imbued with the responsible, caring values of the farming families who cultivate the American soil.

Somehow, the act of slaughter comes to symbolize the whole package: the caring heart, the spirit of self-improvement, and the disciplined pursuit of betterment for everybody's ultimate benefit. Paradoxically and contrary to reason, by killing not only animals but people, and by despoiling nature, the hero is supposedly creating and sustaining civilized life.[21]

What are the consequences of this peculiar logic, one inherited by modern America? Slotkin's answer is as follows:

> The myth of the hunter ... is one of self-renewal or self-creation through acts of violence. ... Believing in the myth of regeneration through the violence of the hunt, the American hunters eventually destroyed the natural conditions that made possible their economic and social freedom, their democracy of social mobility. Yet the mythology and the value system it supported remained. ... We have, I think, continued to associate democracy and progress with perpetual social mobility (both horizontal and vertical) and with the continual expansion of our power into new fields or new levels of exploitation. ... The archetypal enemy of the American hero is the red Indian, and to some degree all groups or nations that threaten us are seen in terms derived from our early myths. (Slotkin 1973, 557–8)

The strange logic of the regenerative hunt, reinforced by the captivity myth, permits Americans to undertake repeated acts of violence against any convenient target in revenge for the historical past. In other words, when they strike out violently, they are getting their own back and feel they have a right to do it.

The past they are avenging is a time when forces in the world around them trapped, constrained, humiliated and victimized the Americans' ancestors. The American urge to dominate and destroy is a consequence of the way the original escape across the Atlantic occurred. It is fuelled by 'the emigrant's sense of guilt for having broken the family circle by his departure' (Slotkin 1973, 563). It also gives vent to a desperate feeling of vulnerability. This was strongest in the earliest days of the American Republic but it has left a strong residue of anxiety in the culture. When Slotkin states that the Americans' deep-ingrained sense of their own history makes them feel they can take revenge for the past in repeated acts of violence against any convenient target, he is describing a psyche that is quite similar to that expressed in Bin Laden's broadcasts justifying 9/11.

Resentment and virtue

So far we have investigated the dialectic between escape and domination within the settler syndrome. Interwoven with this is the dialectic between the stimulus of resentment and the pursuit of virtue. As mentioned aboves, feelings of resentment can lead to destructive violence. How is this related to virtue? The route is indirect and needs explaining.

'Virtue' was originally associated with qualities of strength, courage and intelligence which enable a man to assert himself, to maintain and advance his position in society, and to be effective in looking after his own practical interests, and the interests of those he chooses to protect. In Latin the term *vir* means both 'man' and 'strength', ideas that come together in the notions of 'virility' and 'manliness'. When a man who possesses virtue in this 'honourable' sense asks himself what he 'should' do, the question refers to matters of political or military prudence rather than moral rightness. The key question is 'how can he exercise his manly capacity effectively to look after his own practical interests?' rather than 'what are the standards set by the appropriate ethical rule of behaviour?' In fact, the political culture of the United States has fused together these two considerations by enshrining the assumption that when Americans exercise strength this is a sign of their moral virtue.

At the centre of what might be called 'the American ideology' is the idea that political, economic and military strength are proof of virtue in the sense of moral goodness. This logic runs parallel to the hunter myth. Recall that the structure of the hunter myth is as follows: destructive violence produces a regeneration of social justice and Christian grace and love. Let us turn more directly to the American ideology, both the official myth and to the rules of the game that this myth sanctions.

American ideology

By the 'official myth' I mean the mechanisms supposedly at work shaping Americans and American society. By the 'rules of the game' I mean the way elements of this myth may be drawn upon to explain and justify particular events in real life, history and politics. In the following account, the word 'virtue' carries its modern meaning of 'moral goodness'.

The American 'official myth' states that if a society is free it will create institutions and laws that are rational. It will ensure that those institutions and laws are virtuous ('good') and that the actions of the people guided by them will have righteousness. This righteousness will make them strong and that, in turn, will bring them success. As a result, they will win approval from those who observe what happens. So, freedom brings rationality, which brings virtue, which brings righteousness, which brings strength, which brings success, which brings approval.[22]

There is an unspoken proviso that strength displayed by an enemy will be described as 'tyranny' or 'oppression' to distinguish it from American or democratic 'strength', which in terms of this ideology always carries the connotation of moral rectitude as well as the capacity to act forcefully.

The official myth has a circularity built into it (see box 8.3). 'Success', which is achieved through 'strength', is believed to create new 'freedom' and set the sequence in motion once again. This has many expressions, ranging from philanthropy by powerful plutocrats, classically expressed in the educational institutions for the poor set up by Andrew Carnegie,[23] to the idea that a strong and successful democratic state can 'bring freedom' to other societies by economic and military means. This circularity again recalls the hunter myth: violence successfully carried through has a cleansing effect on the perpetrator, renewing their virtue, righteousness and strength.

As long as the chain of causation is accepted as a set of hard truths, particular effects may be taken as proof of the specific factors that are believed to cause them. These are the 'rules of the game'. For example, success may be taken as a demonstration of one's strength, righteousness and virtue.[24] Similarly, the strength of a country, group or person may be seen as being a result of its freedom, subject to that strength not being 'tyrannical', i.e. anti-American or, even, un-American.

On the other hand, negative criticism (lack of approval) may be taken to indicate failure (lack of success), which may be interpreted as a sign of weakness (lack of strength) and so on. For the more strong-minded, failure may be interpreted as a moral test that may

Box 8.3	**The American ideology**
The official myth	Freedom → Rationality → Virtue → Righteousness → Strength → Success → Approval (→ = 'leads to')
The rules of the game	Approval → Success → Strength → Righteousness → Virtue → Rationality → Freedom (→ = 'is proof of')

engender humility (as in the captivity myth) and strengthen virtue with all the positive things that follow.

Vietnam and after

The rules of the game and the official myth just analysed help make sense of the pattern of American political life, especially its foreign relations, since 1968. This period falls into three phases of roughly equal length. Each phase has a dominant character: respectively, humiliation (1968–79), partial recovery (1979–91) and renewed assertiveness (1991–).

1968–79: humiliation

Beginning in 1968, the United States experienced twelve years of failure, international criticism and internal division.[25] The spectacular Tet offensive in Vietnam in January 1968 was a major humiliation for the US government.[26] North Vietnamese attacks throughout South Vietnam, in conjunction with the Vietcong, caught the Americans by surprise. Twenty Vietcong commandos even captured the American embassy in Saigon for a short while. The Tet offensive was eventually contained but the American political establishment lost its appetite for the war.[27]

In the same year as the Tet offensive, American troops massacred the villagers of Mai Lai, Lyndon Johnson dropped out of the presidential race, massive demonstrations were held against the US government throughout the world, and peace talks began. Finally, in 1975, nine months after Richard Nixon resigned over the Watergate scandal, US officials made an undignified escape from Saigon by helicopter.

That was not all. Nixon had been forced to devalue the US dollar twice, in 1971 and 1973. By the end of the 1970s Japan was challenging America's business dominance. Then on 4 November 1979 a militant Islamic regime in Iran replaced the shah, took over the American embassy in Tehran and held sixty-six people hostage, fifty-two of them until January 1981.

In other words, between 1968 and 1979 Americans experienced a period of deepening humiliation during which approval was withdrawn from them, and they were denied success in key respects; as a result, they began to doubt their strength and, perhaps, even their virtuousness.

1979–91: partial recovery

During the next twelve years, the Japanese economic challenge continued and unemployment was high in the mid-1980s. However, for most of that decade American business enjoyed uninterrupted boom conditions. Ronald Reagan gave Americans renewed self-confidence, telling them they deserved approval. He strengthened their sense of virtue as occupants of 'the city on the hill' confronting an 'evil empire'. Between 1979 and 1989 the Soviet Union was drawn into its own 'Vietnam', the war in Afghanistan, which ended in failure and withdrawal; this was followed by the collapse of the Soviet Union in 1989–91. To summarize, during this second period American society was 'in recovery' and had its self-approval and sense of virtue restored.

1991– : renewed assertiveness

During the next period the United States rediscovered its identity as a 'strong' nation that wanted to be even stronger. The central political question was no longer 'how virtuous can we be?' but 'how strong can we be?'[28] By the early 1990s America's two main rivals, Russia and Japan, had both become very much weaker. The United States was left as the only major player in the global arena. During the 1990s Americans felt 'secure' and unthreatened within their borders. The main political drivers, at home and abroad, were opportunism, profit-taking and score-settling.[29]

*   *   *

So, to summarize, during the first twelve years, up to 1979, the United States experienced disastrous failures in terms of strength, success and approval and this reduced the credibility of the establishment's claim to be champions and exemplars of freedom, virtue and righteousness.

During the second period, from 1979 to 1991, a key part was played by Reagan's prolonged campaign of renewing Americans' belief in their virtue. Luckily for the United States, this was accompanied by the fortuitous weakening of major rivals, Russia and Japan.

While the United States wanted this to happen, it has not yet been convincingly shown that US leaders brought these events about.

During the third period, since 1991, George Bush senior and Bill Clinton both played down 'the vision thing'[30] where Reagan had excelled. Instead, they 'played' the last three elements within the rules of the game. In other words, they tried to use America's strength in a pragmatic way to achieve successes and win approval, both at home and abroad.

When George W. Bush came to office in 2000 he switched emphasis again.[31] His mantra was freedom as the key to keeping America strong.[32] Bush played upon the domestic causes of strength rather than the international rewards of strength. Here is a typical passage from his campaign of 2004 (with italics added):

> This nation is prosperous and *strong*, yet we need to remember the sources of America's greatness. We're *strong* because we love *freedom*. America has a special charge to keep, because we are *freedom*'s home and defender. We believe that *freedom* is the deepest need and hope of every human heart. We believe that *freedom* is the future of every nation, and we know that *freedom* is not America's gift to the world, it is the Almighty God's gift to every man and woman in this world. We also know that the greatest *strength* of this country lies in the hearts and souls of our citizens. We're *strong* because of the values we try to live by – courage and compassion, reverence and integrity. We're *strong* because of the institutions that help to give us direction and purpose – families, and schools, and religious congregations. These values and institutions are fundamental to our lives, and they deserve the respect of our government.'[33]

This is the rhetoric of a born-again fundamentalist Christian with no clear foreign policy agenda and strong corporate links. From his point of view, the best way to keep the links of the chain between freedom and strength well polished was to do two things: create a regulatory framework for American business that allowed the virtue and righteousness of corporate entrepreneurs to produce success; and encourage an American political climate that favoured causes supported by fundamentalist religious groups.

Neo-conservatives

But within nine months of taking office, and as a direct result of 9/11, Bush was in the hands of the neo-conservatives.[34] They had a different ideological agenda, one that began at the point where Bush concluded. Bush trumpeted American freedom as the source of American strength. Freedom was his watchword. The neo-cons began and ended with American strength, its renewal, expansion and protection. Strength was their watchword.

A recent study identified three common themes around which neo-conservatism unite.

1   A belief that human affairs are a struggle between good and evil.
2   A willingness to use military power since this is assumed to be the main factor determining how states relate to each other.
3   A preoccupation with Islam and the Middle East.

The neo-cons persuaded Bush that American strength abroad was necessary to protect American freedom at home. Their mission was to use that strength as an engine of success for corporate America and for themselves: they wanted to be 'the angel [who] rides in the whirlwind and directs [the] storm'.[35]

The spirit of American neo-conservatives is similar to that of Cecil Rhodes, who wrote in 1877: 'I contend that we are the finest race in the world and that the more of the world we inhabit the better it is for the human race.'[36] Rhodes meant the British. The neo-conservatives have a similar ambition for the Americans. They have the advantage of being supported by a leading global figure in the mass media, Rupert Murdoch.[37]

Modern neo-conservatism stems from the defection of a number of Democrats following the victory of Jimmy Carter in the 1976 primary campaign. They were disillusioned with Carter's 'weak' foreign policy. By the mid-1980s they were disenchanted with Reagan also, especially over his administration's reliance on Saudi Arabia rather than having a major military presence of its own.[38] During the 1990s the American interventions in Bosnia and Kosovo convinced the US that working with the Europeans through multilateral institutions such as NATO wasted everybody's time and was a drag on the efficiency of the US military machine.[39] By September 2002 this point of view had been enshrined in official policy.

The new National Security Strategy inaugurated what Halper and Clarke have called 'a kind of global Monroe Doctrine' (Halper and Clarke 2004, 142). The US assumed a global responsibility to defend, preserve and extend a peace that was, it was claimed, under constant threat from terrorism. The policy document made it clear that

America was willing and prepared to act both unilaterally and pre-emptively.

The alliance between Bush and the neo-cons brings together an extreme form of Jacksonianism with an extreme form of Wilsonianism.[40] The Jacksonian approach, adopted by Bush, is to steer clear of foreign entanglements unless someone else bothers you. At that point the strategy is to go after them without mercy, to destroy or disable them as quickly and thoroughly as possible, then get back home as soon as possible.[41] By contrast, the Wilsonian approach is to give the American democratic model to the rest of the world, good and hard, whether they like it or not. The idea is: do it through multilateral institutions if that is easy and convenient; otherwise go it alone, using force as necessary.[42]

Neo-conservatism rests on a contradiction. On the one hand, it is claimed that the United States exemplifies the 'one true way', that America is exceptional, the land *par excellence* of freedom and justice, that it is different and better. On the other hand, America's claim to have its own way is based on the fact that it has superior military capacity and the assertion that any power with such strength would use it to dominate others, irrespective of what the others wanted. In other words, on the one hand: 'We are different and better than you are'; on the other, 'You are the same as we are and would act in the same way if you got the chance.'

Neo-conservatism's central thesis – 'we should dominate' – is treated as non-negotiable. Bush's impassioned Jacksonianism, with its claims for freedom, virtue and rightness, provides good political cover, especially in dealing with the domestic audience. However, even more interesting than the arguments presented by neo-conservatives to justify their position is the style in which they are presented. There is a constant tone of tense resentment, of being unfairly held back, of wanting to humiliate others and to avoid being humiliated by them. For example, Robert Kagan's *Paradise and Power* (2003) adopts a teasing tone, fundamentally accusing Europe of 'unmanliness'.[43]

On 9 April 2001, just three month's into Bush's first term, Robert Kagan and William Kristol wrote an article headed 'National Humiliation' for the *Weekly Standard*. Bush was faced with his first major crisis following a collision between a Chinese fighter plane and an American surveillance aircraft in the South China Sea. As they put it:

> The profound national humiliation that President Bush has brought upon the United States may be forgotten temporarily when the American aircrew . . . return home. But when we finish celebrating, it will

be time to assess the damage done, and the dangers invited, by the administration's behavior. . . . It is hardly surprising that the Chinese government boarded the plane and searched it. . . . What was a good deal more surprising was the Chinese government's announcement of the conditions for the crew's release: The American government would have to make a formal apology. The broader purpose of the Chinese demand was to inflict upon the United States a public international humiliation.

Kagan and Kristol argued that 'By demanding a public apology from the United States, therefore, the Chinese government was not only saving its own face, it was consciously and deliberately forcing the United States to lose face, and thereby to admit its weakness.' There was a 'partial capitulation' by Colin Powell who expressed 'regret' for the incident. However, 'Having brought the United States to one knee, the Chinese government kept up the pressure. Now it was time for the United States to go all the way, to "adopt a cooperative attitude, admit its mistakes and make a formal apology." As Lenin used to say, when your spear hits iron withdraw it, when it hits flesh press forward.' They concluded

> The United States is on the path to humiliation, and for a great power – not to mention the world's "sole superpower" – humiliation is not a matter to be taken lightly. . . . As the Chinese understand better than American leaders, President Bush has revealed weakness. And he has revealed fear: fear of the political, strategic, and economic consequences of meeting a Chinese challenge. Having exposed this weakness and fear, the Chinese will try to exploit it again and again, most likely in a future confrontation over Taiwan. (Kagan and Kristol 2001, 10–17)

This is an expression of the psychological dynamics that were at work, a few months later, in the US government's response to 9/11. In that case, fear of the degrading consequences of humiliation overcame fear of the unforeseeable costs of military engagement with the outside world. The outcome was the proclamation of a war on terror.

Paradise and power

One of the most lucid testaments seeking to justify the war on terror and the way it is being conducted is Robert Kagan's *Paradise and Power* (2003), discussed above (see chapter 6). Kagan's central argument is that the United States refuses to be bound by international laws and treaties because it has the power to ignore them. It has the military capacity to look after its own interests and in so doing it provides a framework of order, which benefits those who are not America's enemies, especially those, like Europe, who are its friends.

According to Kagan, America lives in a Hobbesian world, one where force prevails. Europeans, who enjoy this protected environment, have the luxury of making high-minded laws for themselves in a Kantian spirit and would like, if they could, to impose them on the rest of the world, especially America. For a while this disparity of purpose and attitude was hidden by the Cold War, which kept Europe in the front line and 'involved'. Since 1989, Europe has had the luxury of criticizing the United States while making very little contribution to its own protection.

This argument has been met by both American and European responses. Robert Cooper, a senior British diplomat,[44] suggests that when one state is able to enforce its will in pursuit of its own interests, it is difficult for it to acquire legitimacy in the eyes of others (Cooper 2003). Furthermore, when it is in constant fear of attack it is liable to act in ways that diminish its practical commitment to democratic practices. Multilateralism and international law are intrinsically valuable, asserts Cooper, rather than simply being a means to reduce risk and uncertainty. He expresses, in measured tones, Europe's real sense of shock at the way the US government has reduced its commitment to, and dependence on, NATO. His recommendation is that Europe should continue to build up and coordinate its military capacity so that it can give practical support to multilateralism.[45]

Benjamin Barber, who lives in New York City, homes in on the fear cycle that is activated in Kagan's 'Hobbesian' world when the fear of terrorism motivates and sanctions American military violence against others. As Barber puts it: 'The logic of preventive war is meant to deter adversaries from hostility. Instead it provokes them to it. America uses harsh moralizing words justifying preemptive interdiction to subdue adversaries and is surprised to find that they are aroused' (Barber 2003, 140). This situation has arisen because the 'eagles' (neo-conservatives) say that 'If America can not longer insulate itself from the planet . . . then it must, in effect, rule the planet' (67). This, Barber comments, is the product of misguided 'romantic enthusiasm' (43). For his part, Barber is with the 'owls', those who recognize the realities of global interdependence, the value of international law, and the futility of trying to deter religious fanatics by using military force as they feel sure that after such a death they will go straight to paradise.[46] Here, in fact, is a quest for paradise that power cannot dismiss with contempt.

Barber is right to draw attention to the role of fear in American foreign policy. It expresses itself in the wagon-train circle mentality mentioned at the end of chapter 7. Remember also Slotkin's analysis of the dynamics of resentment. Fear and resentment are a potent mixture, which often leads those who experience them to strike out against their supposed enemies.

Striking out may take two forms:

- *striking first* out of fear in order to pre-empt trouble; and
- *striking back* out of resentment to take revenge on those who have hurt you.

The first response, the pre-emptive strike, is liable to recur whenever new potential threats are perceived. This pattern of repetition may be described as a fear cycle.

The second response, striking back, is liable to fuel a revenge cycle. When this happens, the perpetrators of humiliation later become victims at the hands of those they have damaged, and then become perpetrators themselves once more.

Each episode within a fear cycle is liable to trigger a revenge cycle if the victim has the capacity to strike back.

Revenge cycles are discussed in chapter 10. For the moment, let us concentrate on fear cycles.

Fear cycles

The fear cycle is a repeating sequence of actions and reactions stimulated by the escape response to humiliation. It has the following elements (see box 8.4):

(i)   those who have escaped humiliation, carrying the wounds that made them want to escape, withdraw from the wider world, where more humiliation threatens, into a treasured special place where they may be 'reborn' and achieve success and happiness;[47]

(ii) in this situation they are acutely sensitive to criticism and intolerant of others, fearing real or imagined threats that seem likely to violate, undermine or throw doubt upon the viability or worthiness of their project;

(iii)   those who have escaped strike out against 'threats' and 'enemies', real and imagined, and this causes feelings of humiliation, outrage and resentment among the groups targeted;

(iv)   as a result, the escapees get drawn into complex, lengthy, embarrassing and often humiliating dealings with those affected by their attacks and look for an opportunity to escape from this situation, thus returning to (i).[48]

Fear cycles are certainly not an American monopoly. Nor are they exclusive to settler societies. They are likely to be triggered whenever a powerful group fears it will be successfully challenged in a way that would undermine its identity, authority and rationale. Such was the case of the British in India by the end of World War I. The British massacre of peaceful demonstrators at Amritsar in 1919 was the product of fear that British rule would be effectively challenged. According to the general responsible, it was intended 'to strike terror into the whole of the Punjab'. During the following two decades and again, after World War II, such offences were frequently repeated.[49]

The dynamics of escape were important in the European empires. According to Hannah Arendt, the culture of expatriate communities within the European empires reflected the fact that much of the daily dirty work of empire-building was carried out by the rejects of Europe, those who could not make it 'back home' and therefore got out. Who would willingly risk the dangers of colonial life? Of course, there were practical idealists who wished to take their part in bringing civilization to the rest of the world.[50] However, as Arendt argues, many colonials were escapees from the metropolitan society searching for something less humiliating.

Box 8.4 The fear cycle	
(i) hurt withdrawal into treasured home/homeland ↓	(iv) embarrassing ← entanglements with outraged victims
(ii) anxiety about threat of → violation	↑ (iii) attack upon supposed source of real or imagined threat

These 'rejects' left their own degradations behind, settled in the colonies, and looked around for groups even weaker than themselves to dominate and oppress. Arendt remarks that many such people 'had not stepped out of society but had been spat out by it. . . . [T]he more gifted were walking incarnations of resentment like the German Carl Peters . . . who openly admitted that he "was fed up with being counted among the pariahs and wanted to belong to a master race"' (Arendt 1976, 189). Carl Peters used cruel but effective methods to build up German colonial power in East Africa.[51]

Such facts as these put in historical context the long-running American fear cycle, which includes massacres of Native Americans, lynchings of Southern blacks, the Mai Lai massacre in Vietnam and the mass killing of Iraqi conscripts in battle during the Gulf War of 1990–1. Such happenings are not in themselves more shocking than anything the Europeans have done. However, they stem from a promised land that presents itself as better than the corrupt old world.

The bitter fruits of victory

Dean Acheson once said, famously, that Britain had lost an empire and failed to find a new role.[52] The United States in the first decade of the twenty-first century is in a different situation. It has gained a new empire, or at least a quasi-imperial position, but it has lost its old role.[53]

America is struggling to come to terms with the consequences for itself of the geo-political victories it achieved during the twentieth century. The United States prevented the European empires from re-establishing themselves when they fragmented as a result of the two world wars. It also scored decisive victories over German nazism and Russian communism.

Furthermore, America has shown the rest of the world how to make capitalism generate wealth for national societies. Over the past half-century the rest of the world has responded to this lesson, some more eagerly than others, although it is not clear yet how many countries can also pull off America's other trick of turning itself into a relatively peaceful democracy.[54]

America must now watch Europe and China as well as a resurgent Japan and Russia become wealthier, more politically powerful and better equipped with technologically advanced military systems. Its own military bases and surveillance systems covering Eurasia will meet stronger objections from local populations and their leaders.[55]

The risk of humiliation for the US leadership increases year by year. 9/11 dramatized this situation. The United States has yet to find a way of responding to this plight that does not:

- intensify the climate of humiliation through the generation of fear and revenge cycles;
- weaken its legitimacy by asserting imperial privileges that conflict with its own democratic tradition; or
- undermine political freedom by reducing the rights of its own inhabitants through measures such as the Patriot Act.[56]

If the United States becomes a potential threat to world order and peace, it will be because it is becoming weaker and finds this prospect 'unacceptable'. The difficulties it faces are intensified by the fact that its political culture has been shaped by its history as a settler society that escaped the 'old' world with the intention of dominating the 'new' world coming into being.

Americans thought the 'old' world they left behind would disappear below the horizon. Instead it has turned into a global 'new' world surrounding the United States. The 'Indians' are whooping round the wagon-train circle. This is a dangerous situation. Unable either to escape or dominate this global new world, will the United States try and destroy it? Faced with this prospect, the task of global diplomacy is to persuade the United States to join the new globalized world it did so much to create – to join it as a sibling, not a tyrannical father prepared, like Saturn, to eat his children.

*   *   *

In this chapter we have: surveyed the disagreements concerning the strength, viability and moral worth of the American empire; argued that, as a settler society which has acquired a global empire, the United States is prey to the contradiction between the desire to escape and the desire to dominate the world; traced the origins of this conflict to the European Reformation; compared other settler societies in Ireland and South Africa; examined the psycho-cultural responses of Americans to their settler condition, especially in the themes of resentment and virtue; seen their expression in American political ideology and the dynamics of American foreign policy since Vietnam; analysed the neo-conservative approach; linked it to fear cycles; and noted American fear of renewed humiliation.

9

Acceptance

Freedom and slavery

As we have seen, the reverse side of escape is domination and/or destruction. Escapees 'on the run' do not want to be trapped and turned into victims once more. In order to remain free and in control of their lives they will impose domination on others if they have to and when and where they can. They will inflict destruction where they find it necessary or convenient. This is how those who escape from humiliation turn themselves into agents of humiliation.

But let us now look at the dominated ones, those who have been conquered or hemmed in and cannot escape. Take the case of Africans forced into slavery and shipped to America, or Native Americans forced to share their hunting grounds with intruders from across the sea. What strategies are available to people in such situations?

Their first response is a disabling shock at being overpowered and humiliated. This is neither acceptance nor rejection but acquiescence. However, what happens next? All action is risky. What if acceptance is unrewarded? What if rejection is unsuccessful?

Alexis de Tocqueville found both acceptance and rejection in America during the 1830s. For example:

> The negro makes a thousand fruitless efforts to insinuate himself into a society that repulses him; he adapts himself to his oppressors' tastes, adopting their opinions and hoping by imitation to join their community. From birth he has been told that his race is naturally inferior to

the white man and almost believing that, he holds himself in contempt. (Tocqueville 1968, 394)

African slaves were not saved by this attitude of acceptance. On the contrary, they were subjected to intense oppression.[1] This is not surprising. They were brought to America for precisely that purpose.[2] The conforming, surrendering consciousness noticed by Tocqueville was not the only form of adaptation to humiliation. The Native Americans resisted. Many of them allied with the British in the War of 1812. In response, the white settlers treated Native Americans with a mixture of seduction and repression. Treaties were signed, then broken. Reservations were set aside, then taken back again.[3]

Tocqueville is utterly scathing. He notes that the Spaniards, for all their 'unparalleled atrocities', did not succeed in 'exterminating the Indian race' or 'prevent them from sharing their rights'. However:

the Americans of the United States have attained both these results with wonderful ease, quietly, legally, and philanthropically, without spilling blood, and without violating a single one of the great principles of morality in the eyes of the world. It is impossible to destroy men with more respect to the laws of humanity. (Tocqueville 1968, 421)

Tocqueville was, of course, writing before the massacres at Sand Creek (1864) and Wounded Knee (1890).[4]

Acquiescence and acceptance

Tocqueville was describing an extreme version of a challenge that faces most of us: how to get or keep whatever you think you have a right to, and avoid becoming a victim. Humiliation poses that challenge because it forces those who suffer it to undergo an *unacceptable* displacement or exclusion from the position in society they think is rightfully their own. It is the unacceptability of this displacement, along with its enforced character, that makes it humiliating and not merely inconvenient or annoying.

In many cases, those placed in humiliating circumstances cannot immediately escape. They find themselves driven, for a while at least, into acquiescence, behaving in ways that conform to their oppressors' degrading view of their identity and interests. They endure the virtual chains in which they are unwillingly locked. They adopt subservient body language and cease to make an outward show of discontent.

But acquiescence is certainly not full acceptance of humiliation. On the contrary, acquiescence is nothing more than partial, conditional and reluctant acceptance. In fact, many people live much of their lives moving in the zone of anxiety that lies between forced acquiescence in humiliation (at work, in the home, in the education system, in the neighbourhood) and the more decisive options of rejection, escape, or, in some circumstances, full acceptance.

In practice, we are usually driven most strongly by the negative desire to avoid being trapped, cornered and caged, in other words, to avoid being forced into complete acceptance of humiliation. Under what conditions will people go into that cage without expressing utter outrage? There are two. They will accept a situation that they would have previously considered unacceptable if:

- the particular humiliation threatened is redefined as something else that is not humiliating; or
- their own interests and identity are redefined as being so insignificant that their subjection to humiliation is of little account.

These considerations apply on a world scale as well as in our personal lives. People and governments in many national states live under conditions of forced acquiescence in humiliation. Meanwhile, they are looking around for opportunities to reject, escape or transform these humiliating circumstances.

Powerful and persuasive interests try to push these states and their peoples into more complete acceptance of their humiliation. For example, over the past few decades neo-liberals and neo-imperialists have been trying to persuade governments all over the world that the 'Washington Consensus' with respect to economic and social policy is not humiliating, as some would describe it, but liberating. In cases where their persuasion is successful, this meets the *first condition* just listed.

Meanwhile, religious fundamentalists have been trying to persuade people that, if they adhere to 'true religion', they will find human existence on earth insignificant compared to the paradise to come. This means, according to the understanding of some, that they may happily sacrifice their lives or risk prolonged imprisonment in the course of carrying out terrorism. In cases where their persuasion is successful, this meets *both the conditions* just listed.

In other words, there are strong pressures trying to push people from mere acquiescence in humiliation to a more complete accept-ance of it. If they succumb, this leaves them more vulnerable to the dangers of victimization. By victimization I mean a condition in which one person or group is at the mercy of another that chooses, for its own purposes and satisfaction, to put them in situations that cause them pain and suffering, however much they deny this fact to themselves and others.

However, whenever individuals and groups are required in the course of everyday life to acquiesce in situations they find personally humiliating, they routinely 'switch on' certain internal disciplinary practices that protect their own identities and interests as far as pos-sible. People normally take as much care as they can to avoid being pushed or pulled into situations where they can be victimized.

Hidden injuries

Most people in humiliating situations find themselves wavering between acceptance and rejection. The road to rejection is never easy, even among people who feel intense disappointment and anger with the way their loyalty has been rewarded.

In *The Hidden Injuries of Class* (1972), a study carried out in Boston, Massachussetts, Richard Sennett and Jonathan Cobb traced some of the tactics and strategies of acquiescence and some of its psy-chological manifestations. They focused mainly on men from Polish, Greek and other ethnic backgrounds, all of whom had made the tran-sition from being blue-collar to white-collar workers. These men had gone up in the world but still felt disappointed and dissatisfied. They were, to use the title of Mike Davis's book (1986), 'prisoners of the American dream', seduced by its promise or, at least, not aware of any feasible alternative. They conformed as far as they could to its expectations, working hard in a disciplined way to improve themselves.

They were caught 'in between', in two respects:

- on the one hand, they were in between the fraternal values of the ethnic extended family and the individualistic independence they craved; and
- on the other, they were caught between the desire to conform with and surrender themselves to the system, and the need to defend themselves against the system.

Conformity left these working men unsatisfied, stranded in an alien informal culture whose secret springs did not flow through their own veins. When they tried to solve the problem by withholding personal involvement at work (what I call 'the tactic of separation'), this made them feel ashamed. To compensate, as discussed further below, they took refuge in the micropolitics of victimhood, making their wives and children feel guilty because they, the breadwinners, were sacrificing their time and energy in frustrating and exhausting jobs for the benefit of their close relatives.[5] The *Hidden Injuries of Class* ends with a call for a classless society, one that does not humiliate its members, making them feel inadequate at work while selling them consumer goods to salve their psychic wounds.[6]

At about the same time as Sennett and Cobb were planning their Boston-based study, the works of Frantz Fanon, author of *The Wretched of the Earth* and *Black Skin, White Masks* (both 1967) were beginning to appear in English translation. Fanon, born in Martinique and educated in Paris, drew on his experiences both as a soldier fighting for the Free French during World War II and a clinical psychiatrist in Algeria during the 1950s.[7] His books deal with the anguish of acquiescence in a humiliating system and the question of how to put things right.[8] He found that black Africans were, like Boston's ethnic white-collar workers, caught 'in between'. Their dilemmas were similar, but not the same:

- on the one hand, Africans were caught between accepting the myth of 'negritude', which would confine them to a depoliticized cultural ghetto, and engaging more fully with the political challenge posed by the dominant colonial power; and
- on the other, they were caught between the indignity of having a 'colonized personality' (hyper-sensitive and self-doubting), and the chance to regain their respect by reconstructing their personalities and attacking colonial oppression directly with violence.[9]

Fanon's basic analysis is very similar to that of Sennett and Cobb. Acquiescence in a humiliating socio-political order produces pain. Ultimately, the only way to overcome the humiliation is to transform the socio-political order, liberating those who are oppressed by it.

The solution proposed by Sennett and Cobb is that American citizens should make their society classless, even at the cost of some inefficiency.[10] In effect, they want something like an 'emancipation proclamation' for all workers, backed up with institutional change.

Fanon would have none of that. In his view, slaves set free by white people in the nineteenth century had been subjected to undignified and demoralizing treatment. In fact, they gained neither free institutions nor liberated personalities as a result of emancipation 'from above'. To regain their self-respect, the oppressed must liberate themselves, not have freedom handed to them on a plate. They must take what is theirs by force.

Fanon's prescription is truly 'American'. He takes his stand alongside Daniel Boone and Davy Crockett. Like them, he believes in regenerative violence.[11] As surely as any American frontier heroes, Fanon believes that 'violence is a cleansing force'; violence 'frees the native from his inferiority complex and from his despair and inaction: it makes him fearless and restores his self-respect' (Fanon 1967b, 94). The similarity is not surprising, since 'The violence of the colonial regime and the counter-violence of the native balance each other and respond to each other' (1967b, 88).

Edward Said quotes this passage in his *Culture and Imperialism* (1993, 327), in which he provides substance to Fanon's general charge that European culture demeaned its colonial subjects. Said claims that his study of Western literature reveals a victimizing attitude at work within it.[12] In Said's view, by the time of Fanon's birth (in 1925) any fictional person coming from the colonial world was depicted as 'either a victim or a highly constrained character, permanently threatened with severe punishment, despite his or her many virtues, services or achievements'. Such people did not really count. They were 'excluded ontologically for having few of the merits of the conquering, surveying, and civilizing outsider'. They were marginal to the European field of vision. In their own eyes, Europeans were making heroic efforts to keep their noble imperial ventures going in spite of having to deal with such inferior people. As they saw it, the least – and the most – that colonial people could do to help was to give their obedience. The best way to get this was by imposing strong discipline. In other words, 'For the victim, imperialism offers these alternatives: serve or be destroyed' (Said 1993, 204).

According to Joseph Stiglitz, one-time chief economist of the World Bank,[13] this approach had not changed by the end of the twentieth century. As he put it in his *Globalization and its Discontents* (2002, 41): 'All too often, the [International Monetary] Fund's approach to developing countries has had the feel of a colonial ruler.' For example, in a photograph taken in 1998, the head of the IMF, 'a short, neatly dressed former French Treasury bureaucrat, who once claimed to be a Socialist', is shown 'standing with a stern face and crossed arms over the seated and humiliated president of Indonesia'. Stiglitz comments: 'The stance of IMF, like the stance of its leader, was clear: it was the font of wisdom, the purveyor of an orthodoxy too subtle to be grasped by those in the developing world' (41).[14] Like

Sennett's and Cobb's white-collar workers, and like Fanon's Africans, the Indonesian president was drawn into the game but not allowed to 'join the club' in whose interest it was being played. The IMF's decisions 'were made on the basis of what seemed a curious blend of ideology and bad economics, dogma that sometimes seemed to be thinly veiling special interests' (Stiglitz 2002, xiii).

Ways of acquiescing

There are four approaches to acquiescing in humiliation (see box 9.1). A particular person, group or society may adopt more than one of these ways at the same time, and may switch between them.

One set of responses involves *reversal* of the experience or condition. The given person, group or society says: 'While trying to humiliate us, you have partly succeeded but we can make the very scars

Box 9.1 Forms of acquiescence by victims of humiliation			
	Strategies	*Tactics*	*Tendencies*
FORMS OF ACQUIE-SCENCE	REVERSAL	Defiant acceptance	→ REJECTION
		Politics of victimhood	
	SEPARATION	Sabotage	→ ESCAPE
		Inner withdrawal	
		Denial	
	CONFORMITY	Self-abasement	→ ACCEPTANCE
		Elevation of master	
		Stoicism	
	SURRENDER	Self-abandonment	

left by our partial and incomplete humiliation into useful weapons with which to defend and advance ourselves.' By contrast, responses involving *separation* of the self from the experience or condition could be expressed as: 'You think you are humiliating us but even though the part of us you see performs the rituals of abasement for you, in fact that is a screen behind which we are either indifferent to you or engaged in actions that are unfavourable to you.'[15] Another approach is *conformity*, in other words, bringing perceptions of the self and one's group or society into line with the circumstances in which they find themselves following the humiliation. This response could be summarized as: 'Your actions were humiliating us but in fact you have showed us who we really are and/or what our situation really is, and we accept it.'

Finally, there is *surrender* to fate, giving up the effort of coping through reversal, separation or conformity. Here the response in essence is: 'You have tried to humiliate us and you have succeeded but we will not impose upon ourselves the additional burden of confronting or evading you. Mould us as you will.'[16]

Let us go into these four strategies in a little more detail.

Reversal, separation, conformity and surrender

Reversal

One variant of reversal is the defiant acceptance of stereotyping labels that were originally intended to victimize, to make people feel small and keep them cowering. A classic recent example is the institutionalization of 'Queer Studies'.[17]

A second variant of reversal is the politics of victimhood. This involves persuading others that they are undeservedly lucky non-victims, who should feel guilty, ashamed, afraid or sorrowful (or a mixture of these) about your own situation. It means using these feelings in others to get them to act in ways that serve you or inhibit them from acting in ways that oppose you. There are at least five versions of the politics of victimhood:

1   *The demand for compensation*: 'You or others have hurt me in a very unfair way. You must all try your utmost to put this right.'
2   *The demand for indulgence*: 'We have been badly damaged. We are hurting. We are angry. Do not be surprised if we hit out, or

if we hurt others, including you. You have no right to censure us, especially since you are responsible for the fact that we are damaged. You must accept us the way we are.'

3   *The demand for privileged credence*: 'We, the victims, know who our attackers are. You must believe us when we name them and they must be punished in a way that satisfies us.'

4   *The demand for revenge*: 'We have been wronged and we have the right, and feel a strong and justified urge, to purge our anger by hurting someone else very badly, especially someone who can be plausibly blamed for our suffering.'

5   *The demand for respect through strength*: 'We were victimized because we were weak and now we are making ourselves so strong that no one dare touch us. You must keep your distance or come near only on our terms. This is the kind of respect we demand.'

The politics of victimhood are useful as a way of both sustaining individual or group morale and appealing to more powerful third parties. Like defiant acceptance, it turns acquiescence into rejection of humiliation.

Separation

In this case the core tactic is to represent oneself to the humiliating party through words, actions, posture and demeanour that seem to satisfy their wishes and expectations. At the same time, one makes a separation between the compliant and subservient 'self' that is represented in full congeniality to the master standing over you and another 'self' that has its own intentions.

This other self may, for example, conspire to sabotage the oppressor's plans at every opportunity. This is done, hilariously, by the 'good soldier' Švejk in Jaroslav Hašek's novel and, dramatically, by the soldiers who built, then destroyed, the bridge over the River Kwai.[18] While these responses move towards rejection of humiliation, other variants – inner withdrawal ('I am not here') and denial ('this is not happening to me') provide means of psychological escape.

The tactics of reversal and separation try to avoid the oppressor's framing power. They undermine its ability to encage others in categories of its choosing. They subvert its capacity to say 'who you are' and 'where you fit in'. They are attempts to destroy the cage or escape by slipping through its bars.

Conformity and surrender

By contrast, the remaining tactics turn acquiescence into acceptance of the oppressor's victory. The response of conformity conveys the following message to the conqueror: 'We accept your superiority and our own reduced circumstances. In return, please treat us decently.' This is not the same as the response of surrender whose central message, delivered by the defeated to themselves, is: 'Let us stop fighting because this will give us immediate relief from the pain of struggle.' Those surrendering accept that they are cornered, encaged and vulnerable to abuse. However, they are doing what they can to remove at least one source of discomfort.

Conformity and surrender are often combined. There are two basic moves. One is to identify as strongly as possible with the oppressor, 'discovering' that he is a magnificent lord, noble in character and deed. The other is self-belittlement, relegating and diminishing the self so that it is less demanding (due to self-abandonment), more accepting (due to stoicism) or more servile (due to self-abasement), but in any case a smaller obstacle to the lord's intentions, and a less significant loss if degraded or destroyed.

Here we have the fundamental rationales of European (and Japanese) feudalism and Christianity. The defeated warrior kneeling in humiliation before the victor who spares his life has every incentive to glorify his chief. In his new role of vassal his own prestige is a reflection of his master's. The key to a stable adaptation is wholehearted acceptance of a new role and a new self, operating according to new rules. Success depends on being able to leave the destructive feelings of humiliation, of having been displaced, back in the discarded past along with the old role, the old self and the old rules.

So it is with Adam, who aspires for god-like powers in Eden, and then pays for his arrogance with expulsion from Paradise. His successors eventually accept their belittlement, adapt to their new place in the hierarchy of creation, and learn to obey the new rules delivered on tablets of stone. Christ takes upon himself the pain of their humiliation. By accepting the verdict contained in God's humiliation of Adam, human beings discover who they are and where they fit in. Their humiliation is turned into shame: shame for Adam's past sins, shame for failing too often to follow the rules they have been given.

The strategies of conformity and surrender, mixed in varying proportions, are enacted daily throughout the world. This has been going on for centuries: in local settlements buying off Viking raiders by paying Danegeld and accepting Danelaw;[19] on slave plantations in the Old South in the United States where 'Uncle Tom' and 'Sambo' played the game, consciously or not, to make life less agonizing;[20] in the European colonial empires as local bosses came to terms with their 'civilized' administrators; in NATO headquarters in Europe after World War II as each new Washington-briefed American military consul arrived to take command; in Africa, Asia and Latin America when representatives from the IMF or World Bank descend upon national governments; when new top managers install themselves in companies that have been taken over; and in kitchens, dining rooms and bedrooms throughout the world.

To summarize, the 'conformity' and 'surrender'[21] strategies mean that subordinates must:

- work on the self to make it compatible with the ruler's view of the way things are or should be;
- accept that the conditions of their existence are almost completely controlled by the ruler;
- adapt to the ruler's actions and his or her prescriptions and perceptions about the interests and appropriate behaviour of subordinates;
- abandon defence mechanisms built into the 'reversal' and 'separation' strategies of acquiescence;
- try hard to believe the 'official' line and hope it produces some benefits for subordinates, especially those promised from above;
- discover that after a honeymoon period, during which subordinates may feel lifted up and liberated, the dominant mood is likely to become a sense of loss and diminishment; and
- accept an increased vulnerability to victimization and victimization cycles.

Victimization cycles

Victimization cycles are repeating sequences of actions and reactions stimulated by the acceptance response to humiliation. They become possible when people or groups are drawn into a relationship of extreme dependency upon, and vulnerability to, a dominant agent. This may be a result of conquest (the 'Robin Hood/Sheriff of Nottingham' model) or a more subtle process of infiltration combined with attractive oratory and advertising (the 'Pied Piper' model).

Once the conquered or seduced ones are in thrall,[22] there is a 'strong invitation' from above (an 'offer one cannot refuse') to abide by rules and values imposed from the top. Those below become vulnerable to being manipulated by sharp tugs on the lead strings of desire, shame and fear: desire for promised rewards; shame at the thought of disobedience; and fear of punishment.

Victimization cycles have the following elements (see Box 9.2):

(i)   a relationship of high dependence of the weak upon the strong is established or confirmed, either through conquest or seduction;

(ii)   the dominant party makes the rules of the relationship and manipulates it by playing on motives of desire, shame and fear on the part of subordinates;

(iii)   the dominant party abuses and/or estranges the subordinates and rapidly lowers the level of trust in the relationship; and

(iv)   outrage and/or despair on the part of the subordinate is met by a renewal of seduction and/or a renewal of repression, and/or silent contempt.

When this cycle has been played out a few times, acceptance may be replaced by mere acquiescence, or it may turn into rejection.

Box 9.2   The victimization cycle

(i) conquest or seduction creates relationship of high dependency/ vulnerability for the weaker party ↓	(iv) outrage/despair by subordinate is met ← by renewal of seduction and/or repression and/or silent contempt
(ii) dominant party manipulates shame, → fear and desire to ensure obedience to its rules	↑ (iii) dominant party abuses and/or estranges subordinates and rapidly lowers trust level

Japan and Israel

The World Society of Victimology is based in Japan.[23] This is a global organization, founded in 1979, whose president and vice-presidents are, at the time of writing, drawn from the United States, Israel, South Africa, Mexico and the United Kingdom. It is interesting that pioneering work on victimology was done by an Israeli, Benjamin Mendelsohn,[24] and that the society has found its institutional home in Japan – interesting because Israel and Japan have a dual relationship to victimization. Both countries have been accused of victimizing others: in the first case, Palestinians; in the second, Koreans, Chinese, Allied prisoners of war during World War II as well as 'comfort women'. They also identify themselves as victims: in the first case, of anti-Semitism and the Nazi concentration camps; in the second, of nuclear attacks on Hiroshima and Nagasaki as well as continued abuse due to the presence of US military personnel in Okinawa.[25] Israel and Japan have both had the experience of being subjected to passionate hostility from their immediate neighbours; both have been under supervision or protection from the United States; and both have had troubled relations with their patron.[26]

Israel has often offered the world defiant acceptance ('We are who we are') and the politics of victimhood ('Don't expect us to be nice'). These responses have been relatively consistent since the late 1940s. By contrast, over the same half-century, Japanese responses have changed radically.

From surrender to reversal

Surrender

In 1945 total psychological surrender was commonplace in Japan. The emperor had let his people down. The imperialist system he headed lost much of its legitimacy among the people.[27] According to Masao Maruyama, there was 'a feeling of stagnation, of prostration so complete that foreigners were astonished' (Maruyama 1963, 4).

Conformity

The Japanese turned away from nationalism and politics in revulsion. They turned towards 'the household and corporate family' (Thorsten

2004, 3).[28] Their new desire to conform to the American way stimulated feelings of shame at their backwardness but also gave a clear direction for personal effort. Hard work – and overwork – repressed 'the unbearable'. Many Japanese males refocused their loyalty at a lower level, devoting themselves to the business corporations for which they worked, expecting jobs for life.[29] During the early 1990s, however, with the Asian economic crisis, the corporation failed them just as the emperor had failed their parents and grandparents. Jobs for life and the many paternalistic fringe benefits that went with them began to disappear.

Separation

The question now is: where will the Japanese propensity for loyalty be focused? One possible answer is reinvestment in a nationalistic state, although that prospect remains deeply controversial within Japan. One indication of trends at the top (although not necessarily among the population at large) is that in 1989, after over four decades of disuse, the National Diet ordered Japanese schools to display the national flag and sing the national anthem. In 1999 the flag and the anthem were officially reinstated as state symbols. In other words, Japan began to mark out a strong identity clearly separate from the United States.

Reversal

In 1989 Shintaro Ishihara, later Governor of Tokyo, published *The Japan that can say No*, which exists in many translations (e.g. Ishihara 1991). In this essay, the author presents himself as a proud Japanese who has overcome the inhibitions caused by the national habit of self-effacement. His title is a sardonic comment on the stereotypical Japanese normally encountered by Americans, 'Japanese who smile and agree with them' (142). Here is a strong move towards the 'reversal' strategy for coping with unwilling acquiescence in humiliation; in other words, the strategy that takes a prevailing image (in this case, the Japan that says yes) and turns it around against the oppressor.[30]

It is Ishihara's evident intention to attack the Japanese sense of shame but to strengthen his country's sense of having been subjected to unjust humiliation.[31] For example, Ishihara accuses the Americans of racism against the Japanese.[32] In this way, and others, he contributes to the politics of victimhood. He recalls, for example, how as a teenager in 1946 he had refused to stand aside as three American GIs walked down the street: 'The new rulers had the street to themselves and that swaggering trio seemed to glory in the deference. I did not like their attitude so I walked straight ahead, pretending not to see them. Just as I was about to pass, one GI hit me in the face with his water ice' (79–80). Ishihara recounts many other anecdotes about how he habitually stood up to the Americans and demanded equality with them.[33]

It is impossible to know to what extent Japanese feelings of being victimized will be stirred up and intensified by a mixture of external pressures and internal political opportunists. Nor whether they will overcome the continuing suspicion of Japan's political elites among the general population. Since World War II, however, there has been a shift in the ways that the Japanese have acquiesced in the social and political condition brought about by their humiliation at the hands of overwhelming American power, a change in the character of their responses to what many have seen as the racial arrogance directed against them. This shift has been:

- from an initial pattern of *surrender* blending into *conformity*;
- to *conformity* blending into *separation*; and now
- to *separation* blending into *reversal*.

Will this eventually turn into rejection?

A new *Jungle Book*

Japan's restlessness under American tutelage is part of a bigger picture. Washington has responsibility for the one remaining global nation-state-empire remaining after the end of the Cold War. Like the European empires that preceded it, this empire is built on a contradiction between the hierarchical principles of the honour code, expressed through the practice of imperial control, and the egalitarian principles of the human rights code.

The logic of the market, explored in chapter 6, carries and conceals this contradiction. As we saw, it contains elements from both the honour code and the human rights code. This is because it:

- glorifies the struggle in the market place;
- stays silent about the unequal conditions in which that struggle occurs;
- ignores the role played by military force in sustaining that inequality; and
- downplays the significance of social rights.

Now Thomas Friedman's *The Lexus and the Olive Tree* (2000), which we briefly touched on earlier, can be placed in its proper context. It is as an aid to accepting humiliation, a set of reasons for being cheerful even though the sky may look dark. Friedman's text is intended to provide reassuring cognitive therapy, although one American reviewer admitted to his compatriots: 'I would be embarrassed to lend this book to friends overseas. Friedman gets very rah-rah as an American apologist, and he poses no serious objections to the worldview that regards globalization as an international extension of Manifest Destiny.'[34] Friedman presents a view of the world that 'dilutes' victimization: he regards it as an unavoidable by-product of the way the global free market simply *has* to work if it is to be efficient and therefore good for us all. His book is conservative, demotic and quietly aggressive.

In some ways Friedman has something in common with Rudyard Kipling, who made the most attractive case he could for the British Empire at its height, speaking in language that would delight and comfort not just lords but also the ordinary British worker. Friedman tries to pull off a similar trick for Americans: echoes of Kipling's *Jungle Book* (Kipling 1994a), first published in 1893, find their way into Friedman's *Lexus and the Olive Tree*, which is full of allusions to long-horn cattle, short-horn cattle, lions, gazelles and turtles, each animal signifying different players in the economic global jungle.[35]

Friedman's basic argument is that openness and transparency are being forced on businesses and government by the democratization of technology, information and finance. Globalization is managed by an 'electronic herd' of investors and business executives that gallops into or out of national economies depending on whether or not those economies are any good for grazing. If those economies adopt the new rules of low tax, low inflation and friendliness to powerful foreign business interests, then the herd will be happy to trample its way in. If they don't, then the herd will find juicier pastures.

The herd imposes a 'golden straitjacket' (Friedman 2000, 101) on companies and countries. It always fits tightly. Friedman gives advice about getting into shape for the fitting. He draws attention to the importance of getting the right system of financial regulation and enforcing accountancy standards;[36] he advocates thinking of a nation as having the characteristics of both a computer (with appropriate soft- and hard-ware) and a publicly traded company that tries to earn a good credit rating. Friedman's main message is: if you cannot get into the straitjacket, this shows you have not got the will or skill to survive. If you cannot get these things, you deserve to go under.[37]

Let us follow Friedman into the middle of his jungle. In a typical passage, he describes meeting the mayor of a small town in the Brazilian rain forest. As the two men walked through the forest together, the mayor 'patted every tree. He knew each tree in the rain forest by its Brazilian name.' Friedman 'took an immediate liking to this Brazilian lumberjack. There was something very solid about him.' As they sat down to picnic together in the forest, the mayor 'explained to me that intellectually he understood that logging was not sustainable anymore', but he knew 'his little town was not ready for life without logging.' After a while, Friedman got ready to leave:

> I thanked him and started to pack up my IBM ThinkPad laptop, when he said to me, "Now I want to ask you something." "Please," I answered, "ask anything you like." The mayor then looked me in the eye and said, "Do we have any future?" The question hit me like a fist in the stomach. It almost brought tears to my eyes, looking across the table at this proud, sturdy man, a mayor no less, asking me if his villagers had any future. . . . I cobbled together an answer, trying to explain in simple terms that he and his people did have a future, but they needed to start making a transition from an agro-economy to a more knowledge-based economy. (Friedman 2000, 330)

In Friedman's terms, this is a meeting between an unusually friendly lion (himself) and a frightened, slow-moving turtle (the mayor) who wishes he could turn himself either into a lion cub or a fast-running gazelle.[38]

Friedman is telling a similar story to that of Robert Kagan's *Power and Paradise* (2003), discussed in Chapter 8. The story is: the world is a jungle, the lion is king and everyone, even the lion-king, has to accept the law of the jungle inscribed in the nature of things. The point of this story is, precisely, to normalize victimization, to make it seem an unavoidable, everyday event, something built into the natural order. *The Lexus and the Olive Tree* also brings back memories of another famous work by Kipling: his *Just So Stories* (Kipling 1994b). In effect, Friedman tells his readers a story about 'How America became the Lion-King'. The message of the story is: 'Sorry, Best Beloved, but this is just the way we are and just the way you are. In fact, that is just the way it is.'[39]

The logic of the global market

Friedman sees business globalization as a largely uncontrolled process driven by herd-like instincts yet bringing beneficial effects. But other commentators are more sensitive to the damage done by this process, and some of them see the partly hidden hand of corporate interests behind it. Zygmunt Bauman, for example, believes that many inhabitants of the contemporary world have been turned into travelling strangers: some are tourists with sizeable wallets and 'well-respected' passports; considerably more are vagabonds scavenging for the means of survival, trying to put together the means of a decent life against the odds.

Not everyone is allowed to be a vagabond. Some groups are judged to be too dangerous or unsightly to be let loose. The rich take every measure they can to tie the poor down, trapping them in slums, stopping them from crossing borders. Whenever possible, they put them in prison where they can do no harm except to themselves.[40]

Society's taste for incarcerating the poor, especially young men, is also noticed by Edward Luttwak.[41] As an American conservative (old-style, not neo-) he comes from a very different part of the political spectrum from Bauman. However Luttwak shares Bauman's vision in three respects: capitalism is out of control; it is creating a sharp division between the top and the bottom of society; and the rich are responding to the growing multitude of discontented poor people by throwing them into jail to an increasing extent.[42] In his study entitled *Turbo-Capitalism* (1999) Luttwak argues that deregulation of capitalism is a bad thing. It has made some people extremely rich and about fifty million Americans better off, mainly because of easy credit, but that still leaves more than sixty million rank-and-file American employees with hourly earnings less than they were in the early 1970s in real terms, taking inflation into account.[43]

Luttwak warns that any government in Africa, Latin America or Eurasia allowing forceful political pressure for deregulation to overwhelm them is in danger of being sold a false prospectus. The reason is that if they tear down all their institutional defences against open competition they will be acquiring an 'American' form of capitalism but without two essential balancing features of American life that make it relatively orderly and decent for those who stick with the system.

One of these features is the American legal system, which gives people with grievances, even poor people, the chance to get restitution in court to a much greater extent than in most countries.[44] The

Box 9.3 Business globalization: good or bad? Controlled or uncontrolled?

	Mainly beneficial for human interests	Mainly damaging for human interests
Process largely controlled	Alan Shipman	Samir Amin Noreena Hertz Naomi Klein Hans-Peter Martin and Harald Schumann Michael Hardt and Antonio Negri
Process largely uncontrolled	Thomas Friedman Charles Leadbetter	Edward Luttwak Zygmunt Bauman

other is the Calvinist ethic. This makes being rich a sign of virtue, which reduces social envy. It also forbids people to enjoy their wealth, which reduces corruption and encourages the rich to plough their money back into the community through charitable trusts.[45]

Unlike Friedman, who sees the existing global political economy as a way of liberating human beings, and Bauman who sees it as an engine of systematic victimization, Luttwak sees a 'great dilemma' (see box 9.4 on next page). His own preference is, fairly clearly, for regulated capitalism. However, he acknowledges that most Western governments have 'no better plan than to allow turbo-capitalism to advance without limit, while hoping that faster growth will remedy all its shortcomings' (Luttwak 1999, 237).

Some critics of the free-market ideology claim it weakens the democratic state which, in turn, reduces the citizens' institutional defences against victimization. This undermines their human rights. This makes social disorder more likely, according to Hans-Peter Martin and Harald Schumann. However, 'It is not the really destitute who are rebelling; rather it is the fear of losing position, a fear now sweeping the middle layers of society, which is politically explosive to an incalculable degree. Not poverty but the fear of poverty is the danger to democracy' (Martin and Schumann 1997, 11). The global race for high efficiency and low wages is a recipe for disorder, fear, xenophobia and irrationality.

To put it another way, the great danger is fear of humiliation and victimization. If the democratic state disappears, if more power is

Box 9.4 Luttwak on turbo-capitalism vs regulated capitalism*	
Turbo-Capitalism	*Regulated Capitalism*
Dominant global tendency	Subordinate global tendency
Society serves the economy	The economy serves society
All capital is allocated according to the rate of economic return obtained	Capital is also allocated to economically unprofitable activities because of felt moral obligations, professional commitments and social ideals
Widening income differentials Moderate economic growth Disintegrates society into small elite of winners, a mass of losers and rebellious law-breakers Erodes social fellowship and family ties Social breakdown leads to harsh laws and widespread imprisonment of offenders	Overburdens employers Suppresses entrepreneurship Retards technological progress Growth slower than with turbo-capitalism Steady impoverishment of nation Reduced opportunities for young people
Making all institutions profit-maximizers perverts their essential content although it improves their economic performance	Resisting the profit motive may eventually lead to impoverishment and annihilation of the institutions concerned

* Based on Luttwak 1999, 236–7.

assumed by multinational companies responsible only to their share-holders, who will care about the citizens' interests? In Noreena Hertz's words: 'We, the people are displaced – and in the one-ideology world of the twenty-first century, if things start going wrong, where can the global citizen go to be granted asylum?' (Hertz 2001, 88).

Naomi Klein has traced her own pathway through the landscape shaped by the 'silent takeover' of the public sphere and public spaces by corporate interests. In her *No Logo* (2000), she tells a story about how citizenship has yielded ground to consumerism although she also reports that a fight-back is underway, a 'fight for the global commons' (439).

The fight for the global commons and the challenge posed by global capitalism are two of the central themes treated by Michael Hardt and Antonio Negri in their books *Empire* (2000) and *Multitude* (2005). Linking these two themes together is the growth of capitalism's global 'network power' (2000, 160). Through this network, 'bio-political' control is exercised over the multitude. Ordinary people, as workers, consumers and members of families, are not dominated from above through military force in the old-fashioned way. Instead, they are 'ruled along internal lines, in production, in exchanges, in culture' (344). This global network is an 'empire' although one that 'has no Rome' (317). This empire has learnt to penetrate the 'immaterial, cooperative, communicative, and affective composition of labor power' (277). In other words, business managers have learned how people are thinking and behaving these days and have turned it to their own advantage. Nevertheless, say Hardt and Negri, the really creative force in society is ordinary people, the multitude.[46]

Samir Amin also believes that globalization is a struggle between democratic and capitalist forces. He sees the IMF and World Bank as being mainly preoccupied with short-term profitability for international business. These institutions are pushing ahead with a programme of weakening states wherever possible so the market can reign (Amin 1997). This has pushed 'the ruling classes of the periphery' into nationalist and ethnic politics. The likely outcome, unless the democratic state can be revived or created, is 'total submission to the logic of capital' (xi).

According to John Gray, however, unregulated markets are an unusual phenomenon, historically, and only strong states can bring them into being and maintain them. Such states are unlikely to be very democratic in spirit or practice because 'democracy and the free market are competitors rather than partners' (Gray 1998, 213).[47] In fact, globalization is not a matter of free markets conquering the world. Instead, it is a product of new information technology abolishing distance to a greater extent than ever before. The result has been to 'throw all types of capitalism – not least the free-market varieties – into flux' (216).

One outcome is a high degree of insecurity that is undermining the institutions and values of the existing socio-cultural order. This insecurity is prolonged by the fact that the United States cannot get its own way globally but can veto projects of global institutional change that do not suit its own interests. Frustration will increase as the struggle for control in Central Asia gathers pace. Gray concludes that in this situation, warfare and anarchy are a likely prospect.

These commentators are all looking at the same world as Friedman but they see it very differently. Friedman sees a shared human condition resulting in a universal jungle law that is, he argues, hugely beneficial in material terms to those who go along with it, one that can be civilized around the edges as long as everyone accepts its basic logic. Many others see loss: especially, the loss of human rights, dignity and security. Luttwak sees the existence of some balancing gains, but it is not clear whether he thinks that they are adequate compensation.

Friedman's work is important because it is a high-selling attempt at persuasion. It tries to make us accept that victimization, and the humiliation that brings it about, are natural events like thunderstorms or 'kills' in the jungle. This is a rhetorical strategy that leads back towards the honour code, inviting one to accept it as a mantra. It is an attempt to neutralize the impulse to reject victimization on the grounds that it diminishes our human rights.

*   *   *

In this chapter we have: considered the dilemmas facing those forced to acquiesce in humiliation; identified the strategies of reversal, separation, conformity and surrender; analysed victimization cycles; considered the cases of Israel and Japan; deconstructed the work of Thomas Friedman as an attempt to 'naturalize' victimization and make it acceptable within the framework of the honour code; and compared voices raised for and against the view that business globalization driven by the logic of the market is mainly beneficial for human interests.

10

Rejection

Now we turn to the third type of response to humiliation: rejection. If escape shows a clean pair of heels, and acceptance a pair of widespread arms, what bodily posture represents rejection? At least two possibilities come to mind: the thrusting fist and the parrying arm. Which possibility comes into play first in any particular case may depend on whether we are talking about revenge or resistance.

Revenge or resistance?

Humiliation carries a double punch. It is both *outrageous* and *threatening*.[1] When a person, group or society strikes back against humiliation, what are they doing? Are they trying to signal that the outrage they have experienced is unacceptable? Or are they trying to reduce the practical extent to which their interests and identity are being damaged and/or threatened?

To put it another way (see also box 10.1):

- is the relevant sequence outrage → anger → attempted revenge? Does the outrage generate anger and a desire to strike back at those who can be held responsible for the humiliation, bringing the perpetrators equivalent or greater anguish? Or
- is the relevant sequence threat → fear → attempted resistance? Does the perceived threat generate fear and a desire to strengthen and protect the identity and interests that are being threatened by

Box 10.1	Modes of rejection		
HUMILIATION →	ANGER (because of outrage committed) FEAR (because of threat posed)	REJECTION →	REVENGE PARADOX RESISTANCE PARADOX

    diminishing the capacity or opportunity of others to damage them? Or

• is it both?

Some acts of revenge may undermine efforts at resistance. This was the message contained in the words of Nelson Mandela at Soweto in February 1990 soon after his release from prison. It was a dangerous time, with apartheid in grudging retreat and violence widespread. Mandela told his audience:

> [the] hijacking and setting alight of vehicles, and the harassment of innocent people are criminal acts that have no place in our struggle. We condemn that. Our major weapon of struggle against apartheid, oppression and exploitation is our people organised into mass formations of the Democratic Movement. This is achieved by politically organising our people not through the use of violence against our people. . . . I want to add my voice, therefore, to the call made at the beginning of the year that all students must return to school and learn.

Mandela's message was that making resistance to apartheid effective meant there was no place for revenge. He told his audience in Soweto:

> Go back to your schools, factories, mines and communities. Build on the massive energies that recent events in our country have unleashed by strengthening disciplined mass organisations. We are going forward. The march towards freedom and justice is irreversible. I have spoken about freedom in my lifetime. Your struggles, your commitment and your discipline have released me to stand here before you today. These basic principles will propel us to a free, non-racial, democratic, united South Africa that we have struggled and died for.[2]

For an example of how the spirit of revenge may undermine the politics of resistance, consider the case of Saddam Hussein. According to Said K. Aburish, a well-connected Palestinian journalist who had dealings with Saddam in the 1970s,[3] internal politics within Iraq under Hussein were a synthesis of 'Bedouin guile and Communist method' (Aburish 2000, 8). Saddam Hussein was a master of the bloody 'politics of revenge'[4] that had been characteristic of Iraq's tribal society for many centuries. He was able to manipulate this form of politics effectively, eliminating rivals by torture and execution. His own family became dominant within the Tikriti clan, the Tikriti interest achieved the central position within the Ba'athist party, and the Ba'athists became supreme within Iraq.

For a while, during the 1970s, Saddam was able to combine this with a strategy of using profits from Iraqi oil to modernize the Iraqi economy and its social infrastructure, as well as to build up Iraq's military capacity. In other words, during that decade Saddam was steadily increasing Iraq's ability to resist challenges from other countries in the region that wanted to overthrow him.

Success in conducting the politics of revenge depends on two things: understanding your rivals or enemies, and having the skills and resources needed to humiliate them repeatedly. Within Iraq, Saddam had both. However, outside Iraq's borders his touch was less sure and his resources less adequate.

Take his relationship to Ayatollah Khomeini. This high-ranking cleric became the dominant personality in Iran after the fundamentalist Shia-led revolution of 1979. He was also Saddam's main opponent during the Iran–Iraq war. Ironically, a few months before the Iranian Revolution, Saddam deported Khomeini from Iraq, where he had been living. The previous year Saddam sanctioned the execution of eight Shia clerics, imprisoned two thousand of their co-religionaries and expelled 200,000 others to Iran.[5]

When Saddam deported him, Khomeini moved to Paris and from there, a short while later, he returned to Tehran in triumph. The Iran–Iraq war began in September 1980. Saddam apparently expected it would last no more than a few weeks. In the event, the war lasted nearly eight years. Saddam was trapped by the politics of revenge. It was a very damaging 'grudge fight', wearing both countries down.

According to Aburish, an important factor was that, in this case,

Saddam did not know his enemy. For the believer in revenge not to take into consideration Khomeini's determination to punish him for his military arrogance and for humiliating him by ejecting him from Iraq in 1978 was nothing short of foolish. Khomeini refused to consider any efforts at mediation – to him, what was at stake was the irreducible supremacy of the word of Allah. (Aburish 2000, 195)

Another relevant factor was that the United States and other major powers were very content to see the war prolonged. It weakened two major regional powers, increasing their dependence on America, European or Russian support, while decreasing their capacity to resist pressure from outside. Saddam's capacity to assert his independence outside Iraq and resist outside interference in Iraqi affairs was degraded still further by the Gulf War of 1990–1, repeated bombing campaigns, a lengthy oil embargo, and the invasion that took place in 2003.

These examples make the same point: the urge for revenge, on the one hand, and strategies of resistance, on the other, have to be balanced very carefully indeed and may sometimes work in conflict with each other. Before elaborating and exploring these points further, let us set out some of the possible ways of rejecting humiliation in a little more detail.

The revenge paradox

Revenge belongs to the honour code. It has two related objects (see box 10.1). One object is to express anger and resentment by imposing an appropriate counter-humiliation on a relevant target (e.g. the perpetrator). The second is to restore the lost honour, prestige or 'street credibility' of the revenge-seeker. Within the honour code, demonstrating the capacity to humiliate others is a recognized way to increase personal or group honour.

A paradoxical situation arises. On the one hand, participants in feuds and revenge cycles normally develop a stereotypical view of their opponents, one that depicts them as having very low worth and deserving to be overthrown, degraded and eradicated. On the other, the cultural identity and everyday pattern of activities of many people engaged in the process of humiliation and counter-humiliation are thoroughly bound up with the revenge relationship. They have a strong vested interest in keeping it in existence. If their threats to disable and destroy the hated other were fully realized, they would have to confront a big problem: the loss of an enemy whose existence is central to their own sense of who they are.

Jonathan Lear puts it well in his book on Freud:

> The terrorist thinks it is *because* his people have been humiliated that he is justified in his acts. But might the situation be just the reverse? That is, because he takes a certain pleasure in destructive hatred, he has become attached to his sense of humiliation. Thus while it may be true that the terrorist kills out of a sense of revenge, it is *also* true that he holds onto his sense of humiliation in order that he should be able to go on killing. (Lear 2005, 4).[6]

The *revenge paradox* is that those who most want to defeat the enemy may also be those who most want the struggle to continue.

The resistance paradox

There is a resistance paradox as well. Edward Luttwak mentions it when discussing regulated capitalism and turbo-capitalism. He would like to see the moral obligations, professional commitments, and social ideals embedded in the old ways of Keynesian social-welfare capitalism protected. However, the professionals needed to do this can only get employment if they are prepared to work in institutions adapted to the turbo-capitalist world that seems to undermine those very things.

We have to make a distinction between two things: a group's specific interests, especially its identity and way of life (A in box 10.2) and the institutions, practices and attitudes needed to protect and sustain those group interests (B in box 10.2). For example, landed

---

Box 10.2 Protecting interests, identity and a way of life

A
Institutions, practices and attitudes
needed to protect and sustain B

B
Specific interests,
identity and
way of life

aristocracies that wanted to protect their rural way of life effectively in the nineteenth century found they had to support governments that would encourage urban-industrial growth to generate the wealth and technological advance needed to make the national army powerful enough to defend that rural way of life against foreign aggressors (see box 10.3).

In the end this strategic move by the aristocracies was self-defeating. They were transformed and diminished by the end of the twentieth century because of the overpowering impact of urban-industrial growth on the whole society, including the aristocracy and its way of life. 'Success' in terms of such a strategy is most realistically measured with reference to how slowly this unwelcome change occurred.

The *resistance paradox* states that in order to protect your identity and way of life you may have to change your identity and way

---

Box 10.3 Aristocracies in urban-industrial societies

Aristocracy and its rural way of life are threatened by the military power of rival national states that have industrialized, urbanized and developed an advanced scientific culture ↓	The paradoxical consequence is that having strengthened urban-industrial and scientific interests to defend its rural way of life, the influence of the aristocracy and the strength of the rural way of life are threatened by the new social interests they have encouraged within their own country ↑
Members of the aristocracy realize that to prevent defeat and conquest by these rival national states – which will put an aristocratic way of life under threat – they must encourage urban-industrial and scientific development in their own nation to help make it powerful and capable of resisting attacks →	If urban-industrial and scientific development are successful, the social and political power of the urban working class, the industrial and commercial business class and the scientific professions is increased; all gain greater influence in government and society

Box 10.4 Three ways of coping with the resistance paradox

Last-ditch resistance	Pragmatic adaptation	Calculated reformation
Determination to maintain the old ways at all costs and go down fighting if necessary	Piece-meal shifts under pressure of immediate challenges when survival is at risk	Deliberate remaking of identity and way of life, maintaining key links with the past but also trying to impose an acceptable structure on the new society coming into existence

of life. In other words, in terms of box 10.2, the requirements of A may conflict with the contents of B. As a result, when your identity and way of life are challenged, you may have to decide which aspects to discard in order to protect the 'core'. Which means you have to decide what the 'core' is.

There are at least three ways that a group under threat may respond to this situation. One is pragmatic adjustment. For example, suppose the group is well embedded in the society, resistant to self-analysis, and has substantial access to power resources. Such a group may be able to make flexible, pragmatic shifts in style, tactics and attitudes whenever it is advantageous to do so. This would describe quite well the way in which the English aristocracy responded to the rise of the modern bureaucratic state and the industrial city.

However, as shown in box 10.4, two other responses are a last-ditch resistance and a calculated reformation. Let us explore two examples of these responses from Japan and India as they coped with the challenge of Western imperialism.

The last samurai

In 2003 the film *The Last Samurai*, directed by Edward Zwick and starring Tom Cruise, was a great popular success all over North America. It told the story of a noble Japanese warrior chief who refused to compromise either his traditional way of life or his code of honour when faced with the modern business civilization and modern technology being brought in from the West. This heroic figure refused to take off his sword as the new modern laws demanded. He would not bow down to the new socio-political order that was intended to replace the old feudal hierarchy. This samurai leader tried to put his case to the emperor but could not get a hearing. He felt he had no choice but to stand and fight when the emperor's advisers sent an army to capture or destroy him. He put up a very good fight combining traditional warrior skills with inventive military tactics but in the end the more advanced armaments in the hands of the Japanese state defeated him. Wounded, he committed suicide on the battlefield.

The central message of the film is that it is noble to choose honour above life but tragic to be forced to make that choice. The hero refuses to adopt a strategy of survival that would undermine the only way of life that would make his survival meaningful. In terms of box 10.2, he chooses B (his traditional way of life) because it is honourable and rejects A (in this case, Western-style modernization) because it is humiliating. The doomed act of resistance becomes a performance. It celebrates a culture passing away in the face of Westernization.

The story is loosely based on the rebellion by the Satsuma clan in 1877, led by Saigō Takamori. Saigō was a leading figure in that clan which held power on the island of Kiushiu in the south-west of Japan, close to Korea and China. The film's narrator is an expatriate English gentleman (played by Timothy Spall). This character bears some resemblance to Augustus H. Mounsey, a Fellow of the Royal Geographical Society. His book *The Satsuma Rebellion* (1879), the title-page of which describes him as 'recently Her Britannic Majesty's Secretary of Legation in Japan',[7] is narrated in a tone of quiet amazement that also characterizes the tone of voice in the film.

Mounsey had evidently visited Kiushiu and was no stranger to Japanese history and society. He tells a story that is more complex than the film. Saigō was a major actor in the national politics of Japan before the Meiji Restoration of 1868 when the Shōgun still ruled. The Shōgunate, held by the Tokugawa clan, had been the real power behind the imperial throne for centuries and other clans, including the Satsuma, resented its power.

Saigō, the 'last samurai', was no stranger to rebellion. He took a leading part in the military uprising in 1867 that abolished the Shōgunate and gave power back to the emperor. Many people from the Satsuma clan took positions in national government from that point onward. Others, including Saigō, were not happy with what they were offered. In practice, Saigō seems to have wanted a position almost as powerful as the deposed Shōgun. As a result, the Satsuma clan was divided.

The followers of Saigō were not opposed to all forms of change. They were upset because they were not controlling the pace and direction of change. Nor did they simply turn their back on new ideas and practices in favour of the old way of life and the old identity. A manifesto published in Tokyo newspapers during June 1871 was widely taken to represent Saigō's views.[8] It argued that government should be 'based upon the polity of Japan in the middle ages, but regard being had to the constitution of western states'. In other words, some modernization was acceptable.

But modernization should not be allowed to overwhelm the old Japan. 'We must not attempt to civilise Japan too quickly, and must do first what our resources permit. We must abandon all steam and railroads, &c., and work diligently to perfect our military system. Let us not try to do one hundred things at once, but have patience and go by degrees' (Mounsey 1879, 45). This is not 'No!' but 'Please slow down!' and 'Ask us what we think before you act!' The manifesto said it wanted 'All government measures, small and great, to be well discussed and considered, and then enacted' (42).

Saigō was quite happy to see some changes in the decaying fabric of the old feudal order. For example, abolishing the great feudal lords heading the clans, known as the *daimyo*, would give all samurai more freedom.[9] Abolishing samurai status was a different matter. This happened in 1876.[10] Mounsey described how the most diehard samurai from Kiushiu reacted when imperial troops from the lower orders dressed in Western-style uniforms were sent to their island:

> Dressed in the style of the old Japanese warrior, in helmet and chain armour, and armed with swords and halberds, this band of reckless men surprised the garrison of Kumamoto in the dead of night and butchered or wounded 300 of the Imperial troops in their beds. In the eyes of such men this was a chivalrous exploit, and their subsequent conduct was no less chivalrous, according to Japanese ideas; for after performing this cold-blooded massacre, they retired to the hills, and, finding there was no probability of a general rising in the province, eighty-four of them manifested the sincerity of their intentions by committing hara-kiri, whilst only twenty-nine surrendered to the Imperial troops which soon dispersed or killed the rest of the band. (Mounsey 1879, 92–3)

Followers of Itagaki Taisuke, a leader of the neighbouring Tosa clan, also based in Kiushiu, were less extreme but they also objected to the degradation of their military tradition. Some of the Tosa men had visited the United States and were favourable to Western-style representative institutions in government but they objected to the way the samurai were being dragged down. As quoted by Mounsey, they believed that 'A great mistake has been made in endeavouring to lower the samurai to the level of the common people. Encouragement should have been given to the latter to raise themselves to the level of the samurai.' (260–1)

When Saigō mustered his own highly trained troops for rebellion, he surely had in mind two scenarios, one optimistic, one pessimistic. The optimistic scenario was that the Japanese navy, which was staffed with Satsuma officers, would rise up in sympathy to restore and reinforce the hierarchical principle within Japanese society, implementing the values of the samurai class even though it had been abolished.[11]

The pessimistic scenario was the one romantically enacted in *The Last Samurai*. It was that the emperor and his entourage would feel ashamed when they saw how honourably the samurai from Kiushiu fought for their way of life. In other words, out of a conspicuous collective sacrifice expressing this group's commitment to a certain way of treating human relationships would come a change of heart on the part of those who controlled the nation.[12]

Gandhi

Gandhi's approach of non-violent resistance also deliberately put on display his followers' willingness to suffer for their cause. He intended to instil in his followers a commitment to a certain way of treating human relationships. He also, like the 'last samurai', wanted to bring about a change of heart on the part of those who controlled the nation. Like Saigō and, even more like Itagaki Taisuke (see above), Gandhi was looking for a workable mix between indigenous and imported ideas. However, there are several differences:

- unlike Saigō, who was thoroughly committed to the honour code, Gandhi was much more sympathetic to the idea of universal human rights;
- Gandhi's vision of human relationships emphasized peace rather than violence;
- in Gandhi's eyes, it was much more distasteful to cause or observe humiliation than to be the victim of humiliation;

- Gandhi was working to strengthen the spirit of human solidarity, universal equality and mutual help, not to refurbish the practices of social exclusivity and hierarchy; and
- he was deliberately importing (rather than reluctantly acquiescing in) ideas taken from the West, especially those rooted in Christianity and the visions of social critics such as John Ruskin.

Gandhi was born in India in 1869. As is well known, he trained as a lawyer in England and then spent over twenty years in South Africa. In Natal he became involved in the cause of Indian indentured labourers, founded the Natal Indian Congress and developed his policy of non-violent resistance or *satyagraha* (a Sanskrit word meaning 'truth force'). He went back to India in 1914.

Like Saigō, Gandhi was a man of action, although a very different kind. In his brief account of Gandhi's political philosophy, Bhikhu Parekh gets to the heart of Gandhi's approach as follows:

> Thought came to have no meaning for him unless it was lived out, and life was shallow unless it reflected a carefully thought-out vision. Every time Gandhi came across a new idea, he asked if it was worth living up to. If not, he took no further interest in it. But if the answer was in the affirmative, he integrated it into his way of life, 'experimented' with its 'truth', and explored its moral logic . . . He read little, and only what was practically relevant. (Parekh 2001, 6–7)

Saigō was trying to defend a coherent traditional way of life against a threatened invasion by 'Western civilization'. By contrast, Gandhi was trying to create a coherent new way of life in the face of the British Raj, which was then well installed in India and reluctant to go. For example, he wanted to transform the situation of the 'untouchables' or Dalits.[13] He wanted all individuals to be on patrol duty over themselves, to take personal responsibility for making themselves strong enough to resist attacks on their integrity. Such individuals would be powerful tools for reconstructing Indian society and, eventually, Gandhi hoped, the world. With supreme self-confidence, great organizational powers and a considerable flair for publicity, Gandhi told his followers what kind of reconstruction he thought was necessary.

At the end of *Sarvodaya*, a pamphlet written while in South Africa and inspired by Ruskin's *Unto This Last*, Gandhi sets out his view of the kind of *swaraj* (or self-rule) that India and Indians should aim to achieve. He begins by stating that '*Swaraj* cannot be attained by the sin of killing Englishmen' or by 'the erection of huge factories.

Gold and silver may be accumulated but they will not lead to the establishment of *Swaraj*. Ruskin has proved this to the hilt.' In fact, he adds:

> Western civilization . . . has reduced Europe to a sorry plight. Let us pray that India is saved from the fate that has overtaken Europe. . . . Some day there will be an explosion, and then Europe will be a veritable hell on earth. Non-white races are looked upon as legitimate prey by every European state. What else can we expect where covetousness is the ruling passion in the breasts of men? Europeans pounce upon new territories like crows upon a piece of meat. I am inclined to think that this is due to their mass-production factories. . . . India must indeed have *Swaraj* but she must have it by righteous methods. Our *Swaraj* must be real *Swaraj*, which cannot be attained by either violence or industrialization. India was once a golden land, because Indians then had hearts of gold. The land is still the same but it is a desert because we are corrupt. It can become a land of gold again only if the base metal of our present national character is transmuted into gold. The philosopher's stone which can effect this transformation is a little word of two syllables – *Satya* (Truth). If every Indian sticks to truth, *Swaraj* will come to us of its own accord.[14]

In Japan, the men of Satsuma and Tosa tried to bargain with the Japanese government about the proper trade-off between ends and means, between a valued identity and way of life on the one hand, and, on the other, effective means to make it secure. By contrast, Gandhi refused to consider a trade-off of any kind. In his view, ends and means had an organic connection. As he put it: 'The means may be likened to a seed, the end to a tree; and there is just the same inviolable connection between the means and the end as there is between the seed and the tree' (Gandhi 1951, 10). In terms of box 10.2, B (the valued way of life) had to be not only compatible with A (the means to achieve and defend it) but also closely interwoven with it.

Gandhi continued to recommend and practise his policy of *Satyagraha* (non-violent resistance). He organized mass campaigns of collective disobedience to colonial laws such as the salt tax imposed in 1930. At such demonstrations his followers were required to receive any blows upon their persons by police or military without striking back or breaking the bond of human fellowship that links all people. This proud passivity was, of course, intended to exasperate the authorities and to undermine their self-confidence. These campaigns received enormous publicity. Gandhi's philosophical approach drew upon values very familiar to Europeans, which made it easier for him to elicit feelings of both shame and admiration on the part of the

British and other Westerners. At the same time, by teaching his followers to acquiesce in humiliating punishments without striking back or deviating from their intentions, Ghandi weakened the effectiveness of violence as a means of colonial control.[15]

Gandhi reckoned he had a strategy for national liberation whose 'cost will be insignificant compared to the fabulous sums devoted by nations to armaments'. In 1938 he was confident enough to write that 'even a few true *Satyagrahas* would suffice to bring us freedom'.[16] Gandhi's view of families and clans was very different from Saigō's. For the samurai, the clan was a castle to be held against the attacks of other clans. By contrast, Gandhi believed that when people understood the suffering caused by violence it would melt their hearts. He argued this 'from the analogy of what we do in families or even clans. The humankind is one big family. And if the love expressed is intense enough it must apply to all mankind' (Gandhi 1951, 262–3).

However, Gandhi had no way of handling or even comprehending violence as an expression of inter-communal hatred. Again, Parekh sums up the matter well: 'His theory of human nature could only explain savagery as a temporary loss of humanity capable of being set right by an appropriate surgery of the soul. When he was confronted with the depth and extent of intercommunal brutality, he felt morally disoriented and could not make sense of it' (Parekh 2001, 120).

Nearly a million people died during the savage violence between Hindus and Muslims that occurred when India achieved independence from Britain in 1947, followed by the partition into the modern states of India and Pakistan. Gandhi's enlightened and imaginative politics of resistance helped to loosen the British government's grip upon India. Ironically, as this grip loosened it released another, more deadly, politics, the politics of revenge.

Revenge chains

Revenge may be stimulated by acts of conquest, relegation or expulsion (and by offensively persistent reminders of them). Unlike resistance, the primary object of revenge is not to preserve one's resources and capacity to pursue one's own goals but instead to attack those who are blamed for the humiliation in a way that will hurt and outrage them. It is an act of retaliation, not defence.

The desire for revenge springs from the feeling of outrage. The outrage stems from the perception that one's rightful position and standing have been overthrown or seriously threatened through an act of humiliation. Revenge may be displaced from the actual agent of humiliation – who may be unidentifiable, unreachable or too dangerous to attack – onto a more convenient target that is already, so to speak, 'set up' for humiliation on account of its supposed 'unworthiness' for the place it occupies, according to those seeking to discharge their outrage. In extreme cases, this process of displaced revenge may be repeated several times, moving downward in a hierarchy or 'pecking order' and creating what might be called a revenge chain.

As Elias Canetti puts it: 'No one ever forgets a sudden depreciation of himself, for it is too painful. Unless he can thrust it on to someone else, he carries it with him for the rest of his life' (Canetti 1973, 219). Depreciation is a pushing down, a lowering or diminution that refuses to accord the victim proper recognition of who they are and where they fit into the scheme of things. To put it another way, humiliation is a displacement of the self or group. One response is to displace the humiliation itself, passing it on to others. This helps to re-establish the group or self as an assertive and autonomous agent able to exercise power and do things it wants. In a telling example, Canetti asks his readers to imagine the feelings of Germans during the period of gross monetary inflation between the two world wars. Inflation has depreciated the worth of individuals and put almost everybody in the same boat, feeling diminished. Money has become worthless. This makes people feel worthless. They are desperate to transmit this feeling onto something or someone else. In Canetti's words:

> What is needed is a dynamic process of humiliation. Something must be treated in such a way that it becomes worth less and less as the unit of money did during the inflation. And this process must be continued until its object is reduced to a state of utter worthlessness. Then one can throw it away like paper, or repulp it. The object Hitler found for this process during the German inflation was the Jews. They seemed made for it. (Canetti 1973, 219)

Revenge cycles

For a revenge cycle to occur, both parties must be strong enough to survive the process. At least one (if not both) of the parties involved must regard the other individual, group or society as irredeemably

Box 10.5   The revenge cycle

(i) X blames Y for a humiliating attack upon X, which X survives ↓	(iv) ← the sequence from (i) to (iii) is repeated with X and Y reversed
(ii) X feels outrage against Y, whom they blame → for the attack	↑ (iii) X carries out a humiliating retaliatory attack upon Y to express outrage and even up the score

unworthy. In other words, it must deny that the others have any legitimate right to the position and standing that they 'outrageously' assert. Outrage is caused by the continued existence of the other in the 'inappropriate' place they persist in occupying. The continued and conspicuous presence of the hated other is a running sore, a cause of constant pain (see box 10.5).

Another factor fuelling a revenge cycle is the vested interest that certain participants on both sides – full-time killers, for example – have in continuing the conflict. Ironically, the wounds produced by humiliation eventually get incorporated into the identities of at least some of the people concerned. They begin to 'need' the hatred and to love the revenge. This is part of the revenge paradox.

In order to try and understand revenge cycles better, let us focus briefly on Europe since 1870.

France and Germany

Thomas Scheff and Wolfgang Schivelbusch have both published important studies of revenge. In *Bloody Revenge* (1994), Scheff makes an interesting comparison between international systems and families. He draws on theories developed to understand conflict situation within families to help explain instances of protracted conflict between national states, especially the two world wars in Europe. He argues that instead of blaming particular states or statesmen for specific wars, it is better to look at the system of communications between states in Europe at the time. There was a low level of trust within that system, and widespread use of devious and deceptive techniques such as conspiring with third parties rather than talking in a direct and open way with potential enemies in order to achieve mutual understanding and prevent confrontation.

A pervasive problem, between states as within family relationships, is alienation. This takes two forms: isolation, when the distance from others is too great; and engulfment, when blind loyalty and commitment to a relationship means a submergence of individuality, so that important parts of the self are denied and put out of reach. Intense nationalism carries the danger of individuals being engulfed within the nation while nations are isolated from each other, a situation that comes under the heading of 'bimodial alienation' in Scheff's terminology (Scheff 1994, 2).

Alienation increases the chances that the presence of shame will be unacknowledged. This is unfortunate because shame not only serves as a useful moral arbiter for our behaviour but also provides a good guide as to how well we are balancing closeness and distance, or solidarity and independence, in our relationships. When shame is unacknowledged it may combine with other emotions, such as guilt or fear, to produce 'feeling traps'. Scheff is especially interested in the feeling trap that develops when unacknowledged shame leads to, or results from, anger. When this occurs shame leads to anger, anger to more shame, shame to more anger and so on. This sequence is difficult to stop if the part played by shame is hidden and those involved do not understand what is happening.[17] This factor helps to explain the periods of protracted conflict between states such as France and Germany, carried out in a spirit of vengeance or 'humiliated fury'.[18]

After 1871 France was humiliated by the loss of Alsace and Lorraine. However, Scheff notes, the motive of revenge against Germany 'was seldom publicly avowed, as suggested by Gambetta's advice to the French about the defeat of 1871: "Speak of it never; think of it always," a counsel of obsession, denial and bypassing of shame' (Scheff 1994, 87). After Germany's defeat in 1918, Hitler, who was no stranger to shame-anger in his own life, showed the German people a way to 'interrupt the chain reaction of overt shame and rage' (118). His solution was to project the shame and anger onto the Jews, making them the object of German vengeance.

In *The Culture of Defeat* (2003) Wolfgang Schivelbusch throws light on the socio-cultural character of revenge-seeking after national defeats. By the early nineteenth century history had given a clear answer to two questions: whose interests does the French state represent and defend?; and who stands for France? The parts played by the French aristocracy and monarchy were crucial. The absolutist Bourbon monarchs had humiliated the proud French nobility in the seventeenth century, forcing aristocrats to accept a subordinate place and bend the knee at the royal court. Their uprising, the Fronde, was an early modern version of the Satsuma rebellion. The Fronde was crushed.[19] However, after France's military defeat at the hands of England in 1763, leading members of the aristocracy took the chance to identify themselves with the need to rescue French honour. Lafayette was among those to become patriots.

During the French Revolution, the nobility, like the monarchy, was discredited and 'the Parisian masses became the sole heir and bearer of this aristocratic inheritance, which was recast as the concept of national honour' (Schivelbusch 2003, 133). The French urban working class and peasantry were gradually integrated into the modern French nation during the nineteenth century. Unlike their German counterparts, they acquired a confident sense of nationhood.

It is true that there were deep internal divisions in France. These were exacerbated by military defeats at the hands of the Germans in 1870–1. The French officers regained their sense of pride by bloodily suppressing the revolutionary Paris Commune. They were also lifted by colonial adventures in North Africa. What held the French nation together despite these divisions was a shared sense of itself as a noble but unjustly wounded nation, needing and deserving revenge.

Germany's social divisions after 1918 were much deeper than those in France after 1871. Following World War I, Germany was 'in a free fall', lacking 'France's safety net', its strong sense of national pride that could look back on two centuries of leadership on continental Europe. In Germany, 'The memories of centuries of national inferiority, supposedly relegated to the past by the victory of 1870–71, by the founding of the empire, and by forty years of power politics, now reappeared like an unwelcome guest on Germany's doorstep' (Schivelbusch 2003, 196–7).

The German people joined the nation fully only in August 1914. They were then pitched into a battle supposedly for German *Kultur* against French, British and American 'civilization'. Four years later the nation that they had just joined, the nation for which they had been asked to give everything, fell apart around them. Inflation made things even worse, deepening the social disintegration.

Hitler's achievement was to put this society together again for a while at least, with devastating effects for some, and eventually all, of its members. Schivelbusch shows how much the reconstruction and reintegration of German society in the 1930s depended on techniques of mass production, mass consumerism and mass propaganda borrowed from the United States. The Nazis learned from Henry Ford and the New Deal. Hitler drew the comparison quite explicitly: 'We resemble the Americans in that we have wants and desires' (quoted in Schäfer 1991, 214). Hitler knew how to create and manage these wants and desires. Furthermore, as Schivelbusch comments: 'The extermination of the Indian population influenced Hitler as profoundly as the Monroe Doctrine, which codified America's hegemonic aspirations' (2003, 284).[20]

World on fire

Hitler used the fledgling parliamentary democracy of the Weimar Republic to exploit resentments generated by the capitalistic market and its arbitrary cruelties during the 1920s. He played upon the fact that people felt they had been unfairly treated, degraded, belittled, ignored and treated with contempt. Hitler gave them a target for their revenge: the Jews. Unfortunately, this story did not end in 1945. It is now being replayed throughout the world, although Jews are certainly not the only victims.

In her book *World on Fire* (2003) Amy Chua recounts how her aunt – like her, an ethnic Chinese from a well-off family in the Philippines – died in Manila in 1994. Her aunt's chauffeur, a Filipino, murdered her. In the police report, the 'motive given was not robbery, despite the jewels and money the chauffeur was said to have taken. Instead, for motive, there was just one world – "Revenge"' (Chua 2003, 4–5). This story illustrates the main message of *World on Fire*: do not promote free-market capitalism and votes for all without redistribution measures, the rule of law and effective guarantees for the protection of minorities. Like Edward Luttwak, Amy Chua draws attention to the perils of importing only half the American way, of buying the blueprint without getting the benefits of the historical learning process and the broader socio-cultural context that produced the blueprint and makes it a reasonably decent way of living. Her central point is that:

> for the last twenty years the United States has been promoting through-out the non-Western world raw, laissez-faire capitalism – a form of markets that the West abandoned long ago. . . . It is striking to note that at no point in history did any Western nation ever implement laissez-faire capitalism and overnight universal suffrage at the same time – the precise formula of free market democracy currently being pressed on developing countries around the world. (14)

The problem with this blueprint is that when it is applied two things tend to happen simultaneously. First, minorities become successful, conspicuous and the object of great resentment. Many of these minorities are not just highly talented but also highly exposed and vulnerable to popular discontent. That includes the Chinese in the Philippines, Burma, Malaya and Indonesia, the Bengalis in Assam, the Tamils in Sri Lanka, the Lebanese in West Africa, the Ibo in Nigeria, the Croats in the former Yugoslavia, the Indians in East Africa, Europeans in Zimbabwe and, not least, Americans world-wide.

Second, democratic politics allows the resentful majority to take its revenge on these ethnic minorities, who can easily be labelled arrogant, exploitative and oppressive. Robert Mugabe, for example, is able to direct blame onto the targeted minority (in his case, white settlers) and impose high penalties on them. Sometimes, the political atmosphere created encourages aggrieved individuals or groups to take violent reprisals against members of the minority concerned.[21]

Cycles of revenge are set up. In some cases, these take the form of protests against the workings of the market. For example, reforms imposed on Tanzania by the World Bank and IMF during the 1980s allowed Indians to re-establish themselves as a major economic force. This led to 'bitter anti-Indian brutality' (Chua 2003, 114). In other cases, such as Sierra Leone and Kenya, the beneficiaries of 'crony capitalism' (147) try to protect their interests and reduce their vulnerability by closing down democratic institutions.[22] Sometimes the cycles of revenge lead to genocidal action against hated groups, most notoriously in Rwanda and in the former Yugoslavia.

Amy Chua sets out clearly the formula for generating revenge cycles:

> Take the rawest form of capitalism, slap it together with the rawest form of democracy, and export the two as a package deal to the

poorest, most frustrated, most unstable, and most desperate countries in the world. Add market-dominant minorities to the picture, and the instability inherent in this bareknuckle version of free market democracy is compounded a thousandfold by the manipulable forces of ethnic hatred. (195)

Clash of civilizations

In *The Clash of Civilizations and the Remaking of World Order* (1997), Samuel Huntington is equally impressed by the potential for hatred and revenge since the Cold War. However, his particular lenses focus at a higher level in the system. As far as he is concerned, 'Civilizations are the ultimate human tribes' (Huntington 1997, 207). His list of civilizations includes the Chinese, Japanese, Hindu, Islamic, Orthodox Christian, Western, and Latin American cases.[23] A civilization is 'the highest cultural grouping of people and the broadest level of cultural identity people have short of that which distinguishes humans from other species' forming 'the biggest "we" within which we feel culturally at home as distinguished from all the other "thems" out there' (43).

In Huntington's view, civilizations are the building blocks of global society. Unfortunately, their values are for the most part incompatible or inconsistent with each other. It is difficult for them to understand or agree with each other. Truce or, at best, pragmatic cooperation is the best to be hoped for. Mutual enmity is quite likely.

Huntington argues that the way civilizations relate to each other is the basic framework of world order or disorder. Four factors are especially important: the West is declining, for example, economically, demographically and linguistically (despite the popularity of English); people are turning towards religion all over the world; Islam is resurgent; and, finally, China and, more generally, Asia are becoming more powerful.

Huntington sees four categories of civilization. One is the West, which, he strongly implies, is the only truly 'civilized' civilization.[24] Then there are the 'challenger' civilizations: China (Sinic) and Islam. Third, there are the 'swing' civilizations, those of Japan, Russia (Orthodox) and India (Hindu), whose behaviour or political allegiances could affect the balance of advantage between the West and its challengers. Finally, there are the rest of 'the Rest' (Huntington 1997, 183), i.e. the non-West: these civilizations include the Latin

American, the Buddhist and the African. Between these civilizations he sees two main kinds of clashes. One is 'fault line conflicts' (207) on the boundaries between civilizations. These include the wars in south-eastern Europe, especially in the former Yugoslavia where the Western, Orthodox and Islamic civilizations intersect. In such wars, the core states of the civilizations – in cases where they actually have core states – are drawn in, initially to provide support to their civilizational friends but ultimately to impose constraints and broker peace. The absence of a clear core state in Islam is an important factor prolonging conflict.[25] Using other words, Huntington is describing important aspects of revenge cycles:

> As violence increases, the initial issues at stake tend to get redefined more exclusively as 'us' against 'them' and group cohesion and commitment are enhanced. Political leaders expand and deepen their appeals to ethnic and religious loyalties, and civilization consciousness strengthens in relation to other loyalties. A 'hate dynamic' emerges, comparable to the 'security dilemma' in international relations, in which mutual fears, distrust, and hatred feed on each other. Each side dramatizes and magnifies the distinction between the forces of virtue and the forces of evil and eventually attempt to transform this distinction into the ultimate distinction between the quick and the dead. (Huntington 1997, 266)

The other possible kind of conflict is direct clashes between core states or between whole civilizations. Huntington speculates about the possibility of a war breaking out in the future should, for example, the 'Chinese, eager to revenge their 1979 humiliation,

---

Box 10.6   Huntington's model: the 'clash of civilizations'

The West The 'civilized' civilization	*Challenger civilizations* Sinic Islamic
Swing civilizations Japanese Orthodox Hindu	*The rest of 'The Rest'* Latin America Buddhist African

invade Vietnam' (313).[26] He invents a scenario in which the Americans, Indians, Pakistanis and Indonesians are all involved, dragging Europe in behind them. More generally, he suggests, such wars are most likely to occur if one core state intervenes in the business of another core state in another civilization, making the latter feel that an attempt 'to humiliate and browbeat' (316) them is under way. Huntington's advice to core states faced with this kind of temptation to intervene is: keep out, steer clear and mind your own business.

Huntington's analysis diminishes the perceived threat posed by the rise of Asia by arguing that it contains five or six civilizations and, as a result, will be unable to organize cooperation between its constituent countries such as China, Japan, India and Russia.[27] The likely result, he implies, will be outbreaks of vengeful violence among them. At the same time, Huntington warns against an influx of minorities into the West, especially the United States, from other civilizations, in which category he includes Latin Americans from Mexico and all points south.[28]

By depicting global society as a collection of adjacent, competing and closed civilizations, Huntington revives the nineteenth-century picture of bounded national states, each presenting stereotypical versions of its rivals and enemies to its own people. For example, Huntington gives us 'bloody' Islam, and revenge-seeking China, and suggests that it would be unwise to allow too many 'un-American' Mexicans into the United States.

The tone of voice in *The Clash of Civilizations* is a mixture of reasonableness, anxiety and half-concealed contempt for supposedly less 'civilized' people inclined to violence. One can find a similar tone in an essay by John Stuart Mill, first published in 1859: *On Liberty* (Mill 1964). Mill belonged to a cultured class of property owners in Britain that for generations had been able to rely on the deference of those 'below' them and, as a result, had had no qualms about telling their inferiors how to live their lives. By the late 1850s it was clear that uncultured tradespeople, artisans and even unskilled workers were going to get the vote before many years had passed. The danger was that as a result they might start telling their old masters what to do. The late 1850s was a good time for gentlemen like Mill to rediscover the importance of being able to put a fence around your own culture and way of life and say 'keep out'.[29] A century and a half later, in the late 1990s, it was a good time for at least part of the American establishment to rediscover the importance of the general principle that you should not interfere with someone else's civilization, especially if your own civilization seemed to be the one most at risk. Fear of revenge may be triggering a pre-emptive strategy of cultural resistance.

* * *

In this chapter we have: compared revenge and resistance as responses that reject humiliation; considered the contrasting cases of Mandela and Saddam Hussein; looked at adaptation, last-ditch resistance and calculated reformation as ways of rejecting humiliation, with reference to the British aristocracy, the Japanese samurai and the movement led by Gandhi; examined revenge chains and revenge cycles; reflected on relations between France and Germany; explored revenge cycles between ethnic groups; and investigated the supposed clash of civilizations.

In the last three chapters we have surveyed the escape, acceptance and rejection responses to the experience of humiliation. It is impossible not to notice the hefty profile of the honour code making several appearances. These include the 'virtuous' character of strength and violence as portrayed in the American ideology and in Fanon's writings, the pride in self-sufficiency and capacity to suffer shown by the workers studied by Sennett and Cobb, Friedman's evocation of the globalization's jungle law and the examples of revenge cycles, all foreign to the spirit of the human rights code.

Globalization, as it is developing at present, has the effect of strengthening the honour code. The point is that enforcement of the human rights code depends upon everybody being prepared to follow rules that protect the interests of others. How are those rules enforced? There are three possible ways: by the community where it can exercise strong informal pressure on its members; by the state where the means of surveillance and control are sufficiently developed; and by the self-discipline of individuals who are motivated to behave according in the correct spirit, exercising what Martin Albrow has called 'performative citizenship' (Albrow 1996, 175).

Western influence has disseminated the principles of the human rights code throughout the world. This increased awareness among the global population of these principles has been a major factor raising levels of resentment at 'humiliating' conditions and treatment that do not meet the standards of that code. However, the capacity and willingness of national governments to fund and enforce human rights has not increased to the same extent. Meanwhile, the pressures of globalization often undermine the coherence of local communities, and, in any case, habits of citizenship may not be deeply ingrained at that level compared with the loyalties associated with family and religion.

In these circumstances, feelings of humiliation and resentment that are generated, in part at least, by an increased awareness of one's own human rights frequently lead to action framed by the honour code which says 'fight for yourself and your group'. When fighting is prolonged and widespread, consideration for human rights decreases substantially. If warfare and civil violence become endemic, the honour code is likely to triumph at the expense of human rights.

In the last chapter we will: consider globalization's hidden agenda once more; identify the conditions favouring emancipation cycles and distrust cycles; study the dynamics of European integration since 1945; see the workings of a transatlantic revenge cycle; consider the implications of future global multi-polarity and growing urbanization throughout the world; face up to the possibility of an increase in state-sponsored terror; and ask how the human rights code and honour code are likely to be accommodated within twenty-first-century politics.

11

Decent Democracy or Domineering State?

We have almost completed our exploration of the triple helix of socio-historical processes shaping globalization's hidden agenda. It is time to address that agenda more directly:

1 How will the United States and other leading powers cope with the forthcoming relative decline in America's global influence?
2 How will global governance be managed as American power wanes?
3 Now that capitalism has finally triumphed, what *kind* of capitalist political order will become dominant? Whose interests will it serve, and how?
4 What are the future global prospects for the version of human rights supported by the European Union with its emphasis upon strong social rights?
5 As the world's population becomes increasingly urbanized with practically half its people in cities already, and half the developing world's population due to be urbanized by 2030, how will this newly urbanized population be incorporated within national and global socio-political orders and whose political lead will they follow?

This final chapter deals with these issues, making a journey in two stages: from optimism to pessimism, and from pessimism to realism. We begin in Europe in 1914.

Europe's 'clash of civilizations'

World War I was 'a clash of civilizations'. German officers leading their men in the trenches 'knew' they were fighting for German *Kultur*. Their enemy was French/Anglo-Saxon/Jewish 'civilization', which, in their view, was shallow, materialistic and liable to corrode more profound values.[1] Meanwhile, in November 1914 the religious authorities in Istanbul, capital of the Ottoman Empire, issued a *fatwa* declaring a *jihad* against all Christians.[2]

Over ninety years later, there is good and bad news to tell. The bad news is that between 1914 and the present time, multi-polar rivalries in Europe and around the globe led to two world wars. The first war cost over nine million lives. The second killed over fifty million people. A much larger number of people were wounded. Ironically, most of the major participants got outcomes they certainly did not bargain for. In 1914 the leaders in Vienna, Petrograd (now St Petersburg), Istanbul and Berlin did not aim to see their empires broken up. Neither the Nazis in 1939 nor the Japanese in 1941 were aiming to create an American 'global monarchy'.

The good news is that Germany and France are no longer enemies but are bound together peacefully at the centre of the European Union. Meanwhile, the Turkish government has made an application to become a member of the EU and this application is being seriously considered. Here the optimism begins. Let us see how far it takes us.

Emancipation cycles

Relations between the European powers are far more cooperative than they used to be before 1945. Is this an instance of the emancipatory reworking of humiliating relationships? Does the EU represent a fourth response to humiliation – not escape, acceptance or rejection, but *transformation*?

By transformation, I mean a process during which those involved in imposing and suffering humiliation redefine their relationship in such a way that humiliation is progressively removed from it. Transformation is a kind of collective renewal. One way transformation might be achieved is through an *emancipation cycle*, which involves:

- truce;
- dialogue;

- a new language of peace-seeking as a shared enterprise; and
- the gradual creation of a new set of joint interests.

An emancipation cycle requires a combination of truce and dialogue. This may make possible a 'decommissioning' of negative stereotypes, which are a kind of reinforcement humiliation, a way of making others feel inferior and excluded. This may make it possible to develop a new language of peace-seeking as a shared enterprise; and the gradual creation of a new set of joint interests which does not necessarily imply a merging or submerging of existing interests. The process may involve building attachments to new collective symbols that encompass existing loyalties.

Truce and dialogue may establish a pattern of repetition. A covert truce among key participants may get this pattern established by permitting a process of dialogue within which the work of building trust may begin, shaping attitudes sufficiently to permit an overt truce from hostilities. If successfully implemented, such a truce may provide space for dialogue to deepen and broaden and for trust to increase further.[3] If the transformation envisaged within the dialogue runs ahead of the participants' willingness or capacity to accept it, there may be a truce from dialogue itself, a breathing space for persuasion and adjustment to occur within each side before dialogue is resumed once more. [4]

Such a process is greatly helped if certain background conditions are present. For example:

- if the parties concerned are weary and disenchanted with the existing situation, perhaps suffering the costs of a prolonged revenge cycle;
- if the leaders of each party are able to enter into truce and dialogue on behalf of their followers and deliver on agreements reached;
- if there is a powerful authority respected by both the parties concerned that is willing to take part in an attempted transformation process; and
- if resources are available to help make possible the construction of new interpersonal, inter-group and/or socio-political arrangements within which conflicts may be conducted in a more peaceful manner.

One of the intentions of intermediaries in such negotiations might be gradually to build up enthusiasm for, commitment to and pride in the new arrangements being developed. If this is done effectively, such

Box 11.1 The emancipation cycle	
(i) exhaustion leads to truce from either conflict or dialogue, and this permits reflection and the renewal of energy ↓	(iv) gradual transformation ← of attitudes, behaviour and structures reduce levels of humiliation
(ii) dialogue moves beyond stereotypical → thinking	↑ (iii) jointly created meanings and intentions increase trust between dialogue partners

pride might help to modify the feelings of fear and anger the parties initially bring to the discussions.

Distrust cycles

On the other hand, exhausted opponents may grasp the chance of a truce so that they can rebuild their capacity to fight. They might not want to cast aside the emotional reassurance provided by stereotypical thinking with its protection against the need to expend mental energy on thinking things out afresh.[5] In those circumstances, the dialogue enabled by the truce is liable to be restricted, giving as little as possible away, getting as much as possible for your own side; in fact, bargaining for short-term advantage as distinct from engaging in a mutual sharing of ideas and problems.

The result will be a distrust cycle (see box 11.2). In some contexts, such as those in Northern Ireland or within Israeli–Palestinian relations, both the emancipation cycle and the distrust cycle seem to be operating simultaneously.

The European story

So, what does the European Union tell us about the dynamics of the emancipation cycle? The first thing to notice is that this new polity

Box 11.2 The distrust cycle	
(i) exhaustion leads to truce from either conflict or dialogue, permitting reflection and the renewal of energy ↓	(iv) as the agenda moves beyond points of mutual pragmatic convenience, further ← bargaining arouses distrust, fear of deception, increased mutual antagonism and a renewal of hostilities ↑
(ii) dialogue fails to move beyond stereotypical → thinking	(iii) dialogue restricted to contingent areas of pragmatic mutual concern, for example, establishing the boundaries of aggression

is as strange and challenging to its global neighbours as the United States was in the nineteenth century. The political experiment on the other side of the Atlantic contradicted the old ways since it was not a monarchy and had no aristocracy. Many people in aristocratic, monarchical Europe looked on with quiet satisfaction as the American Republic tore itself apart during the Civil War.

The European Union is also a political experiment in that it is not in itself a state. Outsiders find it reassuring that the European Union now seems destined to undergo a period of inner turmoil as, like the United States in the mid-nineteenth century, it strains to manage the problems of territorial expansion.

During the American Civil War, the American experiment had sometimes seemed to be in danger of failing. However, three decades after the war's end, the United States was busy forcing its way into Latin America and the Far East, pushing aside the European colonial powers. Where will the EU be thirty years from now? There are grounds for optimism that by 2035 it will have overcome its structural problems and be much more coherent and powerful in the global arena.

Despite its recent difficulties, the EU has articulate admirers. Will Hutton finds the EU a more admirable phenomenon than the United

States under the control of neo-conservatives. Hutton likes Europe's clear commitment to three ideas: 'the obligations of the propertied to society, the need for a social contract and the centrality of a public realm and government to a happy community' (Hutton 2003, 21).[6] Jeremy Rifkin is entranced by the 'European Dream', which he discovers is a mixture of civilization, civil society and 'network governance' (Rifkin 2004, 223).[7] Tzvetan Todorov hails Europe's defence of rationality, justice, democracy, individual freedom and secularism: he likes the adaptability of this 'tranquil power' (Todorov 2005, 51) and hopes it will expand its influence geographically.

Zygmunt Bauman is more narrow-eyed. He thinks Europeans have been pulled too far along the road from the 'social state' to the 'security state' (Bauman 2004, 91), which cultivates its citizens' fears. However, Bauman hopes Europe will be outward-looking rather than inward-looking, ready to put aside 'the logic of local entrenchment' in favour of 'the logic of global responsibility (which) ushers us into unknown territory' (137).

In fact, these analyses do not quite get to the heart of the European story. This story is best told in a transatlantic context and with a historical sweep. When the Americans took effective control of Europe in 1945, they put an end to the cycle of 'bloody revenge' that had torn the continent apart repeatedly during previous decades (Scheff 1994, as discussed in chapter 10). America was, for a while, the unchallenged global monarch. It behaved like a sovereign subduing its unruly nobility. In Europe, for a few years the word of the Americans was law.

Europe in the mid-1940s was devastated. Loss of agricultural stock, disruption of trade, rising prices, capital shortage and debt were just a few of the problems. The American response was Marshall Aid. The Economic Recovery Program, to use the official title, injected nearly $12.5 billion into Europe between 1948 and 1952. During the decade after 1945 the total amount of support for Europe added up to nearly twice that amount, directed to Britain, France, West Germany and Italy, in other words to old friends and old enemies alike.

Part of the deal was that European countries would reform their institutions to achieve financial and monetary stability, reduce trade barriers and integrate their national economies with each other. One of the leading American officials, Paul Hoffman, told the Europeans in 1949 that the United States wanted to see 'the formation of a single large market in which quantitative restrictions on the movement of goods, monetary barriers to the flow of payments and, eventually, all tariffs are permanently swept away' (quoted in Walker 1994, 87).

The European movement was given a very decisive shove forward by the United States in the late 1940s, partly because they wanted Western Europe to be a strong barrier against the expansion of the Soviet Union's influence and partly because they wanted a thriving market for their own products, services and investments.[8]

Looking back on this period, Michel Jobert (French foreign minister, 1973–4) recalled that Western Europe just after the war was 'lined up in one camp, under strict US control, taking orders and reporting for duty' (Le Monde, 10 August 1991). Not surprisingly, there was resistance. In 1953 the Americans failed to force through the idea of a European Defence Community. Three years later came the Suez campaign.

Transatlantic power relations became more evenly balanced after the oil shock of the early 1970s, which forced the United States to suspend the convertibility of the dollar into gold, a great blow to its prestige.[9] The Europeans responded in three ways. They moved towards a single internal market. They made plans for a common currency. They made the European Union (then Community) more like a developmental state, with a regional development fund, direct elections to the European Parliament and qualified voting in the Council of Ministers.

The fall of the Berlin Wall in 1989 created a much larger, reunited Germany, which agreed to abolish its separate currency and support the Maastricht Treaty, implemented in 1993. This treaty aims to provide a coordinated foreign and security policy within the EU, as well as inter-governmental cooperation with respect to justice and home affairs. It set up the Committee for the Regions and the Cohesion Fund; it created EU citizenship and increased the powers of the European Parliament. Economic and monetary union was established in 1999. The EU is busy absorbing new countries, its total membership having expanded to twenty-five in 2004 and with further expansion planned.[10]

The European Union faces large problems, although no more serious than those faced, and surmounted, by the United States as it developed, historically. Europe's leaders have been buoyed up by the existence of this huge, if still underdeveloped, power base, which clearly has the potential to rival the United States. In November 1999 Jacques Chirac declared that 'The European Union itself [must] become a major pole of international equilibrium, endowing itself with the instruments of a true power.'[11] In October 2000 Tony Blair argued that 'Europe's citizens need Europe to be strong and united. They need it to be a power in the world. Whatever its origin, Europe today is no longer just about peace. It is about projecting collective power.'[12]

In some respects, the European Union is a classic case of successful transformation.[13] It has emancipated its members from the violent and humiliating revenge cycle into which France, Germany and their close neighbours were locked during the decades before 1945. It has also emancipated the 'subordinate' nations of Western Europe (and, later, Eastern Europe) from their previous position of inferiority. The most obvious beneficiaries are Ireland and Spain; more recently, Poland's leaders enjoyed a similar effect as they achieved EU membership.[14]

By 2004, the EU's population had grown to 450 million, about 175 million more than the United States. In that year its economy was over 40 per cent larger than the US in terms of GDP, although if account is taken of differences in living standards and costs, the US and the expanded EU of twenty-five countries are practically equal.[15] According to such figures, the European Union is a tremendous success, especially if one considers the wrecked condition of Europe four decades before.

However, things are not as simple as that. Transformation carried a cost. The two processes of emancipation from humiliation just described coincided with the creation of two new humiliation processes.

The first was triggered by an example of exclusion humiliation. The European movement has largely been a matter for political, professional and business elites. It has excluded ordinary people from its key decision-making processes.[16] For a few decades, referenda and parliamentary votes were won by appealing to the motives of fear and gratitude: fear of the communist east, gratitude for the absence of war. Now both fear and gratitude are considerably diminished. There is a tide of resentment surging from below. Citizens are beginning to take revenge on their 'betters' through the ballot box. Europe's leaders, in France and elsewhere, will have to find ways to mend the broken bond with their electors.[17]

The second humiliation process was stimulated by the conquest and relegation experienced by Europe's political leadership during the mid- and late 1940s. It was degrading for the old masters of the world to be made into indigent beggars at the court in Washington. As Europeans regained their wealth and strength, they hit back. The result was a transatlantic revenge cycle that has lasted over half a century.

An early event within this revenge cycle was the Suez debacle of 1956, vigorously opposed and exposed by the American government. This affair resulted in the shaming of the British and French governments before the United Nations. Europe's restless subjection to American dominance in the 1950s and early 1960s was answered during the following decade by European attacks on American motives and character during the Vietnam War.[18] The Americans repaid these attacks by determined self-assertion under Reagan's presidential leadership. They engaged in aggressive neo-liberalism during the 1980s, abetted by Britain. This was followed by a period of self-glorification during the 1990s after the collapse of the Soviet Union. 'Old Europe'[19] minus Britain retaliated by overtly opposing the American plan to invade Iraq in 2003, culminating in the French declaration that it would use its UN Security Council veto against the United States for the first time since the Suez crisis in 1956.

Multi-polarity

Here the pessimism begins. The West is divided. It has not got over the shock of losing its old Soviet enemy, which provided a convenient focus for unity. It is difficult to find a replacement. Many have been considered but each has major disadvantages: the Chinese are too capitalist, the Japanese too Americanized, the Russians too accommodating and Islam too diverse (although this remains Washington's favoured candidate for the job of 'necessary enemy').

In the event, the two halves of the West, Europe and America, have turned on each other: not directly but discreetly, punctuating emollient back-scratching with venomous back-biting. This is not simply a matter of nursing historical wounds. The US and EU leadership are divided on three fundamental matters, with the United Kingdom hovering uneasily between the two:

1   The current American administration is inclined to *unilateralism* where possible, while the Europeans much prefer *multilateral* approaches.
2   The Americans are broadly happy with a *uni-polar* world, but the Europeans are evidently looking forward to a time when *multipolarity* will more fully restore their capacity to have an independent voice in the world.

3   The Americans are inclined to favour *militaristic* approaches to troublesome issues of foreign policy, while the Europeans are more inclined to favour *peaceful diplomacy*.[20]

These divisions within the West are part of a steady drift towards multi-polarity at the global level. China's national income has been doubling every eight years during the past two decades. OECD predicts that China's share of total world exports will increase from 6 per cent in 2005 to 10 per cent by 2010, by which time it is likely to be the world's leading exporter.[21]

With increased economic power comes increased capacity to become militarily powerful. That can be turned into actual fighting power quite quickly if a country puts its mind to it. The United States has shown how to do it: you buy brains, skills, information and, where necessary, hardware and software; and you persuade your citizens, rich and poor, that building up armaments is not only a good idea, but worth paying for.

Box 11.3 is a guess at how the global order might look in 2035. It seems quite likely that by then the United States will no longer be the only global super-power, having been joined by China and the European Union. There will be other global-regional players, probably with aspirations to have increasing global influence. Russia, Japan and India all come to mind.

It is possible that by that time fundamentalist terrorism carried out by non-state actors such as Al-Qaeda may have declined, especially if the political uncertainty in Central Asia and the Middle East has diminished. The parts played by Turkey and Iran could be crucial, providing a moderating influence on fellow Muslims that is likely to be more effective than 'infidel' fire power.

However, there is no reason to expect a smooth transition from uni-polarity to multi-polarity. Consider the possibility that the decline of loosely coordinated *freelance or franchised terrorism* of the Al-Qaeda kind may well coincide with the spread of *state-sponsored terror*, not

Box 11.3 How the global order might look in 2035			
Global giants	China	United States	European Union
Leading global-regional players	Japan	Russia	India

especially linked to Islamist causes. This term refers to regimes that employ a mixture of military force and demagoguery to victimize unpopular minorities and attack nearby nations. State brutality against citizens and neighbouring countries is certainly not a specifically Middle Eastern or Muslim phenomenon. It encompasses all manner of brutal regimes employing violence and fear to get their way.

State-sponsored terror could spring up anywhere where there are rapidly growing cities containing many educated or semi-educated young people without paid employment. This is the case especially if such societies harbour enterprising politicians ready to work on the people's resentments as a means of building political movements or even of seizing state power.

According to Immanuel Wallerstein, we have entered a 'transformational TimeSpace' (Wallerstein 1998, 3). In other words, we are arriving at 'a structurally chaotic situation that will be both unpleasant to live through and thoroughly unpredictable in its trajectory.' He believes 'a new order will emerge out of this chaos over a period of fifty years, and this new order will be shaped as a function of what everyone does in the interval – those with power in the present system, and those without it' (89–90).[22]

Put beside this the assessment of Timothy Garton Ash, who argues:

> Unless China's economic growth falters dramatically, perhaps due to political turmoil, China in 2025 will be such a major power – with Japan still formidable and India coming up as well – that there will be no point in conceiving a political strategy for Europe and Asia separately from the intentions and dynamics of Asia. So the old Atlantic-centred West, which has been shaping the world since about 1500, probably has no more than twenty years left in which it will be the main world-shaper. (Ash 2004, 192)

Add a further consideration, which is that all the actors involved, whether politicians, business people, electorates, customers or congregations, are likely to be highly influenced by feelings of fear and vengefulness, and all will have a strong desire to avoid being victimized even if this means becoming victimizers.

The challenge of the slums

The situation is intensified by the fact that a high proportion of the global population is on the move. It is undergoing the difficult and major transition from life in the countryside to an urban existence.

It is a well-known fact that one out of every two people in the world lives on $2 a day or less. It is less well known that the poor are becoming an urbanized phenomenon. They are no longer mainly scattered in villages. The recent United Nations report entitled *The Challenge of Slums* (UN-Habitat 2003) makes it clear that over the next two decades the world's urban population will double from 2.5 billion to 5 billion people.[23]

About half the global population are already town- or city-dwellers. At the moment the world's urban population is growing by the equivalent of thirty-three new cities each with two million people every year and this can be expected to continue for the next thirty years.[24] In 1950 the poor in the developing world were mainly rural. Only 18 per cent of them lived in cities. This is changing rapidly. By 2030 over half this population will be city people.

City life brings people face to face with extremes of inequality. In Armenia, Russia, Tajikistan and Ukraine, levels of inequality have almost doubled over the last ten years. In Hungary between 1992 and 1996 the proportion of people existing below the minimum subsistence level increased by half. By 1999 more than half the population in the Commonwealth of Independent States were living in poverty.[25]

Will religious leaders and local politicians tell their followers to accept the logic of the market and make the best of it? The answer is: probably not. People in cities are powerful when they are organized or become mobilized as crowds. Whether or not urbanites have the vote, they can ruin property, take lives and break governments. That is what the rich found in nineteenth-century Europe.

In the early nineteenth century, the rich, egged on by publications such as Thomas Malthus's *Essay on the Principle of Population* (1798), tried telling the poor they deserved to be poor and could expect no help (Malthus 1999). By the late nineteenth century, after several revolutionary upheavals, the rich concluded, a little reluctantly, that the best way to 'defuse' the threat was to make sure that the poor could get a decent livelihood in a decent environment.

Support was required on such a scale that the welfare state began to evolve supported by tax revenue taken from those who could afford to pay. The advance of the welfare state in Europe was a long, drawn-out business, reaching back at least to Bismarck's social legislation during the 1880s, which gave German workers compensation for industrial injuries and old age pensions, and continuing into the 1960s. The knowledge that led to the introduction of the welfare state was won the hard way.[26] It was one half of a double lesson that is still valid. To make the cities safe and reasonably content two things have to be done:

- poverty must be eliminated; and
- humiliation has to diminish radically.

In late nineteenth- and early twentieth-century Europe, progress was made on the first front but much less was done on the second. In fact, the advance of human rights in the form of citizenship made people even more acutely resentful of the humiliations to which they were still subjected.

At the beginning of the twenty-first century, *The Challenge of Slums* (UN-Habitat 2003) does not say very much about the economic costs of confronting urban poverty. If this report's proposed solutions are to be adopted widely, however, massive political commitment and substantial financial support from the rich will be needed. The report calls for 'good urban governance' within 'inclusive cities' which have

> sustainability, subsidiarity, . . . equality of access to decision-making processes and the basic necessities of urban life, . . . efficiency in the delivery of public services and in promoting local economic development, . . . transparency and accountability of decision-makers and stakeholders, . . . civic engagement and citizenship . . . [and] security of individuals and their living environment. (182–3)

If this is what the urban poor need, then a little bit of intellectual 'reverse engineering' applied to that list will tell us what they have got now. By implication, what they have got now is:

- forbidding and socially excluding cities;
- political leaders who are thoughtless, centralized and distant;[27]
- inefficiently delivered public services;
- no-one to take local economic development seriously;
- secrecy and corruption;
- lack of participation by poor citizens; and
- unsafe environments.[28]

Put it another way: these people are being humiliated, excluded and relegated, either deliberately or through ignorance and neglect.

The ghost of Hitler

Hitler inherited a political culture ridden with humiliation as a consequence of the snobbish and militaristic ethos of the upper class of the German Empire, an ethos that permeated downward through German society. The Nazi leader found a population used to feeling resentment.[29] His strategy was to cultivate this feeling and use it as a reservoir of political energy for his own purposes. The message he conveyed was that other nations had cast down the Germans. He challenged his audience to make Germany strong again, asking: 'Who yields voluntarily? No one! So the strength which each people possesses decides the day. Always before God and the world the stronger has the right to carry through what he wills.'[30] The right to lead was based on 'the authority of personality', he proclaimed; under his leadership the German people would 'champion their right to live'. This meant having the strength to win and not being afraid to use it. England and France pretended to be morally superior but were not. Hitler invited his audience to ask themselves 'By what means have the virtuous nations obtained for themselves this quarter of the world' and added: 'They did not apply virtuous methods!' His message was: 'Do not deceive yourselves about the most important precondition in life – namely, the necessity to be strong.'

Hitler was able to work on a demoralized and disoriented German population that was simultaneously experiencing the humiliating effects of:

- the imperial impulse (which Hitler identified with England and France);
- the logic of the market (which Hitler personified in the stereotype of the Jew); and
- the cosmopolitan condition (in other words, a world of weakened national states facing the prospect of being disciplined from 'outside' and 'above' which Hitler dramatized as the so-called international Jewish conspiracy).

Compare the global situation in the first years of the twenty-first century. As we saw in chapters 5, 6 and 7, the imperial impulse, the logic of the market and the cosmopolitan condition are all in play. They create feelings of humiliation in many societies, even in the United States, where in 2005 President Bush was busy cultivating fears of 'a radical Islamic empire that spreads from Spain to Indonesia'.[31] The danger of a return to Fascism remains high on all continents.[32]

Fusing the two codes of modernity

It is time to undertake the second stage of this journey, from pessimism to realism. How can we protect the gains won for human rights and advance them further? We need to build strong institutions of governance at the global-regional and global level that can codify and enforce those rights. The point is that it was the strength of central governments in national states that turned human rights, usually in the form of citizenship, into a practical reality during the nineteenth and twentieth centuries.

Something similar has to happen at the global-regional and global levels in the twenty-first century. The EU has made a good start. It offers one model for progress at the global level, as Peter Singer has pointed out.[33] How differently the Iraq invasion of 2003 would have been regarded by the world if it had been a police operation sanctioned by a global body accepted as legitimate by the vast majority of national states.

The most important ingredient needed for building strong global and global-regional institutions is political will. To create it must surely involve engaging the interest and commitment of the strategically crucial urban populations coming into being throughout Eurasia, America and Africa. What they want, and what they will endure, counts very heavily indeed.

These rapidly expanding urban populations are caught between the tribal, dynastic or communal honour codes of their old villages and the strengthened dose of human rights thinking they receive in the cities where trade-union, political and business activity all speak the language of 'rights' and 'opportunities'. New urbanites bring with them, and find within the city, religious frameworks for interpreting the world. These convey ideas about the worthiness of every soul and the majesty of God, ideas that can be deployed to reinforce viewpoints based on both honour and human rights.

People in such situations do not make a complete switch from the honour code to the human rights code. They look for a mixture of them both. The question is: which mixture works best for the world and for them? Which amalgam of the honour and human rights codes will be most favourable to building strong forms of governance at the national, global-regional and global levels, creating institutions that are thoroughly committed to maintaining a decent standard of material existence and fair treatment for all citizens?

At least three options exist (see box 11.4). We have already met the first: *liberated capitalism*. Driven by the logic of the market,

Box 11.4 Fusing the honour code with the human rights code

	Option 1	*Option 2*	*Option 3*
	Liberated capitalism	The domineering state	Decent democracy
From human rights code	Everyone has the right to aspire to a decent life and should be free (unless a nuisance to the rich); violence should be eliminated as much as possible (except in defence of property)	A powerful and successful state can and will keep those it favours comfortable and secure, providing them with social rights	Everyone has the right to become equipped for, to enter and to be fairly treated in the social competition, benefit from a duty of care, and receive life-enhancing benefits such as access to culture
From honour code	Humiliation is a fact of life and must be borne or overcome; life is a struggle in which the winners are those who know how to look after themselves	'Might is right': strength is admirable; all that counts is conquest, victory and success by any means	Strength, loyalty, courage, steadfastness and ambition are to be admired if they are displayed within the context of the human rights code

which has one foot firmly planted in each of the two codes, it says: 'Life is a humiliating struggle but let us keep the struggle open, non-violent and free for all to enter. That is the best you can expect. That is as democratic as life gets.' The second option, the *domineering state*, carries another message: 'The state is going to use its strength to look after those it favours at whatever cost to others. Steer clear. We can hurt you.' The third option is *decent democracy*. At its heart is the following proposition: 'The implementation of the human rights code by states and citizens has the object of making sure that everyone gets a decent life insofar as that is possible. It is not permissible to break the human rights code on the grounds that you are promoting it or defending it.' This option responds positively to the honour code's core values of strength, loyalty, courage, steadfastness and striving for success, but also says: 'These values must never be implemented to undermine the human rights code and the laws that enforce it, only to promote or defend them. That way we all benefit.'

Decent democracy is not the cowardly and resentful creature attacked by Nietzsche in his campaign against slave morality. Nor is it the vision of an endless, restless line of welfare cases conjured up to keep government lean, mean and business-friendly. Decent democracy looks to a strong and active (but not brutally 'domineering') state and a vigorous and innovative (but not recklessly 'liberated') capitalist economy as powerful means in the challenge of engaging all citizens and all communities in the task of living together without poverty and humiliation. Reaching paradise is not on the agenda of decent democracy. Eliminating avoidable misery certainly is.

Enlightened self-interest

Decent democracy is the same thing as enlightened self-interest, if that is properly understood. The benefits to the majority of the global population are obvious: more opportunity, less misery, better lives. The benefits to the rich and powerful minority are equally obvious as soon as we begin to consider the matter seriously.

The predominance of the logic of the market since the 1970s has encouraged a climate in the West that denies recognition to the special problems of countries outside the charmed circle of wealth and political strength. This is justified by saying that they have the freedom to improve themselves if they choose to do so. In response, anti-Western politics has mainly been transmitting the message that the West should adopt a new mind-set that gives greater practical recognition to the interests of others.

As is well known, the main tactic followed by Washington has been to recruit local political and business allies in strategically relevant Eurasian, African and Latin American countries. These individuals are chosen because they are prepared to cooperate with Western strategies based on the domineering state (driven by the residual imperial impulse) and liberated capitalism (implementing the logic of the market). Contemporary Iraq is the latest example of this approach.

However, as the global influence of the West diminishes over the next few decades, these local allies will be left stranded. For their own safety, many of them are likely to adopt an anti-Western political stance at that point. The Western investment in such individuals will probably turn out to have been largely wasted.

Instead of just 'buying' a few key people, a sounder, long-term approach would be to invest heavily in providing education, training, material resources, knowledge and skills in these societies. The object of that investment would be to create the conditions for stable decent democracies. Even better, the West should find ways of sharing the burden and commitment with its major global neighbours in Eurasia. That would be a strategy of enlightened self-interest. However, at the moment it seems unlikely to be put into effect.

Choices

Let us consider the choices available from the point of view of two key actors. One is the US government in the early twenty-first century. The other is the poor or nearly poor city-dweller almost anywhere in the world.

The United States straddles all three options set out in box 11.5:

1   There is no doubt that current American policy is strongly in favour of liberated capitalism, both at home and abroad. It works on the assumption that the domination of capitalist business interests in a country is a powerful indicator that this country is 'free' and therefore has the basic ingredient of democracy;

2   When the US government attacks other countries, its spokespeople usually say they are defending or establishing the human rights basic to a decent democracy. It is embarrassing when video footage or photographic evidence gets into the mass media showing prisoners being tortured or the bodies of enemies burned.

3   In practice, some Americans and some of their critics regard such atrocities as an inevitable by-product of the fact that the United

Box 11.5   Is this what we are choosing for the twenty-first century?

	US government	The world's cities
First preference	Liberated capitalism	Decent democracy
Second preference	Domineering state	Domineering state
Third preference	Decent democracy	Liberated capitalism

States is doing what it takes to show that might is right; in other words, behaving according to the norms of the domineering state.[34]

New city-dwellers have a different set of viewpoints:

1   As they usually have a relatively low level of resources at their command, the rational choice is decent democracy, as long it is capable of being implemented through efficient and effective governance of the kind recommended in *The Challenge of Slums* (UN-Habitat 2003). However, this option is often not available.
2   There is a strong pull towards the domineering state, especially if 'their' ethnic, tribal or religious group is strongly represented in government.
3   The least favoured choice is liberated capitalism as it provides rewards to a minority only, especially in the short and medium term, and its implementation may, in any case, be undermined if the government in question is behaving like a domineering state.

Whenever the United States behaves like a domineering state, saying, in effect, that 'might is right', it strengthens the hands of those throughout the world who favour that option for themselves, from Israel to Zimbabwe. The American government may argue that applying a strategy of 'might is right' is a way of introducing 'freedom', implying human rights. However, most poor or nearly poor urban dwellers (and outside the West that means the majority) are unlikely to be convinced by this argument as they realize that 'freedom' means liberated capitalism, which does not solve their problems.

The official agenda of globalization tells us that the world is faced by a choice between 'Islamic terrorism' and freedom in the form of liberated capitalism. This is untrue. It is not on the real agenda. That real agenda has been hidden from our eyes. It asks us to choose between decent democracy and the domineering state.

In the next decade or so the choices that will be available to the world, and especially to the world's city-dwellers, will depend on the choices being made by the West now. The West, albeit divided, has the capacity at the moment to adopt *any one of the three options* set out in box 11.5.

The European Union has gone much further than the United States in envisaging and partly implementing decent democracy. It has not been an easy ride. The people have often objected. Why? In part, hostility has arisen because many ordinary people think the EU's practices are too generous to 'outsider' groups such as asylum seekers. Another reason is that people believe that life in Brussels has become something of a gravy train for politicians. Many of those who represent the EU are too obviously failing to live up to the standards of honourable behaviour expected in a decent democracy. Remedying the second problem will give politicians more authority in dealing with the first.

Perhaps, in time, decent democracy will once more become an option within American politics also. Meanwhile, a struggle is going on within the EU between the options of decent democracy and liberated capitalism. If liberated capitalism wins outright, if the EU and the US move much closer together politically once again, and if the militaristic approach of the Americans prevails, the world will draw its conclusions. People elsewhere will then see Europe as a major beneficiary of the domineering state option, kept secure and comfortable while American strength keeps the poor people outside the club at bay.[35]

If in the next few years the West rules out the option of decent democracy as its goal for itself and others, this will mean the EU has failed to assert its independence within the transatlantic arena. In those circumstances, the most likely outcome is that Washington will continue using the strategy of the domineering state as a means of establishing liberated capitalism over an expanding global area as long as it is able to do so.

If the West abandons decent democracy as a genuine option, if it abandons the duty of care, if it says the market will cure all ills, what will happen then? Who then will make the case for embedding decent democracy and human rights in the working practices of strong global-regional and global institutions of governance? Probably no-one.

In that case, our global city-dwellers will be left with the choice between liberated capitalism and the domineering state, each offered to them by a different set of local politicians. They are likely to favour the latter. It offers them a chance to avoid being victimized while turning some other group into victims (see box 11.5).

If that happens, the world will be denied the opportunity of building decent, prospering, non-humiliated and non-humiliating societies, which is the prospect potentially offered by the option of decent democracy.

What will be left? If people cannot have the decent democracy they really want, with the domineering state they at least have the chance to enjoy the satisfaction of revenge and some of the spoils of possible victory. That was more or less what Hitler offered. The eventual cost was fifty million deaths in World War II.

The future of our world will be settled in the big cities of Eurasia, Africa, Latin America – and the United States. Mohamed Atta, who piloted the first aeroplane on 9/11, was an urban planner. If Atta and the others had discovered a more meaningful and satisfying future in the cities they inhabited, they might not have become terrorists.

The choices being made by the West now are shaping how the world will be in thirty years' time, when the West will no longer be as powerful as it was. These choices are being made in the dark, without much consideration about where they lead. It is time the hidden consequences of globalization's agenda were brought to light.

The story of the twenty-first century will be this: the West shuffled the pack but the world dealt the cards.

At the moment the West means Washington, which strongly favours liberated capitalism enforced, with a show of reluctance, by the domineering state. Washington does not want decent democracy. Business leaders and politicians have taught the American people not to want it. They have told them it puts taxes up too high.

If the European Union bows down to the Washington Consensus (big capital, weak state, obedient populations, US militarism as required), then decent democracy, the card most likely to bring us all relative peace and relative prosperity, will be thrown out of the pack. Everyone will get the second option, according to which: 'Might is right. Strength is admirable. All that counts is conquest, victory and success by any means.'

As the American empire wanes it will be replaced by domineering states confronted with urban chaos on every continent. That will almost certainly lead to war. How bad will it be? In a disorderly and aggressive multi-polar world, the possibility of a third world war can hardly be ruled out.[36]

Notes

Chapter 1   Key Themes

1   Figure 1.1 contains the results of a survey of social science journals recorded in Social Sciences Citation Index that I carried out in May 2005. I found that 'globalization' (or 'globalisation') appeared as a term in 7355 articles written between January 1981 and December 2004, 89 per cent of them published since the beginning of 1997. Over the same period the number of references in the Arts and Humanities Citation Index rose from zero to 219. There is some overlap between this index and the Social Sciences Citation Index and this would make it slightly misleading to aggregate the two series.
2   See Beck 1992; Bauman 2000; Giddens 2000.
3   See previous note and also Castells 1997–2000; Huntington 1997; Friedman 2000.
4   For background see, for example, Maddison 2003; Ponting 2001.
5   The business interests of Venice financed the Fourth Crusade (1202–4) in return for a share of the anticipated profits. The Doge of Venice offered the crusaders easier terms on their debts to the city if they would begin their military campaign by helping Venice to conquer Zara, a Roman Catholic town on the Adriatic that had revolted against Venetian domination. This was hardly a 'natural' target for a Christian crusade. However, the deed was done, even though the pope, quite naturally, objected.
6   In practice, the local village-based structures and the globalized economy took shape before national economies and national states. See, for example, Braudel 1981–4.

7   As in the previous note, it has to be emphasized that the shaping of the global often preceded the crystallization of the national. In other words, transcontinental empires were common a long time before national citizenship became widespread.

8   My intellectual interest in humiliation originally stemmed from becoming familiar with research being done by Evelin Lindner.

9   See also Smith 1990, 19–29, 35–6.

10 On these points: America's rise to global power in the 1940s had a tremendously liberating impact, although this liberation was delivered by humiliating existing political regimes, not just the rulers of Japan and Germany but also the British and French governments who were prevented from rebuilding their colonial empires. To take another case, Irish society has a much greater air of prosperity since that country joined the European Union and attracted a great deal of foreign direct investment. (For a critical view on Ireland as a 'Celtic tiger', see O'Hearn 1998). It is possible to manage transformations in a person or group's social location in a way that helps them to accept and even welcome their new location. That is one objective of special courses preparing people for retirement. Special counsellors may be employed to help workers facing the run-down of their industry (e.g. mining or fishing) prepare for new types of employment.

11 See Adams 1991; Beattie 2002; Elias 1994; Spierenburg 1991; Foucault 1967; Foucault 1977; Maravall 1986; Oestreich 1982; Pike 1983; van Horn Melton 1988.

12 For discussions of the hermeneutic circle, see, for example, Gadamer 1975; Habermas 1977.

Chapter 2   Codes of Modernity

1   Building began in 1966. The first tower opened in 1970, the second in 1972. See *http://www.skyscraper.org/TALLEST_TOWERS/t_wtc.htm*

2   For other details, see *http://www.9-11commission.gov/*

3   On Bin Laden, see, for example, Bodansky 2001.

4   Italics added. Bin Laden's words were transmitted on 7 October 2001. See *http://www.robert-fisk.com/text_of_usama_video_7october2001.htm*

5   For background on the Ottoman Empire, see Faroqhi 2004; see also Lieven 2003, 128–57.

6   The Turkish siege of Vienna was lifted by the Poles in 1683. The Treaty of Karlowitz in 1699, when the Turks ceded Hungary, marked the end of the Turkish threat to Europe. The last vestige of credibility for the argument that a European feudal aristocracy was needed to defeat the Turks had disappeared by 1789. See Anderson 1966.

7   See Norwich 1982, esp. Part I.

8   As Commandante Zebedo of the Zapatista Army of National Libera-
    tion, speaking in Oventik, Chiapas, Mexico, on 9 August 2003, put it:
    'These times of globalization are imposing a new Holy Inquisition in
    another way. Today, the sins of poor people are not being paid with
    whips. We are paying with sophisticated weapons which have been
    specially made for those who rebel against globalization's plans. All of
    us are paying for this, including children and old persons. World glob-
    alization, with its new world order, is the same as saying: "World humil-
    iation of the peoples of the world." See *http://www.zmag.org/content/
    showarticle.cfm?SectionID=8&ItemID=4046* (1 April 2005).
9   George W. Bush, 'Address to a joint session of Congress and the
    American people', 20 September 2001, White House, Washington DC;
    see   *http://www.whitehouse.gov/news/releases/2001/09/20010920-8.
    html*
10 This account is influenced by works such as the following: Tilly 1990;
    Tilly 2004; Mann 1993; Elias 1994; Poggi 1978; Poggi 2000; Ander-
    son 1974a; Anderson 1974b; Gellner 1991; Smith 1991.
11 For recent discussions see, for example, Lister 2003; Lister 2004; Wood-
    iwiss 2003.

Chapter 3   Modes of Humiliation

1   The day set aside was 30 April 1863. The proclamation was issued on
    30 March 1863. See 'Proclamation appointing a national fast day',
    in Lincoln 1953, 156–7, or at *http://www.leaderu.com/bpf/pathways/
    lincoln.html*
2   See,   for   example,   *http://english.people.com.cn/200409/19/eng
    20040919_157545.html* (28 March 2005).
3   See also the papers in Held and McGrew (eds) 2002; Held and Koenig-
    Archibugi (eds) 2003.
4   For his part, Norbert Elias thinks that the disciplining effect of dis-
    courses can produce individuals with 'civilized' ways of thinking, feeling
    and behaving, These self-disciplined and rational people are able to
    build more rational societies. They will not be prey to fantasy-filled
    ideological discourses but will act on the basis of objective knowledge.
    For a discussion on Elias, see Smith 2000.
5   Joseph Stiglitz calls for more transparency at the IMF, more concern for
    debtors as opposed to creditors, and better awareness of the social and
    political damage done by its existing policies. He notes: 'Those, such as
    in east Asia, that have avoided the strictures of the IMF, have grown
    faster, with greater equality and poverty reduction than those who have
    obeyed its commandments' (Stiglitz 2002, 248). Georg Soros thinks

along similar lines and also has a political agenda, a plan to foster a global 'open society', especially by encouraging civil society in south-eastern Europe (Soros 2000, 301–60).

6 Less radical than Arendt, Martin Albrow emphasizes the importance of 'performative citizenship', (Albrow 1996, 175), in other words, a readiness to enact the skills learned within nation-states even when acting outside that political realm.

7 Singer 2004, 43. Singer also discusses issues such as the organization of the WTO, international monitoring of elections and the role of national sovereignty. On the issue of global security, Zbigniew Brzezinski nods towards a 'Trans-Eurasian Security System' with an expanded NATO, involving Russia, China and Japan. TESS might 'gradually relieve America of some of its burdens, even while perpetuating its decisive role as Eurasia's stabilizer and arbitrator' (Brzezinski 1997, 209).

8 For further details, see Singer 2004, 126.

9 On 'rational authority', see Moore 1972, 52–6.

10 Thompson 1963; Thompson 1991. For a discussion of Thompson, see Smith 1991.

11 According to Adam Phillips, parent-child relations cannot be free of humiliation. In his *Beast in the Nursery* (1998) he argues that every child has to learn the uncomfortable lesson that 'the viable self is a diminished self' (Phillips 1998, 48), a self that is less than the one it wishes to be. In Phillips's view, 'Once you know who or what humiliates you, you know what it is about yourself that you truly value, that you worship' (96). The child's rage evoked by humiliation stems from its angry recognition that it depends on others who can choose not to satisfy it: 'there is an inevitable element of humiliation in simply being a child' (101). To get along in society, the child has to learn, partly through language, to want what it does not really want. Phillips contributes to a debate that leads not only towards Freud and Foucault but also towards Richard Rorty and his remarks on ironism and theory: 'Redescription often humiliates' (Rorty 1989, 90). See also Shklar 1984; Scarry 1987.

12 Other writers, such as Jacques Lacan, in turn influenced by Alexander Kojève, have drawn on Hegel's discussion of recognition. See, for example, Roth 1988, Kojève 1969, Lacan 1977.

13 Recognition may be uncomfortable to handle and in some cases may not be nurturing but destructive or embarrassing. Harold Garfinkel has examined the conditions of what he calls 'status degradation ceremonies' (Garfinkel 1956, 420) such as show trials through which people are stereotyped, denounced and belittled. In *Stigma* (1968), Erving Goffman explores how interactions between 'normal' people and people with 'spoiled identities' are managed so as to avoid humiliating situations.

14 See also Margalit 2002 and a special issue of *Social Research* (64, 1, September 1997), devoted to a discussion of Margalit's *Decent Society* (1996). Turning to 'recognition' in the global context, Robbie Robertson and Martin Albrow argue that a change of mental attitude is crucial. Robertson described the gradual development of a 'global consciousness' (Robertson 2003, 3) over three waves of globalization stretching across several centuries. Albrow stresses the need to be open to both pre-modern and non-Western concepts as we enter the global age. Jonathan Sacks makes a plea for respectful open-minded conversation, education, and the market as a source of diversity (Sacks 2002).

15 On Bauman, see Smith 1999a.

16 Humiliation means: knocking someone off their pedestal, stopping them getting above themselves, asking them who they think they are (before showing them who they *really* are), cutting them down to size, putting them in their place, grinding them into the dust, kicking them out, giving them the cold shoulder. The victims of humiliation feel they have been sat upon, flattened, kicked in the teeth, let down, put out, shown the door, and told where to get off.

17 Caution is required since the experience and understanding of conditions such as fear and anger seem to be influenced in very complex ways by the historically produced and always subtly shifting configurations of social bonds in which they occur. See, for example, Rosenwein (ed.) 1998; Rosenwein 2002; James 1997; Barbalet 2002; Barbalet 2005; Miller 1993; Scheff 1990; Scheff 1997; Greenblatt 1980.

18 Or when a monarch succeeds in pacifying feudal warriors and turning them into pacified courtiers. For an insightful study, see Norbert Elias's *Court Society* (1983) and, more generally, his *Civilizing Process* (1994).

19 Also relevant is empirical evidence of the ill-health associated with the inequalities created in hierarchical societies. See Wilkinson 2005. The impact of globalization on inequality is the subject of debate. See, for example, Firebaugh and Goesling 2004; Milanovic 2002; Ravallion 2003; Ravallion 2004; Sutcliffe 2004; Wade 2004.

20 Liminal individuals or entities are 'neither here nor there; they are betwixt and between the positions assigned and arrayed by law, custom, convention, and ceremony' (Turner 1969, 95). On liminality, see *http:// www.liminality.org/about/whatisliminality/*

21 See, for example, Turner 1969, 82–98, 158–60.

22 Max Scheler, writing just before World War I, provided an acute phenomenological analysis of *ressentiment* as a 'unit of experience and action' (Scheler 1961, 39). Scheler found this response especially among social groups that had been relegated socially, driven down the status order. *Ressentiment* is not the same as 'resentment'. Resentment is a feeling of angry indignation that occurs within a specific relationship in response to particular events. By contrast, *ressentiment* is a long-lasting

frame of mind, an emotional climate and even a physical state that permeates the whole being of a person or group. It influences feelings, attitudes and behaviour in a wide range of relationships. *Ressentiment* is felt by those who have been displaced, those who have lost out in ways that undermine their identity. Scheler sees *ressentiment* as a compound: on the one hand, hatred, envy and vengefulness; on the other, a feeling of impotence, of being able neither to escape humiliation nor to strike back against its source. *Ressentiment* grows when the state of humiliation has to be accepted as a permanent condition of existence: 'the injury is experienced as a destiny' (50). Being humiliated becomes part of an individual or group's identity. This identity is expressed and reinforced by a constant stream of complaints against real and imagined oppressors. This discourse of '*ressentiment* criticism' (51) constructs a specific worldview, one that castigates those historical events, social structures and cultural values that led to the victims' humiliation. The main object of attack was the old aristocratic social order. The discourse of the humiliated attacked feudal hierarchy, wasteful pleasure-seeking, and good fellowship. In their place, it recommended the 'modern' values of equality, asceticism, utility and universal distrust. See also Scheler 1961, 71, 143, 152–4.

23 I now prefer the term 'exclusion' to 'expulsion', as used in Smith 2001 and Smith 2002.

24 For an analysis of 'big women' in the South Pacific, see Lepowsky 1993.

25 For another account of life within the grid, especially the urban grid, see Sennett 1994.

26 Humiliation is at the heart of Max Weber's *Protestant Ethic* (1905; Weber 2002). According to the doctrine of predestination, human beings were sinners who had 'wholly lost all ability of will to any spiritual good accompanying salvation'. They had given up control over their own destinies. They had no choice but to accept God's power 'to ordain them to dishonour and wrath', however worthy their lives were in human terms (Weber 2002, 71–2, quoting the Westminster Confession of 1647). Weber goes on to say that 'The humanly comprehensible "Father in Heaven" of the New Testament, who rejoiced at the return of a sinner . . . , has here become a transcendental being remote from any human understanding, a being who had allotted to each individual his destiny according to his entirely unfathomable decrees, and who controlled the tiniest detail of the cosmos' (Weber 2002, 73). In other words, human beings have lost the freedom to chart their own course towards Heaven or Hell. God has taken over that task. At the same time, God has done a disappearing act, leaving the faithful behind. Puritans had to cope with the feeling of being thrust away from God, denied his presence. This was, above all, exclusion humiliation, manifesting itself in tremendous 'inner loneliness' (73) in this life reinforced by the threat of eternal damnation in the next.

27 See Hirschman 1970 for another approach to 'escape' or 'exit.' Mammon has a different take on things. He wants his colleagues to improve their situation by *transforming* Hell into a better place and waiting for the chance to make their relationship to God less humiliating. He puts his faith in a combination of creative action and a form of cognitive therapy. He says, let us look around, look at ourselves, and realize that we can make things better. Beneath Hell's surface, he reckons, will be found gold and gems. The place can be made magnificent, somewhere that enhances, not diminishes its demonic inhabitants. I return to the possibility of transformation as a response to humiliation in the final chapter.

28 The use of the term 'mastery' signified the masculine character of the honour code.

29 See Kaplan 2002.

30 For other illustrations, less graphically described, see Thucydides, *History of the Peloponnesian War*, written in the fifth century BCE (Thucydides 1972).

31 For an interesting take on conflict, hierarchy and equality, see Gould 2003.

Chapter 4 Frames of Globalization

1 For interesting viewpoints on globalization, including its political dimension, see, among many others, Held et al. 1999; Giddens 2000; Scholte 2000; Habermas 2001; Halliday 2001; Halliday 2002; Henderson 1999; Hobsbawm 2000; Monbiot 2003; Urry 1999; Urry 2002; Chandler and Mazlish (eds) 2005; Mazlish and Iriye (eds) 2005; Sassen 1996; Sassen 1998.

2 See, for example, Bowen et al. (eds) 2004.

3 Not to be mistaken for Michael Moore, author of *Dude, Where's my Country?* (2004).

4 Mike Moore was speaking to the US Chamber of Commerce in Florida on 25 February 2002. See *http://www.wto.org/english/news_e/spmm_e/spmm77_e.htm* (1 April 2005).

5 Cosmopolitan anxieties about personal values and cultural identity arise not just among freed colonial subjects but also in the ranks of the imperial power when the scent of decline is in the air. This is especially so if the servants of empire have doubts about the worthiness of their mission, and if the absolutist practices of imperial repression are in conflict with their own beliefs either in human rights and citizenship or, more vaguely, in the fundamental equality and dignity of all human beings. The career and writings of T. E. Lawrence (1888–1935), 'Lawrence of Arabia', would make a relevant case study. See Brown 2005.

6 On the *intifada* see, for example, Jamal 2005.

Chapter 5   The Imperial Impulse

1   The speech was on 17 March 2003. The invasion began the following day.

2   For some documentation of Rupert Murdoch's close relationship with the neo-conservatives, see Halper and Clarke 2004, 184–90.

3   The classic example is the 'Mongol horde' led by Genghis Khan (1167–1227). See Man 2005.

4   See, for example, Panter-Brick et al. 2001.

5   'Shaming' involves exposing rule-breakers to signs of the strong disapproval of the group to which they belong. The reason is that they have failed to maintain standards which, as members of that group, they are supposedly committed to maintaining. One object of shaming is to make rule-breakers reform their ways. By contrast, the object of deliberate humiliation is to displace offenders from their old position within the group. Where there is no hierarchy, the only possible forms of displacement are death or separation from the group, which in the case of a hunter-gatherer band, would normally lead to death because of the loss of relationships on which the abandoned individual depends to sustain his or her life.

6   Although some hunter-gatherer bands were 'affluent'. See Sahlins 1972.

7   Ibn Khaldūn (1332–1406) was an active court politician in North Africa and Islamic Spain. Like Hobbes and Milton he saw politics and war at close hand. See Ibn Khaldūn 1969; Fischel 1967; Lacoste 1984; Alatas 1993; Alatas 2006.

8   For a vivid statement of Milton's political views in 1660, see his letter to General Monk calling for the election of a permanent general council of talented men to exercise government in England (Milton 1660). Milton was an urban man through and through, born in London and making his career there. By contrast, Hobbes, the son of a country vicar, came from Malmesbury in the Cotswolds, the oldest borough in England, and spent much of his life working in great country houses, tutoring the aristocracy. By 1651, the parliamentary side had won the Civil War. Hobbes presented an argument that was relevant both to his defeated royalist colleagues, faced with pressure to swear allegiance to the government, and to the new regime. That same year, Milton became secretary for foreign languages in Cromwell's government. In that capacity, he wrote a number of works to advance and defend the parliamentary cause. Sixteen years later, the crown had been restored and Milton was writing in retirement. *Paradise Lost* (1667, rev. edn 1674) gives an account of the rationale implicit in the way God dealt with humankind. On Hobbes and Milton, see Kow 2004; Lewalski 2002; Malcolm 2002. Hobbes is a key figure for neo-conservatives; see Strauss 1952. For a different view, see Skinner 1978; Skinner 1997; see also Hobbes 1998.

9 See Walzer 1965.

10 See Hobbes 1996, 62–75.

11 Nietzsche 1956, 160–5.

12 Compare Scheler 1961.

13 Its most prominent expression was Christianity, although Nietzsche also attacks Judaism as a precursor of Christianity and modernity. Fired up by slave morality, the masses, 'impotent and oppressed' but 'full of bottled-up aggressions' (Nietzsche 1956, 172), took symbolic revenge on the rich and powerful. They condemned their 'evil' ways for which they would be punished in Hell. For their own part, the poor and weak lived lives of 'quiet virtuous resignation' (179), becoming 'expert . . . in . . . self-depreciation, and in self-humiliation' (172).

14 The passage continues: 'Whatever the good is, it is there to be contrasted with the bad. Man has a profound need to arrange and rearrange in groups all the human beings he knows or can imagine. . . . The frontiers of goodness are marked out exactly and woe to any of the bad who cross them. They have no business among the good and must be destroyed' (Canetti 1973, 346–7).

15 On Veblen, see, for example, Smith 1988, especially 47–74; Smith 1990, 77–97.

16 Augustus preferred the title *princeps*. See 'Res Gestae Divi Augusti' (written *c*.14 CE), cited in Davis (ed.) 1912–13, 166–72; Wells 1992.

17 Hitler and his associates were trying to build a new European order (possibly a world order) glorifying the supposed superiority of the 'Aryan race'. As Hannah Arendt argued in *Origins of Totalitarianism* (1951, 1976), this approach took to an extreme limit the bureaucratic enforcement of 'white supremacy' within the European colonial empires.

18 Christian missionaries were not especially welcomed by pragmatic traders but they fought back. See, for example, Ferguson 2004, chapter 3.

19 In the context of *conquistadors*, a *hidalgo* is the 'son of somebody', a man of genteel breeding, usually translated as 'nobleman'. The word also applies to noblewomen.

20 See, for example, Stasiulis and Yuval-Davies (eds) 1995.

21 On Gandhi, see Parekh 2001; on Collins, see Coogan 1991.

22 See May 1975; Thorne 1979; Thorne 1986.

23 For a readable account of these conflicts, see Ferguson 2004b. On Gallipoli, see Carlyon 2003.

24 As a result of the Versailles peace settlement after World War I, the British Empire acquired an additional 1.8 million square miles of territory and about thirteen million new subjects. Ferguson 2004b, 315.

25 For details, see Taylor 1965, 253–4.

26 It would be an exaggeration to say that its global role was a little like that played by the Holy Roman Empire in Europe during the seventeenth century, but the comparison is suggestive.

27 In fact, each of the three contenders had an ideology that drew upon ideas associated with one of the three key interests within the old imperial compromise. The Nazis had a vision of the Aryans as a kind of global aristocracy. The Bolsheviks trumpeted the forthcoming dictatorship of the proletariat. The United States put its faith in the global mission of big business allied to big science, both acting as the vanguard for Demos.

28 V. I. Lenin, 'Speech at the First Congress of Economic Councils, 26 May, 1918', in Lenin 1972, 408–15. Also at *http://www.marxists.org/archive/lenin/works/1918/may/26b.htm* (6 July 2005).

29 Criticizing the market's bad social consequences was a risky business, requiring skill and tact. The sociologists of the Chicago School made a successful attempt to do this; see Smith 1988.

30 The Statue of Liberty was a gift from France in 1886. The phrases just quoted are from the poem 'The New Colossus' (1883) by Emma Lazarus, lines from which are inscribed on the statue. Lazarus contrasts the Colossus of Rhodes, a symbol of conquest and oppression from the ancient world, with the Statue of Liberty, a 'mighty woman with a torch' whose 'beacon-hand glows world-wide welcome' to the 'homeless' and 'tempest-tost'. See *http://www.libertystatpark.com/emma.htm* (24 October 2005).

31 There was high principle involved, of course, and the cause was a good one, but there was the added advantage that it would stir up the slaves and cause disruption in the enemy camp.

32 For background, see, for example, Cox 1994; Ransom 1989; Schwabe 1985; Macmillan 2002; Roosevelt 1946; Thompson 2004; Thorne 1979; Thorne 1986.

33 See, for example, Williams 1980.

34 See, for example, Porter 2005, chapter 1.

35 See Coll 2005.

36 On the unexpected end of World War I, see Johnson 1998.

37 The German navy deliberately sank five cruisers and thirty-one other ships at Scapa Flow as the war finished. See *http://www.firstworldwar.com/features/scapaflow_scuttling.htm* (15 Oct 2005).

38 See Baun 1995; Middlemas 1995.

39 For a recent expression of American concerns in respect of ASEAN, see Dillon and Tkacik 2005.

40 49 per cent of those assets were held in the European Union plus another 4 per cent in Switzerland. Japan held 11 per cent. See Smith and Braein 2003, 20–1.

41 The two great powers mainly used their military might to overawe rebellious governments on their own side and fight proxy wars against

clients supported by the other side, as in Vietnam and Afghanistan. These military adventures always carried a very heavy cost in terms of the big powers' international reputation.

42 Since the fall of the Berlin Wall Russia has been much less destabilized than China was after the fall of its empire in 1911. For Russia, there has been no civil war and no foreign invasion.

43 The aftermath of New York in 2001 has an uncanny resemblance to the aftermath of Gallipoli in 1915: Gallipoli was a case of humiliation being caused by the failure of the British state to make a decisive incursion into the territory of a Muslim enemy who is considered to be weak and who turns out to be far stronger and more organized than had been suspected; 9/11 was a case of humiliation being caused by the failure of the American state to prevent a decisive incursion into home territory by a Muslim enemy who is considered to be weak and who turns out to be far stronger and more organized than had been suspected. In both cases, the threatened imperial power tried to rescue their position with spectacular victories in Iraq. In both cases, the 'easy victories' turned into a prolonged humiliation cycle in which the 'conquering' army was sometimes the victim, sometimes the perpetrator.

44 See, for example, Sardar and Davies 2002.

45 This was 'the biggest gathering of world leaders in history', according to Rossella Lorenzi of *Discovery News* on 4 April 2005, reporting the words of Rome's mayor, Walter Vetroni. 'Pope's funeral gathers world leaders', *http://dsc.discovery.com/news/briefs/20050404/popefuneral. html*

Chapter 6   The Logic of the Market

1 Chris Mooney, for example, writing in *American Prospect*, predicted the disaster three months before the event. See 'Thinking big about hurricanes: It's time to get serious about saving New Orleans', 23 May 2005, at *http://www.prospect.org/web/printfriendly-view.ww?id=9754* (5 September 2005).

2 'Troops begin combat operations in New Orleans', *Army Times*, 2 September 2005. See *http://www.armytimes.com/story.php?f=1–292925–1077495.php* (5 September 2005).

3 On the 'shock and awe' strategy, see Ullman and Wade 1996 and *http://www.shockandawe.com/index1.htm*

4 According to the US Census Bureau, in 2000 the population of New Orleans stood at 485,000, of whom 326,000 were African American. See *http://factfinder.census.gov/* (5 September 2005).

5 See Nisbett and Cohen 1996.

6 When Barbara Bush appeared on television as part of a fund-raising effort to help evacuees from New Orleans to Houston, she made some

unguarded comments about the 'scary' possibility of the incomers remaining in Texas. She also commented that the disaster was 'working very well' for some of its victims by giving them new opportunities. See *http://www.editorandpublisher.com/eandp/news/article_display.jsp?vnu _content_id=1001054719* (5 September 2005).

7   Broussard made this comment on NBC on 4 September 2002. See *http://www. msnbc.msn.com/id/9179790/* (5 February 2006).

8   For the text of the letter and a number of responses, see *http:// www.jacksonfreepress.com/comments.php?id=7074070C* (5 February 2006).

9   See   *http://www.nola.com/weblogs/print.ssf?/mtlogs/nola_tporleans/ archives/print076766.html* (6 February 2006).

10   US Census 2000; see n. 4 above.

11   See, for example, Davidson and Rees-Mogg 1997.

12   As is well known, the right to bear arms is enshrined in the American Constitution.

13   See Veblen 1970, discussed in Smith 1988, 47–56, 65–70; Smith 1990, 77–97.

14   Interesting material may be found in, for example, Blustein 2005; Galbraith 1963; Gowan 1999; Micklethwait and Wooldridge 2004; Palast 2002; Peet et al. 2004; Schwartz, Leyden and Hyatt 2000; Slater and Taylor (eds) 1999. For a longer historical context, see Arrighi 1994; Beard 1913.

15   For example, Charles Leadbetter devotes most of his words in *Up the Down Escalator* to criticizing the intellectual case for 'chronic pessimism' (Leadbetter 2003, 10). Then he offers his alternative. Its three main planks are the self-employed and self-reliant worker; public services organized around choice, open communication, decentralization, innovation and flexibility; and high principled hopefulness. Leadbetter tells us to rise above 'the current wave of pessimism' (17), ignore the deceptive dream of a 'great escape' (44), and enter the liberating 'age of self-rule' (199). Alan Shipman, author of *The Globalization Myth* (2002), takes a slightly different tack. His approach is: let the multinationals get on with it because we will all benefit from their skills and judgement. Their role is to help us all by providing a framework for our lives. Believing that pessimists who criticize the market are playing into the hands of multinational corporations, he argues: 'Multinational companies . . . must inhabit a planet made economically unstable and environmentally unsustainable by their uncontrolled activity. . . . Governments' failure to resolve these problems . . . (has) forced big business to find its own solutions to over-production and under-consumption. . . . Corporations have done so by setting up central planning systems that modify, manage or sidestep the market – far more effectively than any form of planning that capitalists or other anti-capitalists could dare contemplate' (Shipman 2002, 227).

16 In *The Republic* Plato describes three parts of the soul: the desiring part, the reasoning part and *thymos*, the desire for recognition by others as being worthy of esteem (Plato 1955, 183–200).

17 Fukuyama notices that 'Dignity and its opposite, humiliation, are the two most common words used by [Václav] Havel in describing life in communist Czechoslovakia. Communism humiliated ordinary people by forcing them to make ... moral compromises with their better natures' (Fukuyama 1992, 168). Havel's first New Year's address to the nation recalled previous times when people saw that 'The state, which calls itself a state of the working people, is humiliating workers. ... Throughout the world, people are surprised that the acquiescent, humiliated, skeptical Czechoslovak people who apparently no longer believed in anything suddenly found the enormous strength in the space of a few weeks to shake off the totalitarian system in a completely decent and peaceful way' (quoted in *Foreign Broadcast Information Service* FBIS-EU, 2 January 1990, 9–10, and cited in Fukuyama 1992, 368, n. 12). Havel was the first president of Czechosolvakia following the collapse of the Soviet Union in 1989.

18 In Fukuyama's opinion, the remaining problem is as follows: the desire for satisfying recognition makes some of us discontented with the rewards that our rights bring us under capitalism. This is both because continuing economic inequality means some get less recognition than others (the diagnosis of the Left) and because political equality has reduced opportunities for some to stand out above the crowd (the diagnosis of the Right).

19 Historians have moved back into global issues in a big way in recent years. For example, Bruce Mazlish and his colleagues in the New Global History project are asking 'What are the forces of globalization shaping our world (for better or worse)?' For Mazlish, at least, if the opportunities for constructive dialogue between civilizations are taken up, the prospects for humankind look good. This is conveyed in the challenging title of his *Civilization and its Contents* (Mazlish 2004). See Gibbon 1993, Herodotus 1998; Braudel 1972; Braudel 1981–4; Mazlish and Iriye (eds) 2005; Chandler and Mazlish (eds) 2005. See also *http://www.newglobalhistory.com/* (20 May 2005); *http://www. newglobalhistory.com/mission.html*

20 Martin Albrow, for example, reckons that the modern project of expansionist Western nation-states has run into insurmountable difficulties (Albrow 1996). They have tried to dominate and exploit the social and natural world, but failed. Social energies and cultural forces are slipping free from their control but we have not yet got the language to describe what is happening. Nor will it be easy to adapt or remake ourselves for the coming global era.

21 See also, for example, Beck 1992; Beck 1997; Beck 1999a; Beck 1999b.

22 Joffe is leader writer for *Süddeutsche Zeitung* based in Munich.
23 Harvey lists nine nuclear powers (US, Russia, Britain, France, China, India, Pakistan, Israel and North Korea), and seven countries that could assemble a nuclear arsenal at short notice (Japan, Germany, Brazil, Argentina, South Africa, Taiwan and South Korea). Libya, Iraq and Iran have made serious moves in a nuclear direction in the recent past. See Harvey 2003, 177.
24 See Harvey 2003, 177–213.
25 See Kaplan 1996, 354–68.
26 It is possible that someone who voluntarily accepts help from another may initially feel a sense of shame about losing some of their independence. They may become angry at feeling ashamed and, in retrospect, develop a sense that they were unjustly forced to accept the help they took. In these circumstances, their sense of shame may be transformed into a feeling of humiliation, which they may feel justified in rejecting by taking violent revenge on the supposed perpetrator.
27 On the term 'market fundamentalism', see Soros 2000, xxiii–xxiv.
28 See Bauman 1988; Smith 1999a, 105–9.
29 On his visit to Mumbai in 2001, along with many Indian admirals, Barnett attended a celebration of the Indian Navy's fiftieth anniversary. He 'noted that most of these men had studied in the United States, with almost half of them being graduates of the Naval War College. I wasn't talking to a bunch of foreigners; it was more like a college reunion' (Barnett 2004, 233).

Chapter 7   The Cosmopolitan Condition

1 The *Shorter Oxford English Dictionary* defines a denizen as: 'One who lives habitually in a country but is not a native-born citizen.' The term thus implies residents who do not have strong or deep roots, who have a tinge of alienation about them, and whose rights are a little insecure.
2 National Commission on Terrorist Attacks on the United States, 2004, 162.
3 See, for example, Arthur 1999; Bouwsma 1988; MacCulloch 2004.
4 On the Gunpowder Plot, see, for example, Hogge 2006; Haynes 1994; Fraser 2002. It seems likely the government knew about the plot and allowed it to proceed so that when it was 'discovered' there would be wide public support for persecution of Catholics in England. All the conspirators, save for one, Francis Tresham, were executed. Tresham died while a prisoner in the Tower of London. This might have been

arranged to conceal his possible role in uncovering the plot. It is widely suspected that he shared the secret with his brother-in-law, Lord Monteagle, and that they tried to inform the authorities in a way that would prevent the explosion from taking place but still allow the plotters to escape. See *http://www.gunpowder-plot.org/people/g_fawkes.htm* (22 May 2005).

5 Catesby's father had made plans, with the approval of Elizabeth I, to set up a Catholic colony in North America. The Spanish disapproved and it was not done. See *http://www.gunpowder-plot.org/people/ rcatesby.htm* (22 May 2005).

6 The extent of urban growth throughout Europe as a whole should not be exaggerated. However, the proportion of the population in the North and West of Europe in cities of over 10,000 people increased from about 6 per cent in 1500 to about 13 per cent in 1700. See Hohenberg and Lees 1985, 110; De Vries 1981, 88.

7 See Walzer 1965.

8 For an introduction to this world of spymasters and torturers, see, for example, Bossy 1991; Green 2003; Nicholl 1994; Plowden 1991; Read 1925.

9 This was also the case in many large US cities during the nineteenth and twentieth centuries. See, for example, the discussion of the work of Robert Park and Louis Wirth in Smith 1988.

10 On some aspects of the complex interweaving of urbanization and globalization, see, for example, Bairoch 1988; Castells 1989; Chase-Dunn 1989; Sassen 1991; Sassen 1998; Taylor 1999.

11 Cosmopolitanism has become a focus of debate in the social sciences. Recent contributions (among many important studies) include Archibugi and Held (eds) 1995; Breckenridge et al. (eds) 2002; Cohen and Vertovec 2002; Delanty 2000; Fine 2003; Hardt and Negri 2005; Held 1995; Toulmin 1990. For a dialogue and commentary in *Current Sociology* on globalization, cosmopolitanism and transnationality involving Bruce Mazlish, Victor Roudometof and Dennis Smith, see Mazlish 2005a; Mazlish 2005b; Roudometof 2005a; Roudometof 2005b; Smith 2005.

12 It is true that warriors and weapons of war are also non-fixed assets, which are important power resources. Territorial rulers attempt to maintain a monopoly over control of the most effective and efficient warriors and weapons, especially weapons of mass destruction.

13 For an insightful comparison of these processes, see Moore 1969; Moore 1978; see also Smith 1983.

14 It is an interesting coincidence that 1517, the year in which the split in Christianity began, was also the year when the Ottoman Sultan assumed the title of Caliph, thus becoming Islam's spiritual head and temporal ruler.

15 It was a little easier to survive with dignity in the preceding Elizabethan period. See Holmes 1982.

16 See *http://www.abc.net.au/4corners/atta/interviews/hauth.htm* (7 October 2004).

17 Zygmunt Bauman has explored these dilemmas in recent decades. See, for example, Bauman1992; Bauman 1997; Bauman 2000; Bauman 2005. See also Beilharz 2000; Smith 1999a; Toulmin 1990.

18 For contrasting approaches to Islam in recent times, see Lewis 2004; Ahmed 2003; Rashid 2003.

19 The International Institute for Democracy and Electoral Assistance reports that although 'Overall participation in competitive elections across the globe rose steadily between 1945 and 1990 . . . with the influx of a host of competitive elections in newly democratizing states, the average for elections held since 1990 has dipped back.' The drop is relatively small, but definite. They add that while the participation rate of all eligible voters has dropped only marginally, the drop in the participation rate of those actually registered to vote has been more pronounced. The average global trend contains some wide disparities. In India, for example, participation rates in parliamentary elections have fluctuated within a range of 54–67 per cent since the late 1940s. However, the fall is very clear in the cases of parliamentary elections, for example, in the United Kingdom (81.4 per cent in 1951, 57.6 per cent in 2001), France (74.3 per cent in 1956, 59.9 per cent in 1997) and Japan (77.4 per cent in 1952, 44.9 per cent in 1995, rising back to 59 per cent in 2000). In the United States, the proportion of the eligible population voting in presidential elections fell from 63.1 per cent in 1960 to 49.3 per cent in 2000. These data and the quotation are from the IDEA website. See *http://www.idea.int/vt/survey/voter_turnout1.cfm* (19 May 2005).

20 As is well known, during the past three decades, the increasing power and sophistication of information and communication technologies have greatly increased the state's ability to keep an eye (and an ear) on its national population. Electronic banking and credit, mobile phone records, image recognition technology and the use of television cameras along national highways and in city streets and shopping centres have all made it easier for government to engage in systematic surveillance, or at least monitor video tapes and other records for evidence after incidents have occurred. See Gibb 2005.

21 On current religious trends, see, for example, Armstrong 2004; Corten and Marshall-Fratani (eds) 2001; Freston 2004; Milton-Edwards 2005; Parratt (ed.) 2004; Rashid 2003; Ruthven 2005; Sarkar 2003; Vasquez and Marquardt 2003.

22 See also Hirschman 1982.

23 The classic reference has become Hochschild 1983.

24 See Klare 2002.

Chapter 8 Escape

1 See Ignatieff 2000, especially 179–211.
2 Kissinger takes this thought from Coral Bell. For Bell on Kissinger, see Bell 1977.
3 See also Ikenberry (ed.) 2002; Odom and Dujarric 2004.
4 For an attempt to deal with this, see Kagan 2004.
5 As is well known, Galileo was asked to choose between his scientific theories and continuing membership of the Church; see Drake 2001. Giordano Bruno was jailed for eight years and then burned at the stake in 1600 for refusing to abandon his freethinking denial of Church doctrine; see White 2002.
6 These words are taken from *Nunc lento sonitu dicunt, Morieris*, Meditation XVII of Donne's private meditations, entitled *Devotions upon Emergent Occasions*, written while he was convalescing from a serious illness, and published in 1624; see Donne 1975, 122. The text of the entire meditation is also available at *http://www.global-language. com/devotion.html* (22 May 2005).
7 Donne was born into a Catholic family but became an Anglican in 1615, serving briefly as Dean of St Paul's; see Edwards 2002. Descartes was brought up a Catholic in Poitou, a Huguenot (Protestant) stronghold. He later served briefly in the army of Maurice, Prince of Orange, a Protestant ruler; see Gaukroger 1995.
8 Donne's *Biathanatos*, written in 1607–8, was published posthumously in 1644. Shakespeare's *Hamlet* dates from 1600–01.
9 Of course, if one accepted uncertainty, there was another way, which was to relax, enjoy the cosmopolitan variety offered by the world, continually learn from it, and keep your mind open. See Toulmin 1990, 65–6. This approach influenced writers such as Montaigne and Pascal.
10 Besides the American colonies, Ireland and South Africa, there is also Israel.
11 Many of the 'Scotch-Irish' migrated to the American colonies during the eighteenth century. At least three American presidents – Andrew Jackson, James Polk and Andrew Johnson – came from this stock. So did Davy Crockett. See *http://www.scotch-irishsociety.org/about.html* (13 March 2005).
12 See Prendergast 1997.
13 De Kiewiet 1941, 19, cited in Arendt 1976, 193.
14 For a fascinating take on the Boers, see Arendt 1976, 191–207.
15 See Thompson 2001.
16 See, especially, Slotkin 1973, 146–7, 179, 555–65. See also Wilkinson 1984.
17 Slotkin adds that the book 'begins with a "Lecture" delivered at Boston on "*2 Chron. XII.7. They have HUMBLED themselves, I will not*

destroy them but I will grant them some Deliverance." In the lecture
... [Mather] sketches the steps towards that necessary humiliation
before God, beginning with a confession revealing our consciousness of
sin. There follows a list of the social vices of New England, including
drinking, swearing, foreign fashions, and the overzealous persecution
of dissenters' (Slotkin 1973, 113).

18 This is an example of the 'old' use of the word humiliation to mean the
process through which we are taught to cast off our pride and be
humble before God and our fellow human beings. Through humiliation, in this sense, an individual or society may become worthy to be
saved.

19 See *http://www.ulsternation.org.uk/ulster's%20contribution%20to%20
america.htm* (20 March 2005).

20 Quoted in Slotkin 1973, 555.

21 For a contrasting argument about the Western taste for systematic
slaughter, one going back to the ancient Greeks, see Hanson 2001

22 Gil Troy, a Canadian historian specializing in presidential politics,
discussed the Clinton–Lewinsky affair in an interview with Janice
Castro, an editor of *Time*. Troy comments: 'While citizens in other
countries might mock Americans for being so concerned with their
presidents' personal lives, as an historian I see this as another chapter
in America's search for virtue, going back to the founding of the
Republic. . . . Americans have always believed that a virtuous nation, a
virtuous citizenry requires virtuous leaders.' Janice Castro added: 'And
that doesn't make us weak. It makes us strong.' Troy summed up: 'And
even as the news gets more and more depressing, let's hope that we still
hold to some ideals and continue our quest for virtue.' Taken from a
transcript of the interview on 28 January 1998. See *http://www.
time.com/time/community/transcripts/chattr012298.html* (21 March
2005).

23 On Carnegie see Smith 1991, 37–57.

24 Many political ideologies work in a similar way in the real world. They
use evidence of an 'effect' to claim that a supposed 'cause' is at work.

25 An earlier humiliation, the disastrous attempted invasion of Cuba at
the Bay of Pigs (1961), was quickly overtaken by the Cuban missile
crisis (1962), presented as a victory for the US government, and by the
assassination of President Kennedy (1963), which evoked worldwide
sympathy. The urban riots in Watts (1965) and in Newark and Detroit
(1967) caused more persistent anxiety, although they could be thought
of as 'internal' matters which did not impinge directly on relations
between the United States and other societies.

26 For the politics that led up to this uncomfortable situation, see
Halberstam 1992.

27 For a discussion of the military significance of the Tet offensive, see
Hanson 2001.

28 Strength was a central theme of the 2004 presidential election. One of John Kerry's slogans was: 'Together we can build a stronger America.'

29 Inter-party conflict once more became as bitter as in Nixon's day, and there was an attempt to impeach Bill Clinton, a delayed Republican revenge for Watergate. While US diplomats, especially under Clinton (1992–2000), promoted multilateral institutions such as the WTO to regulate global trade and politics, American business leaders and politicians were reluctant to submit themselves to the judgement of other nations. This arrogance was, in part, an 'answer' to the humiliation they had endured between 1968 and 1979.

30 Elisabeth Bumiller, writing in the *New York Times* (12 January 2004), recalled: 'It was in a moment of irritation during the 1988 campaign that the Republican presidential candidate, Vice President George Bush, first derided "the vision thing," as he called it, thus employing an ungainly piece of Bush-speak to describe a leader's ability to set forth inspiring national goals. Mr. Bush, who may have been one of the most self-effacing presidents in recent American history, went on to become a one-term incrementalist with little taste for big schemes.'

31 See, for example, Frum 2003; Lind 2003; Hatfield 2002.

32 In his State of the Union addresses of 2002–4, Bush used the word 'freedom' three times as often as did Clinton in his addresses of 1989–2000. Clinton mentioned 'freedom' once every 1722 words, while Bush mentioned it once every 566 words (author's research).

33 'President Bush frames the clear choice Americans face in the 2004 election', 23 February 2004. See the George W. Bush campaign website at *http://www.georgewbush.com/News/Read.aspx?ID=2261* (19 June 2004).

34 Stefan Halper and Jonathan Clarke, in their study entitled *America Alone* (2004), include the following in a list of prominent neo-conservatives, indicating, where appropriate, their positions in or around the first administration of George W. Bush: I. Lewis Libby (Vice-President's Chief of Staff), Elliott Abrams (Special Advisor to the President), Paul D. Wolfowitz (Deputy Secretary of Defense), John R. Bolton and David Wurmser (State Department), Richard Perle and Eliott A. Cohen (Defense Policy Board), Donald Kagan (at Yale), Bernard Lewis and Aaron Friedberg (at Princeton), James Q. Wilson (at Pepperdine), William Kristol (of the *Weekly Standard*) and Charles Krauthammer (of the *Washington Post*). They also add 'most foreign policy editorialists on the Wall Street Journal editorial pages and the Fox News Channel; in business former CIA Director James Woolsey among others; and in research institutes Max Boot at the Council on Foreign Relations, Norman Podhoretz and Meyrav Wurmser at the Hudson Institute, any member of the Project for the New American Century, and most foreign or defense studies scholars at the American Enterprise Institute' (14). The movement became prominent in associ-

ation with the views of national security taken by the late Senator Henry M. ('Scoop') Jackson and gained strength in alliance with evangelical Protestants and social conservatives. For an example of the neo-conservative analysis, see, for example, Frum and Perle 2003.

35 This phrase is taken from Bush's first inaugural speech. The context is as follows: 'After the Declaration of Independence was signed, Virginia statesman John Page wrote to Thomas Jefferson: "We know the race is not to the swift nor the battle to the strong. Do you not think an angel rides in the whirlwind and directs this storm?" Much time has passed since Jefferson arrived for his inauguration. The years and changes accumulate. But the themes of this day he would know: our nation's grand story of courage and its simple dream of dignity. We are not this story's author, who fills time and eternity with his purpose. Yet his purpose is achieved in our duty, and our duty is fulfilled in service to one another. Never tiring, never yielding, never finishing, we renew that purpose today, to make our country more just and generous, to affirm the dignity of our lives and every life. This work continues. This story goes on. And an angel still rides in the whirlwind and directs this storm. God bless you all, and God bless America.' See *http://www. whitehouse.gov/news/inaugural-address.html*

36 From Rhodes's *Confession of Faith*, 1877. Quoted at *http://husky1. stmarys.ca/~wmills/rhodes_confession.html* (22 March 2005). For Arendt on Rhodes, see Arendt 1976, 207–21.

37 Halper and Clarke 2004, 184–90.

38 Ibid., chapter 2 and 164–7.

39 Ibid., 90–8.

40 See Kissinger 2002, 242–51.

41 See, for example, Halper and Clarke 2004, 121–31.

42 See Mead 2001; Mead 2004. See also *http://globetrotter.berkeley.edu/ people3/Mead/mead-con3.html* (21 March 2005).

43 'Americans are from Mars and Europeans are from Venus', Kagan 2003, 3; cf. Gray 1992.

44 Robert Cooper is a foreign policy specialist who has served as an adviser to Tony Blair and who was, at the time of writing, Director-General of External and Military Affairs for the Council of the European Union.

45 See, especially, Cooper 2003, 163–70.

46 See Barber 2003, 41–6.

47 On escape, see Cohen and Taylor 1992; Phillips 2001.

48 It may be possible to achieve a more successful 'escape', one which acknowledges continuing interdependence with others. In this case, the wounded but reborn victims of humiliation, having made their escape to a protected special place of their own, work to build trust within the relationships upon which they depend for a secure, peaceful, non-humiliated and non-humiliating existence.

49 Examples include the bombing and gassing of villages in Palestine, Sudan and Iraq by the British during the 1920 and 1930s and, since World War II: 'The brutal suppression of the Mau Mau and the detention of thousands of Kenyan peasants in concentration camps are still dimly remembered, as are the Aden killings of the 1960s. But the massacre of communist insurgents by the Scots Guard in Malaya in the 1950s, the decapitation of so-called bandits by the Royal Marine Commandos in Perak and the secret bombing of Malayan villages during the Emergency remain uninvestigated.' Maria Misra, 'The heart of smugness', *The Guardian*, 23 July 2002. See *http://www. guardian.co.uk/comment/story/0,3604,761626,00.html* (15 August 2005).

50 See Arendt 1976, 209–10.

51 See Perras 2004.

52 Acheson, former US Secretary of State, was speaking to a student conference at the Military Academy, West Point, on 5 December 1962; see *Vital Speeches*, 1 January 1963, 163.

53 Compare Robert Harvey: 'With the Soviet Union's disappearance, the United States no longer appeared to be a crusader for good: it simply seemed to stand for its own interest, but on a much larger scale than any other country. It appeared to have lost its moral purpose beyond the making of money. It had lost a role, and found an empire. The crusade against terrorism may be an attempt to rediscover such a role, but as so few outsiders view the problem in such alarmist tones, perhaps because they have long experienced terrorism and wars on their own territories, it seems unlikely to work' (Harvey 2003, 33).

54 Many of these countries are, so to speak, in the '1850s', trying to avoid the bloody civil war through which the United States had to pass in the early 1960s before becoming a capitalist democracy. Some are experiencing the civil war without any clear prospect of becoming decent democracies.

55 For examples, see Johnson 2000; Johnson 2004.

56 See Ewing 2002.

Chapter 9   Acceptance

1 On slavery, see Elkins 1968; Davis 1986; Patterson 1982; Myrdal 1996; Bales 2004; Blackburn 1988; Genovese 1976; Turley 2000; Miles 1987.

2 On the treatment of African Americans, see, for example, Dailey et al. 2000; Klarman 2004.

3 The destruction of the Native Americans involved, first, the intermediate solution of transporting the inconvenient and unwanted population to reservations beyond the territory occupied by the white 'master race' and, then, as the advance of the expanding empire's frontier brought

those dumping grounds back 'inside', the 'final solution' of exterminating the 'nuisance'. See also Arendt 1963; Levi 1987; Levi 1988.

4　On the massacre of the Lakota tribe at Wounded Knee in 1890, see
http://www.dickshovel.com/WKmasscre.html (25 May 2005).

5　On these points, see Sennett and Cobb 1972, 22, 29–31, 37, 75–9,
94–8, 102–13, 117–18, 124–40, 150–7, 171–83, 192–8, 210–19,
256–62. Sennett has returned to, and further developed, some of these
themes (Sennett 1999, Sennett 2004). For another analysis of feelings
of inadequacy among American males, see Susan Faludi's *Stiffed* (1999)
and Stud Terkel's *Hard Times* (1970), especially the section entitled
'Honor and Humiliation' (481–503). For background, see also Terkel
1972; Terkel 1973; Terkel 1982; Terkel 1986.

6　Sennett and Cobb 1972, 256–62. Compare Edward Luttwak's views on
'shopping as therapy'; Luttwak 1999, 204–14.

7　On Fanon's life, see Macey 2000.

8　As far as I know, Sennett and Cobb were not especially influenced by
Fanon's work; there is no reference to Fanon in Sennett and Cobb 1972.

9　Fanon 1967a; Fanon 1967b. See also McCulloch 1983; Perinbam 1982;
Gordon, Sharpley-Whiting and White (eds) 1996.

10　Sennett and Cobb 1972, 261–2.

11　Jinadu 1986, 65–96.

12　See also Moore-Gilbert 1997.

13　Stiglitz won the Nobel Prize for Economics in 2001.

14　In practice, as Georg Soros put it: 'Both the IMF and the United States
Treasury, which calls the tune at the IMF, have gone out of their way
to appease the market-fundamentalist tendencies of [the US] Congress'
(Soros 2000, 280). That is the view of someone who should know. One
consequence of such political bias is that the IMF normally asks weak
countries in need of IMF-brokered loans to reduce budget deficits and
raise interest rates. This systematically imposes the burden of adjustment on the borrowing countries with obvious inequities in the distribution of human costs. As Soros points out, the burden of adjustment
could be shared more equally between borrowers and lenders if trouble
were taken to undertake the necessary institutional reforms.

15　On the costs and benefits of fragmenting the self in this and other ways,
see Sennett and Cobb 1972, 194–8; Sennett 1998, 60–3.

16　All of these strategies except the last build up personal and group disciplines, and a capacity for skilled management that would be invalu-
able if deployed in efforts to transform the humiliating relationship.

17　For example: 'Queer Studies is an emerging interdisciplinary field whose
goal is to analyse antinormative sexual identities, performances, dis-
courses and representations in order ultimately to destabilize the notion
of normative sexuality and gender. Queer studies comes out of a critique of identity politics. It rejects essentialized conceptualization[s] of
sexuality, gender, and sexual identity as innate or fixed. It represents a

deconstruction of hegemonic conceptions of sexual and gender categories within straight, gay and lesbian communities. In queer studies, the interpretation, enactment, and destabilizing of sexual identities is linked to that of gender categories. The queer studies concentration's home in women's studies makes explicit these links between theories of gender and sexuality.' See website of Smith College, Northampton, MA, at: *http://www.smith.edu/wst/queerstudies.html*

18   See Hašek 2005; Boulle 1954.

19   As Rudyard Kipling put it: 'once you have paid him the Dane-geld/You never get rid of the Dane.' His poem ends with the lines: 'For the end of that game is oppression and shame,/And the nation that plays it is lost!' The (untitled) poem was first published in C. R. L. Fletcher's *A School History of England* (1911), in the chapter on Saxon England. See *http://www.theotherpages.org/poems/kipli05.html* (25 May 2005) and *www.kipling.org.uk* (18 February 2006). The phrase 'paying danegeld' has come to mean making concessions to a threatening force in order to buy it off temporarily. It implies vehement conformity verging on surrender.

20   See Elkins 1968.

21   According to Hobbes: 'It is not . . . the victory that giveth the right of dominion over the vanquished but his own covenant. Nor is he obliged because he is conquered; that is to say, beaten and taken, or put to flight; but because he cometh in, and submitteth to the victor; nor is the victor obliged by an enemy's rendering himself (without promise of life), to spare him for this his yielding to discretion; which obliges not the victor longer than in his own discretion he shall think fit' (Hobbes 1996, 141).

22   The word 'thrall' is derived from the Old English *thrāēl* (Old Norse thrāēll), which means 'slave' or one who is in bondage.

23   The objects of the WSV are: 'to promote research on victims and victim assistance; advocacy of their interests throughout the world; to encourage interdisciplinary and comparative research in victimology; to advance the cooperation of international, regional, and local agencies, groups, and individuals concerned with the problems of victims.' See *http://www.worldsocietyofvictimology.org*

24   See Wemmers 1998.

25   According to Chalmers Johnson: 'The condition [in Okinawa] – expropriation of the island's most valuable land for bases, extraterritorial status for American troops who committed crimes against local civilians, bars and brothels crowding around the main gates of bases, endless accidents, noise, sexual violence, drunk-driving crashes, drug use and environmental pollution – are replicated anywhere there are American garrisons' (Johnson 2004, 8). See also Johnson 2000, 34–64.

26   General MacArthur, who led the invasion force that occupied Japan in 1945, is reputed to have expressed the view that 'the mentality of the Japanese is that of a twelve year old' (Kawasaki 1969, 9). In October

1945 President Truman was told by an envoy that, in MacArthur's view, 'Oriental peoples suffer from an inferiority complex which leads them to "childish brutality" when they conquer in war and slavish dependence when they lose' (Dower 1999, 223).

27 See, for example, Dower 1999, 302–8; Wetzler 1998; Lamoot 1944; Maruyama 1963.

28 References to Thorsten 2004 cite the internet version at *https://goliath. ecnext.com/free-scripts/document_view_v3.pl?item_id=0199–18419&f* (12 April 2005), the pagination of which is different from the article as printed in the journal *Alternatives*.

29 For examples of the American influence on Japanese industrial techniques, see Deming 1986; Juran 2004; Landsberg 1999.

30 Ezra Vogel acknowledged that what I have called the 'separation' strategy for coping with forced acquiescence in humiliation was also well established: 'Until recently, Japanese could assume that what they said to each other and wrote to their press would not get picked up by Americans. . . . Among themselves, . . . they could talk of American irrationality, pomposity, ignorance, and inferiority, assuming that it would not be noticed' (Vogel 1991, 8).

31 Ishihara severely criticized a book by Ichiro Kawasaki, a Japanese diplomat, called *Japan Unmasked*, that had expressed shame about many aspects of Japanese society and culture. See Kawasaki 1969; Ishihara 1991, 31.

32 Ishihara 1991, 27–8, 80, 143–5.

33 See, for example, Ishihara 1991, 27–9, 43, 47, 59, 60–1, 76, 80, 142–4, 146. See also Mohamad and Ishihara 1995.

34 Scott Whitney at Salon Books, 19 April 1999. Quoted at *www.salon.com/books.review/1999/04/19/friedman* (16 April 2005).

35 'Short-horn cattle' are short-term traders in stocks, bonds and currencies. 'Long-horn cattle' are the multinationals involved in foreign direct investment (Friedman 2000, 114–15).

36 Friedman's book was written before the Enron scandal and the subsequent criminal investigation.

37 See, especially, Friedman 2000, 7–16, 46–67, 104–11, 112–17, 151–5, 169–74, 187–90, 205–6, 212–13, 250, 271, 281–3, 301–5, 342–3, 355–8, 367–78, 437–40, 444–5, 451–7, 463–8.

38 For more on lions and gazelles, see Friedman 2000, 331. See also Friedman 2003.

39 The *Just So Stories* were written for children (addressed as 'Best Beloved'). They include, for example, 'How the whale got his throat', 'How the camel got his hump', 'How the rhinoceros got his skin' and 'How the leopard got his spots' (Kipling 1994b).

40 See Bauman 1998, for example 64–5, 92–7, 106–18.

41 Edward Luttwak is a senior fellow at the Center for Strategic and International Studies in Washington. He describes himself as 'the son of an

innovative capitalist manufacturer and an entrepreneur [in his own right, who] believe[s] deeply both in the virtues of capitalism and in the need to impose some measure of control over its workings' (Luttwak 1999, ix).

42 Luttwak 1999, 2.

43 Ibid., 3, 218.

44 According to *The Economist*, 16 December 2000, 'America has 281 lawyers for every 100,000 people, compared to Britain with 94, 33 in France and a mere 7 in Japan'.

45 Luttwak 1999, 12–25.

46 The challenge now, say Hardt and Negri, is to turn this into political power in the globalized world. One of the points of conflict where a global political consciousness might develop is immigration: '*The general right to control its own movement is the multitude's ultimate demand for global citizenship*' (Hardt and Negri 2000, 400; italics in original). Also, the multitude's constant creativity, and the empire's dependence on it, should be recognized by '*a social wage and a guaranteed income for all*' (403; italics in original). The 'mobilization of the commons' (Hardt and Negri 2005, 211) will become more widespread as people engaged in struggle in different global locations learn to understand and exploit 'the new network model of the multitude' (217). For other demands, hopes and expectations, see Hardt and Negri 2000; 403–13; Hardt and Negri 2005. For elaborations and critiques, see Balakrishman (ed.) 2003; Negri 2003; Passavant and Dean 2004; Virno 2004.

47 The difficulties of bringing capitalism and democracy together are explored in *Capitalist Democracy on Trial* (Smith 1990).

Chapter 10   Rejection

1 Threatening both in prospect ('will it happen?') and if or when it happens ('can we survive it?').

2 Nelson Mandela, 'Address to rally in Soweto', 13 February 1990, at *http://www.anc.org.za/ancdocs/history/mandela/1990/sp900213.html* (26 April 2005).

3 Said K. Aburish relates that he was managing director of Growth International, a consulting firm, and chairman of its successor, Aburish, James and Associates. In this capacity he helped the Iraqi leader make contact with foreign suppliers who could help develop Iraq as a modern urban-industrial society with a strong arms programme (Aburish 2000, 107).

4 Aburish used the phrase '*politics of revenge*' as the subtitle of his book on Saddam (2000).

5 Aburish 2000, 122, citing Makiya 1989, 316.

6 Lear's comment continues thus: 'But how are we to understand someone who is *motivated* to keep feeling humiliated? On the surface, the terrorist sincerely believes that he hates his humiliation, and would do anything to get rid of it. He would be deeply offended – furious, *humiliated* – at any suggestion that, really, he has a hidden longing to stay connected to his sense of humiliation. Humiliation is nothing he really *wants* – and thus doing anything to promote it is against his own sense of his best interests. Thus it is irrational for him to pursue it. And this goes to the heart of Freud's insight: that humans tend towards certain forms of motivated irrationality of which they have little or no awareness' (Lear 2005, 4; italics in original).

7 Apparently, a 'Mrs. Augustus H. Mounsey' was occupying Lawford Hall, one of Essex's principal country houses, in 1898. See *http://www. essexpub.net/Directories/Seats.htm* (25 April 2005).

8 Saigō had arrived in Tokyo the previous month. The manifesto 'though never proved to come from his pen, was generally believed to contain a statement of his views' (Mounsey 1879, 41).

9 Mounsey 1879, 101–3.

10 Ibid., 88.

11 On Satsuma clan members in the Japanese navy, see Mounsey 1879, 119.

12 On the death of Saigō, see Mounsey 1879, 214–15. It is as heroic as in the film. Mounsey notes that the Japanese government pardoned over thirty-nine thousand of the rebels, imprisoned about three thousand and executed only twenty (226–7).

13 On the topic of Dalits in India, see Gorringe 2005; Mendelsohn and Vicziany 1998.

14 See The Official Mahatma Gandhi Archive at *http://www.mahatma. org.in/books/showbook.jsp?id=48&link=bg&book=bg0029&lang=en &cat=books* (26 April 2005).

15 Ironically, in this latter respect Gandhi was treading a path which, when taken to extremes, would lead to the suicide bomber who is difficult to resist because he or she does not fear death.

16 Unless otherwise stated, the quotations here are taken from a reprint of an article written by Gandhi in the newspaper *Harijan*, 22 October 1938.

17 For further details, see Scheff's website at *www.soc.ucsb.edu/faculty/ scheff/* (4 April 2005).

18 Scheff 1994, 61; see also 61–3.

19 On the Fronde, see Ranum 1994.

20 Gassert 1997, 92, 95, 100, 264, 296ff, cited in Schivelbusch 2003, 284. See also Prinz and Zitelmann 1991.

21 For a case study meant to carry the opposite message, one of hope and reconciliation, see Blumenfeld 2003.

22 See Chua 2003, 147–51, 157–8.

23 To which Huntington adds, 'African (possibly)' (Huntington 1997, 47).
24 See, for example, Huntington 1997, 40–41, 321.
25 Ibid., 176–9.
26 In 1979 China invaded Vietnam and withdrew after about three weeks.
27 For example, 'Multicivilizational international organizations like ASEAN could face increasing difficulty in maintaining their coherence' (Huntington 1997, 128).
28 See also Huntington 2004, especially 221–56.
29 For a broader view of the social and political context, see, among others, Harvie 1976; Collini 1991.

Chapter 11 Decent Democracy or Domineering State?

1 See, for example, Berman 1982, 47; Elias 1994, chapter 1.
2 Its victims included many of Turkey's Armenian population.
3 See Sztompka 2000.
4 For relevant texts on dealing with conflict, see Galtung 2004; Ury 1999.
5 On stereotyping, see Pickering 2001.
6 See also Hutton 2003, 61–106.
7 See also Kupchan 2002, 119–59.
8 On American involvement in these early phases of European integration, see Lundestadt 1998; Smith 1999b.
9 According to Hutton, 'This ranks with the collapse of the Soviet Union in 1991 as a pivotal event in postwar history' (Hutton 2003, 235).
10 See Smith and Wright (eds) 1999a; Smith and Wright 1999b; Smith 1999b.
11 From a speech at Élysée Palace, 4 November 1999. See *www.delegfrance-cd-geneve.org/chapter1/chirac041199.htm* (30 May 2005).
12 'Prime minister's speech to the Polish Stock Exchange', 6 October 2000. See *www.number-10.gov.uk/news.asp?NewsId=1341&Section1d=32.* Quoted in Kupchan 2002, 151.
13 For valuable background, see Axtmann 1998.
14 On Spain, see Jáuregui 1999. On Poland, see the lecture by the Polish foreign minister Wlodzimierz Cimoszewicz, given at Poland's embassy in London on 24 July 2002, at *http://www.poland-embassy.si/eng/politics/londynang.htm* (22 October 2005).
15 These figures are from the US Department of Agric-Economic research service). See *http://www.ers.usda.gov/Briefing/EuropeanUnion/basicinfo.htm*
16 See, for example, Connolly 1995; Siedentop 2001; Smith and Wright (eds) 1999a.
17 The French rejection of the new European Constitution in May 2005 is consistent with Eric Hobsbawm's view, expressed five years earlier:

'Today, in my opinion, the French drive for European integration has abated. They have less interest in the process, now that their centrality has been visibly diminished' (Hobsbawm 2000, 93).

18   There were, of course, also major protests against the war within the United States. These were seen by some Americans as 'anti-establishment'. By contrast, the European protests often seemed 'anti-American'.

19   Meaning France and Germany, castigated as 'old Europe' by Donald Rumsfeld during a press conference on 22 January 2003. See *http://news.bbc.co.uk/2/hi/europe/2687403.stm* (26 May 2005).

20   See Smith 2003a; Smith 2003b.

21   See OECD Economic Survey of China, 2005, summarized at *http://www.oecd.org/document/7/0,2340,en_2649_201185_35343687 _1_1_1_1,00.html*

22   For the broader context of Wallerstein's analysis, see Wallerstein 1974; Wallerstein 1980; Wallerstein 1989; Wallerstein 1997.

23   According to UN Population Division, an urban area is a settlement with a population of at least two thousand people. See *http://www. unhabitat.org/hd/hdv7n2/* (22 October 2005).

24   UN-Habitat 2003, xxxi–xxxii.

25   Ibid., 39.

26   See, for example, Flora and Heidenheimer 1990; Mann 1987.

27   See Reis and Moore 2005.

28   For other points of view, see Aziz 1997; De Soto 2000.

29   See, for example, MacAleer 1994; Elias 1996.

30   The extracts here are from speeches that Hitler gave on 13 April 1923, 27 January 1932 and 1 April 1939. See *http://www.hitler.org/speeches/*

31   See *http://www.whitehouse.gov/news/releases/2005/10/20051006–2. html* (6 October 2005).

32   See, for some evidence, Council of Europe Parliamentary Assembly document 8607, 'Threat posed to democracy by extremist parties and movements in Europe', January 2000, at *http://assembly.coe.int/ Documents/WorkingDocs/doc00/Edoc8607.htm* (30 May 2005). I will not give a long list of citations for other continents. They are easily found, but the term 'fascist', like the term 'humiliation,' has to be handled with caution, especially when used about others. For a more optimistic reading of the situation, see Wright 2001.

33   Singer 2004, 199.

34   For moves in this direction, see Hanson 2001; Bobbitt 2002; Kaplan 2003.

35   Kagan 2003.

36   Kearney 1987.

Bibliography

Aburish, S. K., 2000, *Saddam Hussein: The politics of revenge*, London: Bloomsbury

Adams, T. M., 1991, *Bureaucrats and Beggars: French social policy in the Age of Enlightenment*, Oxford: Oxford University Press

Ahmed, A., 2003, *Islam under Siege*, Cambridge: Polity

Alatas, S. F., 1993, 'A Khaldunian perspective on the dynamics of Asiatic societies', *Comparative Civilization Review*, 29, 29–51

Alatas, F. A., 2006, 'A Khaldunian exemplar for an historical sociology for the south', *Current Sociology*, 53, 4, 397–411

Albrow, M., 1996, *The Global Age: State and society beyond modernity*, Cambridge: Polity

Amin, S., 1997, *Capitalism in the Age of Globalization: The management of contemporary society*, London: Zed Books

Anderson, M. S., 1966, *The Eastern Question, 1774–1923*, London: Macmillan

Anderson, P., 1974a, *Lineages of the Absolutist State*, London: Verso

Anderson, P., 1974b, *Passages from Antiquity to Feudalism*, London: Verso

Archibugi, D., and Held, D. (eds), 1995, *Cosmopolitan Democracy: An agenda for a new world order*, Cambridge: Polity

Arendt, H., 1963, *Eichmann in Jerusalem: A report on the banality of evil*, London: Penguin

Arendt, Hannah, 1976, *The Origins of Totalitarianism*, New York: Harcourt, Brace & Company; originally published 1951

Armstrong, K., 2004, *The Battle for God: Fundamentalism in Judaism, Christianity and Islam*, New York: HarperCollins

Arrighi, G., 1994, *The Long Twentieth Century: Money, power and the origins of our times*, London: Verso

Arthur, A., 1999, *The Tailor King: The rise and fall of the Anabaptist kingdom of Munster*, London: St Martin's Press

Ash, T. G., 2004, *Free World: Why a crisis of the West reveals an opportunity of our time*, Penguin: Allen Lane

Ashcroft, B., and Ahluwalia, P., 1999, *Edward Said: The paradox of identity*, London: Routledge

Axtmann, R. (ed.), 1998, *Globalization and Europe: Theoretical and empirical investigations*, London: Continuum

Aziz, A., 1997, *Miniature Political Economies: The survival strategies of the poor*, New Delhi: M. D. Publications

Bacevich, A. J., 2002, *American Empire: The realities and consequences of US diplomacy*, Cambridge, MA: Harvard University Press

Bairoch, P., 1988, *Cities and Economic Development*, London: Mansell Publishing Limited

Baker, N. D., Hayes, J. H. H., and Straus, R. W., *The American Way: A study of human relations among Protestants, Catholics and Jews*, New York: Willett, Clark and Co.

Balakrishnan, G. (ed.), 2003, *Debating Empire*, London: Verso

Bales, K., 2004, *Disposable People: New slavery in the global economy*, Berkeley, CA: California University Press

Barbalet, J., 2002, *Emotions and Sociology*, Oxford: Blackwell

Barbalet, J., 2005, *Emotion, Social Theory, and Social Structure: A macrosociological approach*, Cambridge: Cambridge University Press

Barber, B. R., 1995, *Jihad vs McWorld: How globalism and tribalism are reshaping the world*, New York: Times Books

Barber, B. R., 2003, *Fear's Empire: War, terrorism and democracy*, New York: W. W. Norton

Barnett, T. P. M., 2004, *The Pentagon's New Map*, New York: G. M. Putnam's Sons

Bauman, Z., 1988, *Freedom*, Milton Keynes: Open University Press

Bauman, Z., 1989, *Modernity and the Holocaust*, Cambridge: Polity

Bauman, Z., 1992, *Intimations of Postmodernity*, London: Routledge

Bauman, Z., 1997, *Postmodernity and its Discontents*, Cambridge: Polity

Bauman, Z., 1998, *Globalization: The human consequences*, Cambridge: Polity

Bauman, Z., 2000, *Liquid Modernity*, Cambridge: Polity

Bauman, Z., 2004, *Europe: An unfinished adventure*, Cambridge: Polity

Bauman, Z., 2005, *Liquid Life*, Cambridge: Polity

Baun, M., 1995, 'The Maastricht Treaty as high politics: Germany, France and European integration', *Political Science Quarterly*, 110, 605–24

Bayoumi, M., and Rubin, A. (eds), 2000, *The Edward Said Reader*, New York: Vintage Books

Beard, C. A., 1913, *An Economic Interpretation of the Constitution of the United States*, New York: Free Press

Beattie, J. M., 2002, *Policing and Punishment in London 1660–1750: Urban crime and the limits of terror*, Oxford: Oxford University Press

Beck, U., 1992, *Risk Society: Towards a new modernity*, London: Sage

Beck, U., 1999a, *The Brave New World of Work*, trans. P. Camiller, Cambridge: Polity

Beck, U., 1999b, *World Risk Society*, Cambridge: Polity

Beck, U., 1999c, *What is Globalization?*, trans. P. Camiller, Cambridge: Polity; German original 1997

Beilharz, P., 2000, *Zygmunt Bauman: Dialectic of modernity*, London: Sage

Bell, C., 1977, *The Diplomacy of Détente: The Kissinger era*, London: Palgrave Macmillan

Bello, W., 2002, *Deglobalization: Ideas for a new world economy*, London: Zed Books

Berman, M., 1982, *All that is Solid Melts into Air: The experience of modernity*, London: Verso

Blackburn, R., 1988, *The Overthrow of Colonial Slavery*, London: Verso

Blumenfeld, L., 2003, *Revenge: A love story*, London: Picador

Blustein, P., 2005, *And the Money Kept Rolling In (and Out): Wall Street, the IMF, and the bankrupting of Argentina*, New York: Public Affairs

Bobbitt, P., 2002, *The Shield of Achilles: War, peace and the course of history*, New York: Alfred A Knopf

Bodansky, Y., 2001, *Bin Laden: The man who declared war on America*, New York: Randon House

Bossy, J., 1991, *Giordano Bruno and the Embassy Affair*, New Haven, CT: Yale University Press

Boulle, P., 1954, *Bridge over the River Kwai*, London: Vanguard

Bouwsma, W. J., 1988, *John Calvin: A sixteenth-century portrait*, Oxford: Oxford University Press

Bowen, H. V., Lincoln, M., and Rigby, N. (eds), 2004, *The Worlds of the East India Company*, Woodbridge: Boydell Press

Braudel, F., 1972, *The Mediterranean and the Mediterranean World in the Age of Philip II*, 2 vols, London: Fontana; French original 1949

Braudel, F., 1981–4, *Civilization and Capitalism 15th–18th Centuries*, 3 vols, London: Collins; French original 1979

Breckenridge, C., et al. (eds), 2002, *Cosmopolitanism*, Durham, NC: Duke University Press

Brown, M., 2005, *Lawrence of Arabia: The life, the legend*, London: Thames and Hudson

Brzezinski, Z., 1997, *The Grand Chessboard: American primacy and its geostrategic imperatives*, New York: Basic Books

Brzezinski, Z., 2004, *The Choice: Global domination or global leadership*, New York: Basic Books

Buchanan, P. J., 2002, *The Death of the West: How dying populations and immigrant invasions imperil our country and civilization*, New York: St Martin's Press

Canetti, E., 1973, *Crowds and Power*, Harmondsworth: London; German original 1960

Carlyon, L. A., 2003, *Gallipoli*, London: Bantam

Castells, M., 1989, *The Informational City: Information technology, economic restructuring, and the urban-regional process*, Oxford: Blackwell

Castells, M., 1997, *The Information Age: Economy, society and culture*, vol. 2: *The Power of Identity*, Oxford: Blackwell

Castells, M., 1998, *The Information Age: Economy, society and culture*, vol. 3: *End of Millennium*, Oxford: Blackwell

Castells, M., 2000, *The Information Age: Economy, society and culture*, vol. 1: *The Rise of the Network Society*, 2nd edn, Oxford: Blackwell

Cervantes, M., 2005, *Don Quixote*, trans. E. Grossman, London: Vintage; Spanish original 1605–15

Chandler, A. D., and Mazlish, B. (eds), 2005, *Leviathans: Multinational corporations and the new global history*, Cambridge: Cambridge University Press

Chase-Dunn, C., 1989, *Global Formation: Structures of the world-economy*, Oxford: Blackwell

Chomsky, N., 2003, *Hegemony or Survival: America's quest for global dominance*, New York: Metropolitan Books

Chua, A., 2003, *World on Fire: How exporting free market democracy breeds ethnic hatred and global instability*, London: Arrow Books

Cohen, R., and Vertovec, S., 2002, *Conceiving Cosmopolitanism*, Oxford: Oxford University Press

Cohen, S., and Taylor, L., 1992, *Escape Attempts: The theory and practice of resistance to everyday life*, London: Routledge

Coll, S., 2005, *Ghost Wars: The secret wars of the CIA, Afghanistan and Osama bin Laden, from the Soviet invasion to September 10th, 2001*, London: Penguin

Collini, S., 1991, *Public Moralists: Political thought and intellectual life in Britain 1850–1930*, Oxford: Clarendon Press

Connolly, B., 1995, *The Rotten Heart of Europe*, London: Faber and Faber

Coogan, T. P., 1991, *Michael Collins: A biography*, London: Arrow

Cooper, R., 2003, *The Breaking of Nations: Order and chaos in the twenty-first century*, London: Atlantic Books

Corten, A., and Marshall-Fratani, R. (eds), 2001, *Between Babel and Pentecost: Transnational Pentecostalism in Africa and Latin America*, Bloomington, IN: Indiana University Press

Cox, L., 1994, *Lincoln and Black Freedom: A study in presidential leadership*, Columbia, SC: University of South Carolina Press

Dailey, J., et al., 2000, *Jumpin' Jim Crow: Southern politics from Civil War to Civil Rights*, Princeton: Princeton University Press

Davidson, J. D., and Rees-Mogg, W., 1997, *The Sovereign Individual: The coming economic revolution and how to survive and prosper in it*, London: Pan Books

Davis, D. B., 1986, *Slavery and Human Progress*, Oxford: Oxford University Press

Davis, M., 1986, *Prisoners of the American Dream*, London: Verso

Davis, W. S. (ed.), 1912–13, *Readings in Ancient History: Illustrative extracts from the sources*, vol. 2: *Rome and the West*, Boston: Allyn and Bacon

De Kiewiet, C. W., 1941, *A History of South Africa, Social and Economic*, Oxford: Oxford University Press

Delanty, G., 2000, *Citizenship in a Global Age*, Buckingham: Open University Press

Deming, W. E., 1986, *Out of the Crisis*, Cambridge, MA: Massachusetts Institute of Technology, Center for Advanced Engineering Study/SPC Press

De Soto, H., 2000, *The Mystery of Capital: Why capitalism triumphs in the West and fails elsewhere*, London: Bantam Press

De Vries, J., 1981, 'Patterns of urbanization in preindustrial Europe, 1500–1800', in Schmal 1981, 77–109

Dillon, D. R., and Tkacik, J. J., 2005, 'China and ASEAN: Endangered American primacy in Southeast Asia,' Backgrounder no. 1886 (19 October 2005), Washington, DC: Heritage Foundation; see *http://www. heritage.org/Research/AsiaandthePacific/bg1886.cfm*

Donne, J., 1975, *Devotions upon Emergent Occasions: A critical edition*, ed. E. Savage, Salzburg: Universität Salzburg Institut für Englische Sprache und Literatur

Douglas, M., 1970, *Natural Symbols*, Harmondsworth: Penguin

Dower, J. W., 1999, *Embracing Defeat: Japan in the wake of World War II*, New York: W. W. Norton and Co.

Drake, S., 2001, *Galileo: A very short introduction*, Oxford: Oxford Paperbacks

Edwards, D. L., 2002, *John Donne: Man of flesh and spirit*, Grand Rapids, MI: Wm. B. Eerdmans Publishing Company

Elias, N., 1983, *The Court Society*, Oxford: Blackwell; German original 1969

Elias, N., 1994, *The Civilizing Process*, trans. E. Jephcott, Oxford: Blackwell; German original 1939

Elias, N., 1996, *The Germans: Power struggles and the development of habitus in the nineteenth and twentieth centuries*, Cambridge: Polity; German original 1989

Elkins, S., 1968, *Slavery: A problem in American institutional and intellectual life*, 2nd edn, Chicago, IL: Chicago University Press

Elliott, J. H., 1968, *Europe Divided 1559–98*, London: Fontana

Ewing, E. B., 2002, *The USA Patriot Act*, Hauppauge, NY: Nova Science Publishers

Faludi, S., 1999, *Stiffed: The betrayal of modern man*, London: Vintage

Fanon, F., 1967a, *Black Skin, White Masks*, trans. C. L. Markmann, London: MacGibbon and Kee

Fanon, F., 1967b, *The Wretched of the Earth*, trans. C. Farrington, London: Penguin

Faroqhi, S., 2004, *The Ottoman Empire and the World Around it*, Cambridge: Cambridge University Press

Ferguson, N., 2004a, *Colossus: The rise and fall of the American empire*, London: Penguin

Ferguson, N., 2004b, *Empire: How Britain made the modern world*, London: Penguin

Field, M., 1945, *Freedom is more than a Word*, Chicago, IL: University of Chicago Press

Fine, R., 2003, 'Taking the "ism" out of cosmopolitanism: An essay in reconstruction', *European Journal of Social Theory*, 6, 4, 451–70

Firebaugh, G., and Goesling, B., 2004, 'Accounting for the Recent Decline in Global Income Inequality', *American Journal of Sociology*, 110, 2, 283–312

Fischel, W., 1967, *Ibn Khaldun in Egypt: His public functions and his historical research, 1382–1406; a study in Islamic historiography*, Berkeley, CA: University of California Press, 1967

Flora, P., and Heidenheimer, A. J., 1990, *The Development of Welfare States in Europe and in America*, New Brunswick and London: Transaction Publishers

Foucault, M., 1967, *Madness and Civilization*, London: Tavistock; trans. R. Howard; French original 1961

Foucault, M., 1973, *The Birth of the Clinic*, trans. A. M. Sheridan, London: Tavistock

Foucault, M., 1977, *Discipline and Punish: The birth of the prison*, trans. A. M. Sheridan, Harmondsworth: Penguin; French original 1975

Foucault, M., 1978, *The History of Sexuality*, vol. 1: *An Introduction*, trans. R. Hurley, Harmondsworth: Penguin; French original 1976

Frank, T., 2004, *What's the Matter with America?: The resistible rise of the American right*, London: Secker and Warburg

Franken, A., 2003, *Lies and the Lying Liars who Tell them: A fair and balanced look at the right*, London: Allen Lane

Fraser, A., 2002, *The Gunpowder Plot: Terror and faith in 1605*, Blaine, WA: Phoenix Publishing

Fraser, N., and Honneth, A., 2003, *Redistribution or Recognition?: A political-philosophical exchange*, London: Verso

Freston, P., 2004, *Evangelicals and Politics in Asia, Africa and Latin America*, Cambridge: Cambridge University Press

Friedman, T., 2000, *The Lexus and the Olive Tree*, London: HarperCollins

Friedman, T., 2003, *Longitudes and Attitudes: Exploring the world before and after September 11*, London: Penguin

Frum, D., 2003, *The Right Man: The surprise presidency of George W. Bush*, New York: Random House

Frum, D., and Perle, R., 2003, *An End to Evil: How to win the war on terror*, New York: Random House

Fukuyama, F., 1992, *The End of History and the Last Man*, London: Penguin

Gadamer, 1975, *Truth and Method*, New York: Seabury Press

Galbraith, J. K., 1963, *American Capitalism: The concept of countervailing power*, Harmondsworth: Penguin

Galbraith, J. K., 1993, *The Culture of Contentment*, London: Penguin

Galtung, J., 2004., *Transcend and Transform: An introduction to conflict work*, London: Pluto Press

Gandhi, M. K., 1951, *Non-Violent Resistance*, New York: Schocken Books

Garfinkel, H., 1956, 'Conditions of successful status degradation ceremonies', *American Journal of Sociology*, 61, 420–4

Gassert, P., 1997, *Amerika im Dritten Reich: Ideologie, Propaganda, und Volksmeinung, 1933–1945*, Stuttgart: Steiner

Gaukroger, S., 1995, *Descartes: An intellectual biography*, Oxford: Oxford University Press

Gellner, E., 1991, *Plough, Sword and Book*, London: Paladin

Genovese, E. O., 1976, *Roll, Jordan, Roll, Roll: The world the slaves made*, New York: Random House

Gibb, J., 2005, *Who's Watching You?*, London: Collins and Brown

Gibbon, E., 1993, *The Decline and Fall of the Roman Empire*, London: Everyman's Library; originally published 1776–88

Giddens, A., 2000, *Runaway World: How globalization is reshaping our lives*, London: Routledge

Glover, J., 2001, *Humanity: A moral history of the twentieth century*, London: Pimlico

Goffman, E., 1968, *Stigma: Notes on the management of spoiled identity*, Harmondsworth: Pelican Books

Gordon, L. R., Sharpley-Whiting, T. D., and White, R. T. (eds), 1996, *Fanon: A critical reader*, Oxford: Blackwell

Gorringe, H., 2005, *Untouchable Citizens: Dalit movements and democratisation in Tamil Nadu*, London: Sage

Gould, R. V., 2003, *Collision of Wills: How ambiguity about social rank breeds conflict*, Chicago, IL: University of Chicago Press

Gowan, P., 1999, *The Global Gamble: Washington's Faustian bid for world dominance*, London: Verso

Gray, J., 1992, *Men are from Mars, Women are from Venus*, London: HarperCollins

Gray, J., 1998, *False Dawn: The delusions of global capitalism*, London: Granta

Gray, J., 2003, *Al Qaeda and what it Means to be Modern*, London: Faber and Faber

Green, D., 2003, *The Double Life of Doctor Lopez: Spies, Shakespeare and the plot to poison Elizabeth I*, Post Falls, ID: Century Publishing

Greenblatt, S., 1980, *Renaissance Self-Fashioning: From More to Shakespeare*, Chicago, IL: University of Chicago Press

Grossberg, L., 1992, *We Gotta Get Out of this Place: Popular conservatism and postmodern culture*, Routledge: London

Gutman, A. (ed.), 1994, *Multiculturalism*, Princeton, NJ: Princeton University Press

Habermas, J., 1977, 'A review of Gadamer's *Truth and Method*', in *Understanding and Social Inquiry*, ed. Fred R. Dallmayr and Thomas A. McCarthy, Notre Dame, IN: University of Notre Dame Press

Habermas, J., 2001, *The Postnational Constellation: Political essays*, Cambridge: Polity

Halberstam, D., 1992, *The Best and the Brightest*, New York: Ballantine Books; originally published 1969

Halliday, F., 2001, *The World at 2000*, New York: Palgrave

Halliday, F., 2002, *Two Hours that Shook the World. September 11, 2001: Causes and consequences*, London: Saqi Books

Halper, S., and Clarke, C., 2004, *America Alone: The neo-conservatives and the global order*, Cambridge: Cambridge University Press

Hanson, V. D., 2001, *Why the West has Won: Carnage and culture from Salamis to Vietnam*, London: Faber and Faber

Hardt, M., and Negri, A., 2000, *Empire*, Cambridge, MA: Harvard University Press

Hardt, M., and Negri, A., 2005, *Multitude*, London: Hamish Hamilton

Harvey, R., 2003, *Global Disorder*, London: Robinson

Harvie, C., 1976, *The Lights of Liberalism: University liberals and the challenge of democracy 1860–86*, London: Allen Lane

Hašek, J., 2005, *The Good Soldier Švejk*, trans. C. Parrott, London: Penguin; Czech original 1922

Hatfield, J., 2002, *Fortunate Son: George W. Bush and the Making of an American President*, London: Vision Paperbacks

Hayek, F. A., 1976, *The Road to Serfdom*, London: Routledge; originally published 1944

Haynes, A., 1994, *The Gunpowder Plot*, Stroud: Sutton Publishing

Held, D., 1995, *Democracy and the Global Order*, Cambridge: Polity

Held, D., et al., 1999, *Global Transformations: Politics, economics, culture*, Cambridge: Polity

Held, D., and McGrew, A. (eds), 2002, *Governing Globalization: Power, authority and global governance*, Cambridge: Polity

Held, D., and Koenig-Archibugi, M. (eds), 2003, *Taming Globalization: Frontiers of governance*, Cambridge: Polity

Henderson, H., 1999, *Beyond Globalization: Shaping a sustainable global economy*, West Hartford, CT: Kumarian Press

Herodotus, 1998, *The Histories*, trans. R. Waterfield, ed. C. Dewald, Oxford: Oxford University Press; written *c.* 430–424 BCE

Hertz, N., 2001, *The Silent Takeover: Global capitalism and the death of democracy*, London: Heinemann

Hirschman, A. O., 1970, *Exit, Voice and Loyalty: Responses to decline in firms, organizations and states*, Cambridge, MA: Harvard University Press

Hirschman, A. O., 1982, *Shifting Involvements: Private interest and public action*, Princeton, NJ: Princeton University Press

Hitler, A., 1992, *Mein Kampf*, trans. R. Manheim, London: Pimlico; German original 1925

Hobbes, T., *Leviathan*, ed. R. Tuck, 1996, Cambridge: Cambridge University Press; originally published 1651

Hobbes, T., 1998, *On the Citizen*, ed. R. Tuck and M. Silverthorne, Cambridge: Cambridge University Press; originally published 1647

Hobsbawm, E., 2000, *The New Century*, London: Abacus

Hobson, B. (ed.), 2003, *Recognition Struggles and Social Movements: Contested identities, agencies and power*, Cambridge: Cambridge University Press

Hochschild, A. R., 1983, *The Managed Heart: Commercialization of human feeling*, Berkeley, CA: University of California Press

Hogge, A., 2006, *God's Secret Agents: Queen Elizabeth's forbidden priests and the hatching of the gunpowder plot*, London: HarperCollins

Hohenberg, P. M., and Lees, L. H., 1985, *The Making of Urban Europe 1000–1950*, Cambridge, MA: Harvard University Press

Holmes, P., 1982, *Resistance and Compromise: The political thought of the Elizabethan Catholics*, Cambridge: Cambridge University Press

Honneth, A., 1996, *The Struggle for Recognition: Moral grammar of social conflicts*, Cambridge: Polity

Huntington, S. P., 1997, *The Clash of Civilizations and the Remaking of World Order*, London: Simon and Schuster

Huntington, S. P., 2004, *Who Are We?: America's great debate,* New York: Free Press

Hutton, W., 2003, *The World We're In*, London: Abacus

Ibn Khaldūn, 1969, *The Muqaddimah: An introduction to history*, trans. F. Rosenthal, ed. N.J. Dawood (abridged), New York: Bollingen

Ignatieff, M., 2000, *Virtual War: Kosovo and beyond*, New York: Metropolitan Books

Ignatieff, M., 2003, *Empire Lite*, London: Penguin

Ikenberry, G. J., 2001, *After Victory: Institutions, strategic restraint, and the rebuilding of order after major wars*, Princeton, NJ: Princeton University Press

Ikenberry, G. J. (ed.), 2002, *America Unrivalled: The future of the balance of power*, Ithaca: Cornell University Press

Ishihara, S., 1991, *The Japan that can say No: Why Japan will be the first among equals*, trans. F. Baldwin, with foreword by E. F. Vogel, New York: Simon and Schuster; Japanese original, with A. Morita, 1989

Jamal, A., 2005, *The Palestinian National Movement: Politics of contention 1967–2003*, Bloomington, IN: Indiana University Press

James, S., 1997, *Passion and Action: The emotions in seventeenth-century philosophy*, Oxford: Oxford University Press

Jáuregui, P., 1999, 'National pride and the meaning of "Europe": A comparative study of Britain and Spain', in Smith and Wright (eds) 1999a, 257–87

Jinadu, L. A., 1986, *Fanon. In search of the African revolution*, London: KPI

Joffe, J., 1998, *The Great Powers*, London: Weidenfeld and Nicolson

Johnson, C., 2000, *Blowback: The costs and consequences of American empire*, New York: Henry Holt and Company

Johnson, C., 2004, *The Sorrows of Empire: Militarism, secrecy and the end of the republic*, London: Verso

Johnson, J. H., 1998, *1918: The unexpected victory*, London: Cassell

Juran, J. M., 2004, *Architect of Quality: The autobiography of Dr. Joseph M. Juran*, New York: McGraw-Hill

Kagan, R., 2003, *Paradise and Power: America and Europe in the new world order*, London: Atlantic Books

Kagan, R., 2004, 'America's crisis of legitimacy', *Foreign Affairs*, 83, 2, 65–87

Kagan, R., and Kristol, W., 2001, 'National humiliation', *Weekly Standard*, 9 April, 10–17

Kaldor, M., 2003, *Global Civil Society: An answer to war*, Cambridge: Polity

Kaplan, R. D., 1996, *The Ends of the Earth: A journey to the frontiers of anarchy*, New York: Vintage

Kaplan, R. D., 2003, *Warrior Politics: Why leadership demands a pagan ethos*, New York: Vintage Books

Kawasaki, I., 1969, *Japan Unmasked*, Rutland, VT: Charles E. Tuttle Company

Kearney, C., 1987, *Nuclear War Survival Skills*, Cave Junction, OR: Oregon Institute of Science & Medicine; also at *http://www.ki4u.com/free_book/s73p904.htm*

Kelley, R., 1969, *The Transatlantic Persuasion: The liberal-democratic mind in the age of Gladstone*, New York: Alfred A Knopf

Kelsey, H., 2000, *Sir Francis Drake: The Queen's pirate*, New Haven, CT: Yale University Press

Kipling, R., 1994a, *The Jungle Book*, London: Everyman; originally published 1893

Kipling, R., 1994b, *Just So Stories*, London: Penguin; originally published 1902

Kissinger, H., 2002, *Does America Need a Foreign Policy?: Toward a diplomacy for the 21st century*, London: Simon and Schuster

Klare, M. T., 2002, *Resource Wars: The new landscape of global conflict*, New York: Henry Holt

Klarman, M. J., 2004, *From Jim Crow to Civil Rights: The Supreme Court and the struggle for racial equality*, New York: Oxford University Press

Klein, D. C., 1991, 'The humiliation dynamic: an overview', *Journal of Primary Prevention*, 2, 2, 93–121

Klein, M., 2000, *No Logo*, London: Flamingo

Kojève, A., 1969, *Introduction to the Reading of Hegel*, trans. J. H. Nichols, Jr., New York: Basic Books; French original 1947

Kow, S., 2004, 'Hobbes' critique of Miltonian independency', *Animus*, 9, December, at *http://www.swgc.mun.ca/animus/current/current.htm*

Kupchan, C. A., 2002, *The End of the American Era: US foreign policy and the geopolitics of the twenty-first century*, New York: Alfred A Knopf

Lacan, J., 1977, *Ecrits: A selection*, trans. A. M. Sheridan, London: Tavistock

Lacoste, Y., 1984, *Ibn Khaldun: The birth of history and the past of the third world*, trans. D. Macy, London: Verso

Lamoot, W., 1944, *Nippon: The crime and punishment of Japan*, New York: The John Day Company

Landsberg, P., 1999, 'In the beginning there were Deming and Juran', *Journal for Quality and Participation*, Nov/Dec

Laver, M., *The Politics of Private Desires: The guide to the politics of rational choice*, Harmondsworth: Penguin

Leadbetter, C., 2003, *Up the Down Escalator: Why the global pessimists are wrong*, London: Penguin

Lear, J., 2005, *Freud*, London: Routledge

Lenin, V. I., 1972, *Collected Works*, vol. 27, Moscow: Progress Publishers

Lepowsky, M., 1993, *Fruit of the Motherland: Gender in an egalitarian society*, New York: Columbia University Press

Levi, P., 1987, *If This is a Man* and *The Truce*, trans. S. Woolf, London: Abacus; Italian originals 1958 and 1963

Levi, P., 1988, *The Drowned and the Saved*, trans R. Rosenthal, London: Abacus; Italian original 1986

Lewalski, B., 2002, *The Life of John Milton: A critical biography*, Oxford: Blackwell

Lewis, B., 2004, *The Crisis of Islam: Holy war and unholy terror*, New York: Random House

Lieven, D., 2003, *Empire: The Russian empire and its rivals from the sixteenth century to the present*, London: Pimlico

Lincoln, A., 1953, *Collected Works of Abraham Lincoln*, vol. 6, New Brunswick, NJ: Rutgers University Press

Lind, M., 2003, *Made in Texas: George W. Bush and the takeover of American politics*, New York: Basic Books

Lindner, E. G., 2001a, 'Humiliation and the human condition: Mapping a minefield', *Human Rights Review*, 2, 2, 46–63

Lindner, E. G., 2001b, 'Humiliation as the source of terrorism: A new paradigm', *Peace Research*, 33, 2, 59–68

Lindner, E. G., 2002, 'Gendercide and humiliation in honor and human rights societies', *Journal of Genocide Research*, 4, 1, March, 137–55

Lister, R., 2003, *Citizenship: feminist perspectives*, 2nd edn, London: Palgrave Macmillan; originally published 1998

Lister, R., 2004, *Poverty*, Cambridge: Polity

Loyola, I., 1950, *Spiritual Exercises*, trans. A. Motolla, London: Bantam; written 1522–4

Lundestadt, G., 1998, *'Empire' by Integration: The United States and European integration, 1945–1997*, Oxford: Oxford University Press

Luttwak, E., 1999, *Turbo-Capitalism: Winners and losers in the global economy*, London: Orion Books

MacAleer, K., 1994, *Duelling: The cult of honor in fin-de-siècle Germany*, Princeton, NJ: Princeton University Press

MacCulloch, D., 2004, *Reformation: Europe's house divided 1490–1700*, London: Penguin

McCulloch, J., 1983, *Black Soul, White Artifact: Fanon's Clinical Psychology and Social Theory*, Cambridge: Cambridge University Press

Macey, D., 2000, *Frantz Fanon: A life*, London: Granta Books

Macmillan, M., 2002, *Peacemakers: The Paris Peace Conference of 1919 and its attempt to end war*, New York: Random House

Maddison, A., 2003, *The World Economy: A millennial perspective*, Paris: OECD

Makiya, K., 1989, *Republic of Fear: The politics of modern Iraq*, Berkeley, CA: University of California Press

Malcolm, N., 2002, *Aspects of Hobbes*, Oxford: Clarendon Press

Malkoff, K., 1977, *Escape from the Self: A study in contemporary American poetry and poetics*, New York: Columbia Press

Malthus, T. R., 1999, *An Essay on the Principle of Population*, Oxford: Oxford University Press; originally published 1798

Man, J., 2005, *Genghis Khan*, London: Bantam

Mann, M., 1986, *The Sources of Social Power*, vol. 1: *A History of Power from the Beginning to AD 1760*, Cambridge: Cambridge University Press

Mann, M., 1987, 'Ruling class strategies and citizenship', *Sociology*, 21, 3 (August), 339–54

Mann, M., 1993, *The Sources of Social Power*, vol. 2: *The Rise of Classes and Nation-states, 1760–1914*, Cambridge: Cambridge University Press

Mann, M., 2003, *Incoherent Empire*, London: Verso

Maravall, J. A., 1986, *Culture of the Baroque: Analysis of a historical structure*, trans. T. Cochran, Minneapolis, MN: University of Minnesota Press

Margalit, A., 1996, *The Decent Society*, Cambridge, MA: Harvard University Press

Margalit, A., 2002, *The Ethics of Memory*, Cambridge, MA: Harvard University Press

Martin, H.-P., and Schumann, H., 1997, *The Global Trap: Globalization and the assault on democracy and prosperity*, trans. P. Camiller, London: Zed Books

Maruyama, M., 1963, 'Nationalism in Japan: Its theoretical background and prospects', in Maruyama, *Thought and Behaviour in Modern Japanese Politics*, Oxford: Oxford University Press

May, E. R., 1975, *The Making of the Monroe Doctrine*, Harvard, MA: Harvard University Press

Mazlish, B., 2004, *Civilization and its Contents*, Stanford, CA: Stanford University Press

Mazlish, B., 2005a, 'The global and the local', *Current Sociology*, 53, 1, 93–111

Mazlish, B., 2005b, 'Roudometof: A dialogue', *Current Sociology*, 53, 1, 137–41

Mazlish, B., and Iriye, A. (eds), 2005, *The Global History Reader*, London: Routledge

Mead, M., 1944, *The American Character*, Harmondsworth: Penguin

Mead, W. R., 2001, *Special Providence: American foreign policy and how it changed the world*, New York: Alfred A. Knopf

Mead, W. R., 2004, *Power, Terror, Peace and War: America's grand strategy in a world at risk*, New York: Alfred A. Knopf

Mendelsohn, O., and Vicziany, M., 1998, *The Untouchables: Subordination, poverty and the state in modern India*, Cambridge: Cambridge University Press

Micklethwait, J., and Wooldridge, A., 2004, *The Right in America: Why America is different*, London: Allen Lane

Middlemas, K., 1995, *Orchestrating Europe: The informal politics of European Union 1973–1995*, London: Fontana

Milanovic, B., 2002, 'True world income distribution, 1988 and 1993: First calculation based on household surveys alone', *Economic Journal*, 112, 476, 51–92

Miles, R., 1987, *Capitalism and Unfree Labour: Anomaly or necessity?*, London: Tavistock

Mill, J. S., 1964, 'On Liberty', in *Utilitarianism, Liberty, Representative Government*, London: Dent, 65–170; essay written 1859

Miller, W. E., 1993, *Humiliation and Other Essays on Honor, Social Discomfort, and Violence*, Ithaca, NY: Cornell University Press

Milton, J., 1660, *The Readie & Easie Way to Establish a Free Commonwealth*, London; see *http://www.shu.ac.uk/emls/iemls/resour/mirrors/rbear/readie.html*

Milton, J., 1982, *Complete Prose Works*, vol 6: *Christian Doctrine*, New Haven, CT: Yale University Press

Milton, J., 1998, *Areopagitica, and Other Political Writings of John Milton*, Indianapolis, IN: Liberty Fund; originally published 1644

Milton, J., 2004, *Paradise Lost*, Oxford: Oxford University Press; originally published 1667, rev. edn 1674

Milton-Edwards, B., 2005, *Islamic Fundamentalism since 1945*, London: Routledge

Mohamad, M., and Ishihara, S., 1995, *The Voice of Asia*, London: Kodansha International

Monbiot, G., 2003, *The Age of Consent: A manifesto for a new world order*, London: HarperCollins

Moore, B., 1969, *Social Origins of Dictatorship and Democracy: Lord and peasant in the making of the modern world*, Harmondsworth: Penguin

Moore, B., 1972, *Reflections on the Causes of Human Misery*, Harmondsworth: Penguin

Moore, B., 1978, *Injustice: The social causes of obedience and revolt*, London: Macmillan

Moore, M., 2002, *Downsize This!*, London: Pan Macmillan

Moore, M., 2004, *Dude, Where's my Country?*, London: Penguin

Moore-Gilbert, B., 1997, *Postcolonial Theory: Contexts, practices, politics*, London: Verso

Mounsey, A. H., 1879, *The Satsuma Rebellion: An episode of modern Japanese history*, London: John Murray

Myrdal, G., 1996, *An American Dilemma: The Negro problem and modern democracy*, 2 vols, New Brunswick: Transaction Books; originally published 1944

Naphy, W. G., and Roberts, P. (eds), 1997, *Fear in Early Modern Society*, Manchester: Manchester University Press

National Commission on Terrorist Attacks on the United States, 2004, *The 9/11 Commission Final Report*, Washington, DC: US Government Printing Office; see *http://www.9-11commission.gov*

Negri, A., 2003, *Time for Revolution*, London: Continuum

Nicholl, C., 1994, *The Reckoning: The murder of Christopher Marlowe*, Orlando, FL: Harcourt

Nietzsche, F., 1956, *The Genealogy of Morals*, trans. F. Golffing, New York: Anchor Books; German original 1887

Nisbett, R. E., and Cohen, D., 1996, *Culture of Honor: The psychology of violence in the South*, Boulder, CO: Westview Press

Norwich, J. J., 1982, *A History of Venice*, London: Penguin

Nussbaum, M., 2000, *Sex and Social Justice*, Oxford: Oxford University Press

Nussbaum, M., 2001, *Women and Human Development: The capabilities approach*, Cambridge: Cambridge University Press

Nussbaum, M., 2006, *Frontiers of Justice: Disability, nationality, species membership*, Cambridge, MA: Belknap Press

Nye, J. S., 2002, *The Paradox of American Power: Why the world's only superpower can't go it alone*, Oxford: Oxford University Press

Odom, W. E., and Dujarric, R., 2004, *America's Inadvertent Empire*, New Haven: Yale University Press

Oestreich, O., 1982, *Neostoicism and the Early Modern State*, trans. D. McLintock, Cambridge: Cambridge University Press

O'Hearn, D., 1998, *Inside the Celtic Tiger: Irish economy and the Asian model*, London: Pluto Press

Palast, G., 2002, *The Best Democracy Money Can Buy*, London: Pluto Press

Panter-Brick, C., Layton, R. H., and Rowley-Conwy, P. (eds), 2001, *Hunter-Gatherers: An interdisciplinary perspective*, Cambridge: Cambridge University Press

Parekh, B., 2001, *Gandhi: A very short introduction*, Oxford: Oxford University Press

Parratt, J. (ed.), 2004, *An Introduction to Third World Theologies*, Cambridge: Cambridge University Press

Parrington, Vernon L., 1930, *Main Currents in American Thought*, 3 vols, New York: Harcourt, Brace and World

Partington, J. S., 2003, *Building Cosmopolis: The political thought of H. G. Wells*, London: Ashgate

Passavant, P. A., and Dean, J., 2004, *Empire's New Clothes: Reading Hardt and Negri*, London: Routledge

Patterson, O., 1982, *Slavery and Social Death: A comparative study*, Cambridge, MA: Harvard University Press

Peet, R., et al., 2004, *The IMF, World Bank and the WTO*, London: Zed Books

Perinbam, B. M., 1982, *Holy Violence: The revolutionary thought of Frantz Fanon*, Washington, DC: Three Continents Press

Perras, A., 2004, *Carl Peters and German Imperialism 1856–1918*, Oxford: Oxford University Press

Phillips, A., 1998, *The Beast in the Nursery*, London: Faber and Faber

Phillips, A., 2001, *Houdini's Box: On the arts of escape*, London: Faber and Faber

Pickering, M., 2001, *Stereotyping: The politics of representation*, London: Palgrave Macmillan

Pike, R., 1983, *Penal Servitude in Early Modern Spain*, Madison, WI: University of Wisconsin Press

Plato, 1955, *The Republic*, trans. H. D. P. Lee, Harmondsworth: Penguin; written *c.* 360 BCE

Plowden, A., 1991, *The Elizabethan Secret Service*, London: Harvester

Poggi, G., 1978, *Development of the Modern State*, London: Hutchinson

Poggi, G., 2000, *Forms of Power*, Cambridge: Polity

Ponting, C., 2001, *World History: A new perspective*, London: Pimlico

Porter, G., 2005, *Perils of Dominance: Imbalance of power and the road to war in Vietnam*, Berkeley, CA: University of California Press

Prendergast, J. P., 1997, *The Cromwellian Settlement of Ireland (1652–1660)*, Baltimore, MD: Clearfield Publishing Company

Prinz, M., and Zitelmann, R. (eds), 1991, *Nationalsozialismus und Modernisierung*, Darmstadt: Wissenschaftlicher Buchgesellschaft

Ransom, E. L., 1989, *Conflict and Compromise: The political economy of slavery, emancipation and the American Civil War*, Cambridge: Cambridge University Press

Ranum, O., 1994, *The Fronde: A French Revolution*, New York: W. W. Norton

Rashid, A., 2003, *Jihad: The rise of militant Islam in Central Asia*, Princeton, NJ: Princeton University Press

Ravallion, M., 2003, 'The debate on globalization, poverty and inequality: Why measurement matters', *World Bank Policy Research Working Paper 3038*, Washington, DC: World Bank

Ravallion, M., 2004, 'Competing concepts of inequality in the globalization debate', *World Bank Policy Research Working Paper 3243*, Washington, DC: World Bank

Read, C., 1925, *Mr. Secretary Walsingham and the Policy of Queen Elizabeth*, Oxford: Clarendon Press

Reis, E. P., and Moore, M., 2005, *Elite Perceptions of Poverty and Inequality*, London: Zed Books

Rifkin, J., 2004, *The European Dream: How Europe's vision of the future is quietly eclipsing the American dream*, Cambridge: Polity

Robertson, A. F., 2001, *Greed: Gut feelings, growth and history*, Cambridge: Polity

Robertson, R., 2003, *The Three Waves of Globalization: A history of a developing global consciousness*, London: Zed Books

Roosevelt, E., 1946, *As He Saw It*, New York: Duell, Sloan and Pearce

Rorty, R., 1989, *Contingency, Irony and Solidarity*, Cambridge: Cambridge University Press

Rosenwein, B. H. (ed.), 1998, *Anger's Past: The social uses of an emotion in the Middle Ages*, Ithaca, NY: Cornell University Press

Rosenwein, B. H., 2002, 'Worrying about emotions in history', *American Historical Review*, 107, 3, 821–45

Roth, M. S., 1988, *Knowing and History: Appropriations of Hegel in twentieth century France*, Ithaca and London: Cornell University Press

Roudometof, V., 2005a, 'Transnationalism, cosmopolitanism and glocalization', *Current Sociology*, 53, 1, 113–35

Roudometof, V., 2005b, 'The moral conundrums of the global age', *Current Sociology*, 53, 1, 143–7

Runciman, W. G., 1966, *Relative Deprivation and Social Justice*, London: Routledge

Ruthven, M., 2005, *Fundamentalism: The search for meaning*, Oxford: Oxford University Press

Sacks, J., 2002, *The Dignity of Difference: How to avoid the clash of civilizations*, London: Continuum

Sahlins, M., 1972, *Stone Age Economics*, Chicago, IL: Chicago University Press

Said, E. W., 1978, *Orientalism: Western conceptions of the Orient*, London: Routledge

Said, E. W., 1993, *Culture and Imperialism*, London: Vintage

Said, E. W., 1999, *Out of Place*, London: Granta

Said, E. W., and Hitchens, C. (eds), 1988, *Blaming the Victims: Spurious scholarship and the Palestinian question*, London: Verso

Sardar, Z., and Davies, M. W., 2002, *Why Do People Hate America?*, Cambridge: Icon Books

Sarkar, S., 2003, *Beyond Nationalist Frames: Postmodernism, Hindu fundamentalism, history*, Bloomington, IN: Indiana University Press

Sassen, S., 1991, *The Global City: New York, London, Tokyo*, Princeton, NJ: Princeton University Press

Sassen, S., 1996, *Losing Control?: Sovereignty in an age of globalization*, New York: Columbia University Press

Sassen, S., 1998, *Globalization and its Discontents*, New York: The New Press

Scarry, E., 1987, *The Body in Pain: The making and unmaking of the world*, Oxford: Oxford University Press

Schäfer, H.-D., 1991, 'Amerikanismus im Dritten Reich', in Prinz and Zitelmann (eds) 1991, 199–215

Scheff, T. J., 1990, *Micosociology: Discourse, emotion, and social structure*, Chicago, IL: University of Chicago Press

Scheff, T. J., 1994, *Bloody Revenge: Emotions, nationalism and war*, Boulder, CO: Westview Press

Scheff, T. J., 1997, *Emotions, the Social Bond and Human Reality: Part/whole analysis*, Cambridge: Cambridge University Press

Scheler, M., 1961, *Ressentiment*, trans. W. W. Holdheim, New York: Free Press of Glencoe; German original 1912

Schivelbusch, W., 2003, *The Culture of Defeat: On national trauma, mourning and recovery*, London: Granta Books

Schmal, H., 1981, *Patterns of European Urbanization since 1500*, London: Croom Helm

Scholte, J. A., 2000, *Globalization: A critical introduction*, New York: Palgrave

Schwabe, K., 1985, *Woodrow Wilson, Revolutionary Germany, and Peacemaking, 1918–1919*, Chapel Hill, NC: University of North Carolina Press

Schwartz, P., Leyden, P., and Hyatt, J., 2000, *The Long Boom: A future history of the world 1980–2020*, London: Texere

Sen, A., 1999, *Development as Freedom*, Oxford: Oxford University Press
Sen, A., 2002, 'How to judge globalism', *American Prospect*, 13, 1 and at *http://www.prospect.org/print/V13/1/sen-a.html*
Sennett, R., 1980, *Authority*, London: Secker and Warburg
Sennett, R., 1986, *The Fall of Public Man*, London: Faber and Faber
Sennett, R., 1994, *Flesh and Stone: The body and the city in Western civilization*, London: Faber and Faber
Sennett, R., 1999, *The Corrosion of Character: The personal consequences of work in the new capitalism*, New York: W. W. Norton and Company
Sennett, R., 2004, *Respect: The formation of character in an age of inequality*, London: Penguin
Sennett, R., and Cobb, R., 1972, *The Hidden Injuries of Class*, New York: Vintage
Shapiro, G., and Markoff, J., 1998, *Revolutionary Demands: A content analysis of the cahiers de doléances of 1789*, Stanford, CA: Stanford University Press
Shaw, M., 2000, *Theory of the Global State: Globality as an unfinished revolution*, Cambridge: Cambridge University Press
Shipman, A., 2002, *The Globalization Myth*, Cambridge: Icon Books
Shklar, J., 1984, *Ordinary Vices*, Cambridge, MA: Harvard University Press
Siedentop, L., 2001, *Democracy in Europe*, London: Penguin
Singer, P., 2004, *One World: The ethics of globalization*, 2nd edn, New Haven, CT: Yale University Press
Skinner, Q. R. D., 1978, *The Foundations of Modern Political Thought*, vol. 1: *The Renaissance*, Cambridge: Cambridge University Press
Skinner, Q. R. D., 1997, *Reason and Rhetoric in the Philosophy of Hobbes*, Cambridge: Cambridge University Press
Slater, D., and Taylor, P. J. (eds), 1999, *The American Century: Consensus and coercion in the projection of American power*, London: Blackwell
Slotkin, R., 1973, *Regeneration through Violence: The mythology of the American frontier, 1600–1860*, Middletown, CT: Wesleyan University Press
Smith, A., 1979, *The Wealth of Nations*, Harmondsworth: Penguin; originally published 1776
Smith, D., 1981, *Conflict and Compromise. Class formation in English society 1830–1914*, London: Routledge
Smith, D., 1983, *Barrington Moore: Violence, morality and political change.* London: Macmillan
Smith, D., 1988, *The Chicago School: A liberal critique of capitalism*, London: Macmillan
Smith, D., 1990, *Capitalist Democracy on Trial: The transatlantic debate from Tocqueville to the present*, London: Routledge
Smith, D., 1991, *The Rise of Historical Sociology*, Cambridge: Polity
Smith, D., 1999a, *Zygmunt Bauman: Prophet of postmodernity*, Cambridge: Polity

Smith, D., 1999b, 'Making Europe: Processes of Europe-formation since 1945', in Smith and Wright (eds) 1999a, 235–56

Smith, D., 2000, *Norbert Elias and Modern Social Theory*, London: Sage

Smith, D., 2001, 'Organizations and humiliation: Looking beyond Elias', *Organization*, 8, 3, 537–60

Smith, D., 2002, 'The humiliating organization: The functions and dysfunctions of humiliation', in Iterson, A. van, Mastenbroek, W., Newton, T., and Smith, D. (eds), *The Civilized Organization: Norbert Elias and the future of organization studies*, Amsterdam: John Benjamins

Smith, D., 2003a, 'Europe and America: Strategies for survival', in Lindahl, R. (ed.), *Whither Europe?: Borders, boundaries and frontiers in a changing world*, Göteborg, Sweden: Centre for European Research at Göteborg University, 57–71

Smith, D., 2003b, 'Europe and America: Reflections on the future of the West', *Politologen*, spring, 33–42

Smith, D., 2005, 'Transnationality and the Trans-Siberian Express: Comments on a dialogue', *Current Sociology*, 53, 1, 149–56

Smith, D., and Braein, A., 2003, *The State of the World Atlas*, London: Earthscan

Smith, D., and Wright, S. (eds), 1999a, *Whose Europe?: The turn towards democracy*, London: Blackwell

Smith, D., and Wright, S., 1999b, 'The turn towards democracy', in Smith and Wright (eds), 1999a, 1–18

Soros, G., 2000, *Open Society: Reforming global capitalism*, London: Little, Brown and Company

Spierenburg, P., 1991, *The Prison Experience: Disciplinary institutions and their inmates in early modern Europe*, New Brunswick, NJ: Rutgers University Press

Stasiulis, D., and Yuval-Davis, N. (eds), 1995, *Unsettling Settler Societies: Articulations of gender, ethnicity and class*, London: Sage

Stiglitz, J., 2002, *Globalization and its Discontents*, London: Penguin

Strauss, L., 1952, *The Political Philosophy of Hobbes: Its genesis and basis*, Cambridge: Cambridge University Press

Sutcliffe, B., 2004, 'World Inequality and Globalization', *Oxford Review of Economic Policy*, 20, 1, 15–37

Sztompka, P., 2000, *Trust: A sociological theory*, Cambridge: Cambridge University Press

Taylor, A. J. P., 1965, *English History 1914–1945*, Oxford: Oxford University Press

Taylor, P. J., 1999, *Political Geography: World-economy, nation-state and geography*, London: Longman

Terkel, S., 1970, *Hard Times: An oral history of the great depression*, New York: Avon Books

Terkel, S., 1972, *Working*, New York: Avon Books

Terkel, S., 1973, *Talking to Myself: A memoir of my times*, New York: Simon and Schuster

Terkel, S., 1982, *American Dreams: Lost and found*, London: Granada

Terkel, S., 1986, *The Good War: An oral history of World War Two*, London: Penguin

Tester, K., 2004, *The Social Thought of Zygmunt Bauman*, London: Palgrave Macmillan

Thomas, C., and Wilkin, P. (eds), 1999, *Globalization, Human Security and the African Experience*, Boulder, CO: Lynne Reiner Publishers

Thomas, K., 1978, *Religion and the Decline of Magic*, London: Peregrine

Thompson, E. P., 1963, *The Making of the English Working Class*, London: Gollancz

Thompson, E. P., 1991, *Customs in Common*, New York: New Press

Thompson, L., 2001, *A History of South Africa*, New Haven, CT: Yale University Press

Thompson, R. S., 2004, *The Eagle Triumphant: How America took over the British Empire*, London: John Wiley and Sons

Thorne, C., 1979, *Allies of a Kind: The United States, Britain and the war against Japan, 1941–1945*, Oxford: Oxford University Press

Thorne, C., 1986, *The Far Eastern War: States and societies 1941–45*, London: Unwin

Thorsten, M., 2004, 'Shame to vengeance: The grand cliché of the Japanese superstate', *Alternatives*, 29, 199–218

Thucydides, 1972, *History of the Peloponnesian War*, London: Penguin; written fifth century BCE

Tilly, C., 1990, *Coercion, Capital and European States AD 990–1990*, Oxford: Blackwell

Tilly, C., 1999, *Durable Inequality*, Berkeley, CA: California University Press

Tilly, C., 2004, *Social Movements*, St Paul, MN: Paradigm

Tocqueville, A. de, 1955, *The Old Regime and the French Revolution*, New Haven, CT: Yale University Press; French original 1856

Tocqueville, A. de, 1958, *Journeys to England and Ireland*, trans. G. Lawrence and K. P. Mayer, London: Faber and Faber; from previously unpublished journals

Tocqueville, A., de, 1968, *Democracy in America*, 2 vols, New York: Collins; French original 1835–40

Tocqueville, A., de, 1985, *Alexis de Tocqueville: Selected letters on politics and society*, ed. R. Boesche, Berkeley, CA: University of California Press

Todd, E., 2003, *After the Empire: The breakdown of the American order*, New York: Columbia University Press

Todorov, T., 1984, *The Conquest of America*, New York: Harper

Todorov, T., 2005, *The New World Disorder*, Cambridge: Polity

Tomlinson, J., 1991, *Cultural Imperialism: A critical introduction*, London: Continuum

Tomlinson, J., 1999, *The Globalization of Culture*, Cambridge: Polity

Toulmin, S., 1990, *Cosmopolis: The hidden agenda of modernity*, Chicago, IL: University of Chicago Press

Turley, D., 2000, *Slavery*, Oxford: Blackwell

Turner, J. H., 2000, *On the Origins of Human Emotions: A sociological inquiry in the evolution of human affect*, Stanford, CA: Stanford University Press

Turner, V. W., 1969, *The Ritual Process*, Harmondsworth: Penguin

Ullman, H. K., and Wade J. P., 1996, *Shock and Awe: Achieving rapid dominance*, Washington, DC: National Defense University Press

UN-Habitat, 2003, *The Challenge of Slums: Global report on human settlements*, London: Earthscan

Urry, J., 1999, *Sociology beyond Societies: Mobilities for the twenty-first century*, London: Routledge

Urry, J., 2002, *Global Complexity*, Cambridge: Polity

Ury, W. L., 1999, *Getting to Peace: Transforming conflict at home, at work and in the world*, London: Viking

Vaissant, K., and Mazumdar, S. (eds), 2003, *Antimonies of Modernity: Essays on race, Orient, nation*, London: Duke University Press

van Horn Melton, J., 1988, *Absolutism and the Eighteenth-century Origins of Compulsory Schooling in Prussia and Austria*, Cambridge: Cambridge University Press

Vasquez, M. A., and Marquardt, M. F., 2003, *Globalizing the Sacred: Religion across the Americas*, Piscataway, NJ: Rutgers University Press

Veblen, T., 1965, *The Theory of Business Enterprise*, New York: Augustus Kelley; originally published 1904

Veblen, T., 1970, *The Theory of the Leisure Class*, London: Allen & Unwin; originally published 1899

Villalon, L. A., and Huxtable, P. A. (eds), 1998, *The African State at a Critical Juncture: Between disintegration and reconfiguration*, Boulder, CO: Lynne Reiner

Virno, P., 2004, *A Grammar of the Multitude*, New York: Semiotext(e)

Vogel, E., 1991, 'Foreword', in Ishihara 1991, 7–10

Wade, R., 2004, 'Is globalization reducing poverty and inequality?', *World Development*, 32, 4, 567–89

Walker, M., 1994, *The Cold War*, London: Vintage

Wallerstein, I., 1974, *The Modern World-System*, vol. 1: *Capitalist Agriculture and the Origins of the World-Economy in the Sixteenth Century*, New York: Academic Press

Wallerstein, I. 1980, *The Modern World-System*, vol. 2: *Mercantilism and the Consolidation of the Capitalist World-Economy 1600–1750*, New York: Academic Press

Wallerstein, I., 1989, *The Modern World-System*, vol. 3: *The Second Era of Great Expansion of the Capitalist World-Economy 1730–1840s*, New York: Academic Press

Wallerstein, I., 1998, *Utopistics: Or, historical choices of the twenty-first century*, New York: New Press

Wallerstein, I., 2003, *The Decline of American Power*, New York: The New Press

Walzer, M., 1965, *The Revolution of the Saints: A study in the origins of radical politics*, Cambridge, MA: Harvard University Press

Weber, M., 2002, *The Protestant Ethic and the Spirit of Capitalism*, Harmondsworth: Penguin; German original 1905

Wells, C. M., 1992, *The Roman Empire*, London: Fontana

Wells, H. G., 1987, *The Future in America: A search after realities*, London: Granville Publishing; originally published 1906

Wells, H. G., 1940, *The Rights of Man, or What are we fighting for?*, Harmondsworth: Penguin

Wemmers, J., 1998, 'In memory of Benjamin Mendelsohn, founder of victimology', *The Victimologist*, 2, 1; also at *http://www.world-society-victimology.de/wsv/index.aspx?page=19&nr=6*

Wetzler, P. M., 1998, *Hirohito and War: Imperial tradition and military decision-making in pre-war Japan*, Honolulu: University of Hawaii Press

Wheatcroft, A., 2004, *Infidels: A history of the conflict between Christendom and Islam*, London: Penguin

White, M., 2002, *The Pope and the Heretic: A true story of courage and murder at the hands of the Inquisition*, London: Little, Brown and Company

Wilkinson, R., 1984, *American Tough: The tough-guy tradition and American character*, London: Greenwood Press

Wilkinson, R., 2005, *The Impact of Inequality: How to make sick societies healthier*, London: Routledge

Williams, W. A., 1980, *Empire as a Way of Life: An essay on the causes and character of America's present predicament along with a few thoughts about an alternative*, Oxford: Oxford University Press

Woodiwiss, A., 2003, *Making Human Rights Work Globally*, London: Glasshouse Press

Wright, R., 2001, *Nonzero: History, evolution and human cooperation*, London: Abacus

Yegenoglu, M., 1998, *Towards a Feminist Reading of Orientalism*, Cambridge: Cambridge University Press

Index

Numbers in italics refer to displayed text boxes.